First Published – 2004

Reprinted – 2024

ISBN: 978-81-7141-818-3

Essentials of Instructional Technology

Published by:

DISCOVERY PUBLISHING HOUSE PVT. LTD.

4383/4B, Ansari Road, Darya Ganj
New Delhi-110 002 (India)
Phone: +91-11-23279245; 23253475; 43596065
Mobile: +91 9811179893 / +91 9871656464
E-mail: discoverypublishinghouse@gmail.com
orderdphbooks@gmail.com
web: www.discoverypublishinggroup.com

Printed at:
Infinity Imaging Systems
Delhi

ESSENTIALS
OF
INSTRUCTIONAL TECHNOL

Edited by

Dr. A R. Rather

Department of Education
Kashmir University
Srinagar

DISCOVERY PUBLISHING HOUS
NEW DELHI-110002

Contents

Preface

Teachers' Training is a vital part of Education. Therefore, all efforts of the educationists, educators and instructors are aimed at the task of providing better training to the 'would be teachers' for their better education and proper growth, as a benefactor. No doubt, this responsibility can only be exercised, if the educators are equipped with the required knowledge of the subject concerned and the trainees develop needed interest in it. That's why, it becomes essential for making adequate provisions for each course to the teachers and as well as trainees. This series is designed for providing a solid practical base for all the papers. The series has been prepared strictly according to the B.Ed. syllabus, prescribed by universities.

Of course there are many a book on the subject, presently available in the market. But every author has his or her own style and way of presentation. The present work also has its own features, characteristics and significance. While preparing this series of books, the editor had to refer to the works of other authors and various sources for information. He expresses a deep gratitude for incorporating their ideas in the text. Hopefully, this series would serve as perfect reference material for all teachers, teacher-students and other readers also. If that much is achieved, the undersigned would feel contented and honoured.

–Editor

Syllabus

ESSENTIALS OF INSTRUCTIONAL TECHNOLOGY

Unit I. Teaching & Its Models

(i) Concept of teaching.

(ii) Characteristics & functions of teaching.

(iii) Phases of teaching (Jackson)

(iv) Principles & maxims of teaching

(v) Concept attainment model (J. Burner)

(vi) Synectics model (W. Gordon)

Each Model is to be discussed along the following :

Syntx; Social System; Principles of Reaction; Support system; Instructional effect and Application.

Unit II. Audio-visual Aids & Teaching Devices

(i) Meaning & advantages of A-V- aids

(ii) Types of Audio-Visual Aids

- (a) Projected : Film, Film Strips, Overhead Projector, Slides
- (b) Non-Projected : Graphics, 3-D aids, Display boards, Audio aids.
- (c) Use of Radio, TV & Newspaper as teaching aids.

(iii) Teaching Devices

- (a) Meaning & Importance
- (b) Home Assignment, Discussion, Dramatization
- (c) Illustration, Lecturing, Narration

(d) Objservation, Source Method, Story Telling

(e) Study habits & Supervised Study.

Unit III. Techniques of Teacher-preparation

(i) Microteaching : Nature & Meaning, Main proposition, Phases, Steps, Merits & Limitations.

(ii) Simulated Teaching : Nature & Meaning, Mechanism, Role Play & T-group, Advantages & Limitations

(iii) Programmed Learning : Meaning & Characteristics, Principles & Development of the Programmed Instructions, Types, Merits & Demerits

Unit IV. Taxonomy of Educational Objectives & Lesson Planning

(i) Blooms, Taxonomy of instructional objectives : Cognitive, Affective & Psychomotor domains

(ii) Formulation of Instructional Objectives (Mager's)

(iii) Meaning & Significance of Lesson Planning

(iv) Approaches to Lesson Planning

(a) The Herbartian Steps

(b) Gloverian approach

(v) Skill lesson & Appreciation lesson

Unit V. A Detailed Disscusion of the Following :

(i) Play way Method

(ii) Dalton Plan

(iii) The Project Method

(iv) Heuristic Method

1
Models of Teaching

For those, who like it and love it, teaching is a very interesting activity. It may be boring for some people who are in the teaching profession due to some compulsions. The teacher who likes teaching wants to continue with teaching forever. Such a teacher has everlasting desire to improve teaching.

Every good teacher is able to establish his own model of teaching in the course of his life-span of teaching. That way good teachers give rise to good models of teaching. Teaching models can improve the activity of teaching in class room situations to a great extent.

Concept of Teaching

Teaching is a process which usually takes place in the class room situations. It is more of a formal process. In the class room situations, we see that the teacher has something in his mind and he wants to convey it to the students. For this purpose, he takes the help of teaching. He makes all efforts to make the students understand it. His teaching is successful if the students are able to grasp it fully. Through teaching, the teacher aims at:

(i) giving some knowledge to the students;

(ii) passing some information to them;

(iii) making the students acquire some skill;

(iv) changing the attitude of the learners;

(v) modifying the behaviour of the students;

(vi) giving some experiences of life; etc.

Teaching in the class depends upon how the teacher performs his duty of teaching. A sincere and hard working teacher always comes out all successful. He makes every effort to achieve the desired ends. He always goes well prepared in every way. In his class room teaching, there is always a very good class room interaction. He faces the class clearly and boldly. He is always face to face with the students while speaking in the class. Naturally, that type of teacher will be able to impress the students fully. Such a teaching can be called effective teaching.

Teaching may also take place outside the class rooms. The students come in contact with their teacher in the corridors, in the staff room, in the canteen, in the play ground, in the school assembly grounds etc. The process of teaching surely goes on there also which is more of informal type. Learning by the students through informal contacts with the teacher is many a time more sound and lasts longer.

In fact, teaching is an art of educating other people. In this age of science and technology when there is explosion of knowledge, the process of teaching has reached new dimensions. It is no longer a simple art of imparting information to the students. It is now tending to become a technology by itself Instructional Television, Computer Assisted Instruction, Teaching Machines, etc.

Teaching is an activity which goes on between the two parties i.e. the giver and the receiver. Here the giver is the teacher more matured person with more experiences of life. The receiver may be an individual, a small group or a big group.

Henry Von Dyke says, "And what is teaching? Ah! There you have the worst paid and best rewarded of all vocations. Dare not to enter it unless you love it. For the vast majority of men and women, it has no promise of wealth and fame, but they to whom it is dear for its own sake, are among the nobility of mankind. I sing the praise of the unknown teacher, king of himself and leader of mankind."

By mercenary standards, teaching is poorly paid, its riches are of another order, less tangible but more lasting-the satisfaction involved in influencing others and of personal fulfilment. There is little reward in teaching for those who worship money. There is much for those who worship God. Teaching is thus not everybody's cup of tea. It is not a soft option, it requires blood, sweat and tears.

Decidedly, teaching is more than standing before a class and applying a few specific techniques. Teaching is not merely presenting textbook information and then testing students' ability to repeat it. There is no magic formula for transforming knowledge from the teachers's mind to the pupils. Teaching is not a mechanical process. It is an intricate, exacting, challenging job. Teaching can't be boiled down to a convenient formula of "telling and testing". It is the complex art of guiding pupils through a variety of selected experiences towards the attainment of a widening field of learning. Teaching is not a simple affair as some people say, it is very comprehensive. The more we dig out of it, the deeper it becomes. Only a small fraction of it has been understood so far.

A Few Definitions of Teaching

(i) According to Rabindra Nath Tagore, "A Teacher can never truly teach unless he is still learning himself. A lamp can never light another lamp unless it continues to burn its own flame."

In the above given definition, Rabindra Nath Tagore has summed up the qualities of a good teacher. A good learner can he a good teacher. One who does not learn and acquire uptodate knowledge cannot teach others. Teacher's job is just like that of a lamp. Unless the lamp is burning, it cannot light another lamp with its name.

(ii) H.C. Morrison (1934) says; "Teaching is an intimate contact between a more mature personality and less mature one which is designed to further the education of the latter."

(iii) Teaching is a matter of helping the child to respond to his environment in an effective manner. John Brubacher and Simpson have rightly remarked that teaching is the means whereby society trains the young in a selected environment as quickly as possible to adjustment lives to the world in which they live.

(iv) John Brubacher (1939) : "Teaching is an arrangement and manipulation of a situation in which there are gaps and obstructions which an individual will seek to overcome and from which he will learn in the course of doing so."

(v) B.D. Smith (1961) : a very leading technologist of education said: "Teaching is a system of actions intended to induce learning."

(vi) N.L, Gage (1962) : "Teaching is a form of interpersonal influence aimed at changing the behaviour potential of another person."

(vii) B.O. Smith (1963) : "Teaching is a system of action involving an agent, and in view a situation including two sets of factors those over which the agent has no control (class size, size of class-room, physical characteristics of pupils etc,) and those that he can modify ways of asking questions almost instruction and ways of structuring information or ideas gleaned."

(viii) Edmund Amidon (1967) : "Teaching is defined as an interactive process, primarily involving class-room talk which takes place between teacher and pupils and occurs during certain definable activities."

(ix) Clarke (1970) : Teaching refers to "activities that are designed and performed to produce change in student (pupil) behaviour."

(x) Thomas F. Green (1971) : "Teaching is the task of teacher which is performed for the development of a child."

(xi) According to Ryburn : "Teaching includes the training of emotions of the child. It is one of the means of giving right feeling to the children."

(xii) In the words of Floyd Weil : "Children are notoriously curious about everything except the things people want them to know. It then remains for us to refrain from forcing any kind of knowledge upon them and they will be curious about everything."

(xiii) John Dewey : "One might as well say he has sold when no one has bought, as to say he has taught when no one has learned."

(xiv) Paul Goodman; "A good teacher feels his way, looking for response."

(xv) William Lyon : "In my mind teaching is not merely a life work, a profession, an occupation a struggle. It is a passion. I love to teach, as a painter loves to paint, as a musician loves to play, as a singer loves to singer, as a strong man rejoices to run a race."

(xvi) According to John Chapman : "The gift of teaching is a peculiar talent, and it implies a need and cravelling in the teacher himself."

(xvii) J. Welton : "To know where the pupils are and where they should try to be are the first two essentials of good teaching."

(xviii) Michael Oakeshort defines teaching as "two-fold activity of communicating information and communicating judgement."

(xix) According to American Educational Research Association Committee on the 'Handbook of research on Teaching', 1962 "Teaching is a form of interpersonal influence aimed at changing the behaviour potential of another person."

(xx) Israel Sheffler says; "Teaching may be characterized as an activity aimed at the achievement of learning and practised in such a manner as to respect the students' intellectual integrity and capacity for independent judgement."

(xxi) Burton has given a very precise but comprehensive definition of teaching as "Teaching is the stimulation, guidance, direction and encouragement of learning."

Out of the definitions enlisted above, it is rather difficult to find out which one out of them is more accurate and suitable. In fact, a good definition can be all aged on the basis of some criterion.

It should clarify:

(i) whether teaching is a process or a product.

(ii) the objectives.

(iii) the structural aspect.

But we find that none of the definitions comes out to be comprehensive. The functional definition can be:

Teaching is a tripolar process which involves active participation of the teacher, the learner and the teaching-learning situation leading to the modification in the behaviour of the learner.

Prof. K.P. Pandey has given a very functional definition "Teaching is an influence- directed activity, it is influencing the learner with a content structure."

Characteristics of Teaching

Nature of teaching is revealed to us fully if we try to enlist its fundamental characteristics. A few characteristics of teaching are discussed here below:

1. Teaching is not One Sided : Any teaching which keeps the teacher active and does not care for the learners is no teaching at all howsoever good the teacher may be. Both the teacher and the learners have to be fully active. It is, therefore, not one sided affair only. The teacher is face to face with the students, they interact with him and cause teaching-learning. The real teacher is able to create something good by his formal and informal contacts with the learners. And above all, teaching which keeps the teacher alone active and the students just passive listeners is no teaching in the real sense of the word though the many so-called teachers and administrators may name it teaching. And what goes on in the routine type of teaching situations may not be teaching really.

Teaching — A Bipolar Process : The saying that 'teaching is a bi-polar process' is true which means it is a two-way traffic. In the process of teaching, both the teacher and the harner are engaged actively. Teaching is not possible in the absence of learner.

Teaching — A Tripolar Process : Now in the context of modern developments, teaching is a tri-polar process because the surroundings, the environment in which teaching-learning goes on cannot be excluded. It plays an equally important role. Any teaching-learning which is devoid of the environment cannot be called good teaching. Through teaching the learner is enabled to exist successfully in his environment play their unique roles in the process of teaching.

Teaching is not an Independent Activity : Teaching is not an independent activity. It does not take place in the vacuum. It takes place in some social set up where the teacher aims at improving the behaviour of the, individual or some social group. He also furthers the physical, cultural, moral, academic growth of the individuals. In this process of all round growth and development of social beings the teacher also comes out to be a far better individual with his knowledge updated 'and' enriched.

Teaching is both Formal and Informal : Teaching may occur formally or it may also be there informally. In both the ways it meets the desired ends by and large. In the class-room, the teacher and the students meet in a formal way and teaching takes place. Outside the class-room also, the teacher and the students meet where teaching does take place but that is informal teaching. Both formal and informal ways help in reaching the desired goals.

Teaching is Related to Time and Place : Teaching is always concerned with the social set up of life and cultural environment of the people. The society-its values, ideals etc. go on changing with the passage of time. Hence teaching also undergoes some changes. In a democratic set up of life, teaching is based on the principles of democracy. The teacher gives importance to democratic values of life. Teaching also varies from place to place. In India, teaching is carried on in a different way. In the U.S.A. or the Russia teaching has to be varied in accordance with the norms of those places.

Teaching is an Art : Every Tom, Dick and Harry cannot be good at teaching. It is an art which is favourite of the selected few. Such persons have craze for teaching. They find themselves fully engrossed in the process of teaching. Surely with them teaching is more a mission than a profession. Addison rightly points out that sculpture is to a block of marble, what education is to the human soul. The teacher unconsciously designs the child entrusted to him. Always and in every case and in every situation, the teacher is proceeding in his teaching with a purpose and accordingly he modifies the child under his charge.

Teaching is both an art as well as science as Silvermal (1966) expresses it in the following words : —

"To be sure-teaching like the practice of medicine- is very much an art which is to say, it calls for exercise of talent and creativity. But like medicine, it is also a science, for it involves a repertoire of techniques, procedures and skills, that can be systematically studied and described and improved. A good teacher like a great doctor is one who adds creativity and inspiration to the bask repertoire."

Teaching an Interactive Process : Teaching is an interactive process which is carried out for the attainment of some specific purposes and objectives. The purpose may be academic growth of the learner, his physical improvement, making him economically sound, making him bold and courageous so that he may resist and exist well in the present conditions of life.

Teaching is Worthy of Observation and Analysis : Teaching can be observed, analysed and assessed. The analysis and assessment may provide essential feed-back for bringing desirable improvement in the process of teaching. The improvement can be brought about in the teacher, in the learner or in the teaching-learning situations.

Teaching is Dominated by the Communication Skills : The various communication skills dominate the process of teaching. The better the communication, the better is the process of teaching. In fact, the communication skills make the process of teaching lively and ultimately a success.

Teaching is both Conscious and an Unconscious Process : The most effective part of it is generally the part of which we are unconscious. In many situations, teaching goes on very unconsciously and then it is as meaningful as otherwise.

Teaching is Task Oriented : Teaching is a process both of conscious and unconscious type. Teaching is a process where task is the objective already fixed up. Teaching has to ensure the attainment of those objectives.

Teaching is a Planned Activity : Teaching is a well planned activity. It is organised in a very systematic way. A lot of thinking is done on it in advance. Once teaching is started by the teacher class room situation, it goes on systematically and smoothly.

Teaching is Intentional : In teaching, there is intentional behaviour of the teacher. It aims at changing the behaviour of others.

Teaching is a Professional Activity : Teaching is an activity which is carried on by the professionals. This activity involves the teacher and the learner and as a result of it, there is development of the student.

Teaching Causes Motivation : The activity of teaching causes motivation. That results into learning.

Teaching is Providing Guidance : Teaching activity guides the learners. As a result of teaching, the students are able to learn the right things, in the right ways and at the right time.

Teaching is Causing to Learn : Teaching is to cause the pupil to learn and acquire the desired knowledge. The pupil is not like an empty vessel in which the teacher is to put knowledge. In fact, the teacher is to help the child in learning. He is expected to make the learner a willing learner. That type of teaching is good which causes the pupil to learn well.

Teaching is Diagnostic : In teaching the teacher acts as a doctor. The process of teaching aims at diagnosing the ills and drawbacks of the learner. These ills are wiped out and suitable remedies are given by the teacher through his process of teaching.

Good Teaching Liberates the Learner : The ideal of good teaching is to develop initiative, independence in thought, self reliance and confidence among the pupils. So as a result of teaching, the learners are able to attack their problems independently and work out solutions. The ideal of good teaching is to liberate the child.

Good Teaching is Democratic : The good teacher always respects the individuality of his pupils. Good teaching attempts to create a democratic environment in which the rights of the individual are respected. In this environment, the teacher thinks that each individual is entitled to equal rights with every other individual in the class and that he is subject to the same rules with respect to equality as other pupils.

The real teacher is wedded to teaching. It is rather impossible to separate him from teaching. In the course of his teaching the teacher mirrors himself into the child, he puts indelible stamp on the young growing plastic mind of the child. That is why every learner reflects the personality of his teacher to a considerable extent. A sincere honest, punctual and hard working student means that his teacher has been of that type. The hard fact is that the child is what his teacher has made him. The nation needs good teachers today. Let the teachers rise to the occasion and come up to the expectations of all concerned by doing their duties towards the children right earnestly.

Teacher's performance is the most crucial input in the field of education. However lofty the aims, however uptodate and abundant the equipment, however effective the administration, whatever the policies may be laid down, in the ultimate analysis these have to be interpreted and implemented by the teachers as much through their personal example as through teaching-learning process.

Only to give knowledge of limited courses is not teaching. Its main aim is to maintain the mind of the child which should not depend upon the choice of the teacher. It also depends upon the liking of the learner. In the words of Finey Peter Dunne : "It does not make much difference what you study as long as you do not like it."

Teaching is a noble profession and the teacher is the architect of the destiny of the nation. Good teaching considerably depends upon the qualities of the teacher. A good teacher:

- inspires others with his ways of teaching and working.
- is neither too harsh nor to lenient.
- helps the weak students to tide over their difficulties.
- maintains his dignity by following a set code of conduct.
- lights many candles with his wisdom and service to the community.

In the words of Rabindra Nath Tagore, "The basis of teaching are love, understanding and care. Freedom should be given to the students in order to express themselves. The teacher is the moving spirit in all this. He is considered a guide and friend who understands the 'child well. One who has lost the child in himself is totally unfit to' undertake the task of educating children."

In teaching, the teacher must pay attention to the entire complex organism. He is concerned with the all round development of the child-intellectually. Emotionally, socially, spiritually and in some degree physically. Therefore, the modern teaching-learning process keeps the learner at the centre.

The child is the focal point on which the whole attention of the teacher is devoted. The teacher has to see that the subject matter is appreciated by the learner. He takes the learner as the starting point and through the process of teaching he is to make the learner go ahead keeping himself with him all through. It may be compared to a race where the learner is the participant competing and the teacher is the referee who is running alongwith the learner taking care of him all through. For the faults, the teacher has to set him right and above all, he is to see that the competitor in the race wins as per his own wishes. In other words, the teacher has to modify his behaviour in terms of the goals already fixed. Teaching, thus, ensures learning in a guaranteed way.

Relation of Teaching with other Related Concepts : The terms like training instructions, conditioning and indoctrination etc. are sometimes taken as synonymous with teaching. In fact, these terms denote one or other type of teaching. The teaching is a broader concept and these are a part or one aspect of it.

Training is concerned with a little more raised level of teaching than conditioning, which is the lowest level of a mode of teaching. A trained person can do a number of jobs on some machines skillfully. Training helps in shaping, conducting and teaching various skills.

As compared to teaching, training requires much less intelligence. Simple behaviour may be produced through training but not complicated behaviour.

Instruction works on higher footing than conditioning and training. Instruction is mainly concerned with the development of knowledge and understanding in an individual. Teaching is much more than the act of acquiring some knowledge and understanding. Instruction cares only for development of intellect and affects the cognitive domain of one's behaviour, while teaching is aimed at shaping a total man. And lastly, the face to face interaction of the teacher and taught is found in teaching. It is not essential in the process of ins-truction. Here, the teacher can be replaced by instructional materials.

Indoctrination represents a fairly higher level of teaching which adds to the establishment or shaping of beliefs and ideas. Higher role of intelligence is required here. It results in bringing quite stable changes in the cognitive and affective domains of one's behaviour. But, indoctrination is only one mode of teaching. Indoctrination may be teaching but the reverse is not true. Teaching is possible without adopting indoctrination as the mode of teaching.

The above mentioned modes of teaching cannot be termed as quite unrelated. They overlap each other in many ways.

Functions of Teaching

The independent and dependent variables perform three major functions which are explained below:

Diagnostic Function : The teacher as an independent variable is more active in this function. He has to diagnose the entering behaviour of the learner. He has also to find out the structure of the content for writing the teaching objectives in behavioural terms. The teacher comes to know fully about the behaviour of the learner and so he is able to proceed in his teaching work according to the requirements of the learners. He analyses the problems that he can foresee in the teaching process and he thinks of their solutions. He also finds out the individual variations in the learners and so he plans strategies of teaching suiting to their requirements. He also analyses the contents into elements and then they are arranged logically in sequence so that they are taught in some easy ways.

The student as a dependent variable also performs the diagnostic functions. The learner comes to know his own speed of perceiving the subject matter and for how long he, can retain that. He is able to know about his language, comprehension, abilities, skills and expression.

Prescriptive Function : Prescriptive function means that in the process of teaching, the teacher has the privilege to prescribe certain things for the leaders. Through diagnosis, he is able to see almost the mental abilities, capability and capacity of the learner-his likes, dislikes, the individual differences of the learners etc. On the basis of all this information the teacher finds it easy to prescribe for the students the contents suitable to their requirements, the different strategies which can work well so as to have the desired goals.

Evaluative Function : What does evaluative function mean? It has its concern with the diagnostic and prescriptive functions. To understand it clearly, let us compare this with the doctor treating the patient. First of all, the doctor makes diagnosis, then he prescribes some medicine and after that evaluation is done to see whether both diagnosis and prescription are all right. In the teaching process, realisation of objectives will indicate the success at the earlier two stages of diagnosing and prescribing. Mistakes in diagnosis or in prescribing are spell out through evaluative functioning of teaching.

The evaluative functioning concerns the teacher as well as the learner. Both of them are able to evaluate for themselves. The teacher has to take the help of various evaluation devices such as tests, observations, interview, rating scales, inventories etc. He prepares all these test items, applies them and then finds out the results. The learner also is able to evaluate himself. He knows definitely and there is no behavioural change, he consults the teacher again so that he is able to make fresh diagnosis and also prescribe again.

Here both the teacher and the learner are active in the evaluative function though the former comparatively is more active as compared to the latter.

Phases of Teaching

Teaching is a quite complex, social, cultural and ethical process designed in a social or cultural context. Therefore, to make this job successful and easy, we have to make a systematic planning. Teaching has to be done in steps. The different steps constituting the process are called the phases of teaching. There are three phases of teaching:

(i) Pre-active Phase of Teaching.

(ii) Inter-active Phase of Teaching.

(iii) Post-active Phase of Teaching.

	1. Pre-active Phase
Teaching	2. Inter-active Phase
	3. Post-active phase

The Pre-active Phase

'Pre-active phase' as the name implies is concerned with the preparation for teaching. It is the preparation in the class-room activity. It is also called the planning stage or the paration stage. This phase consists of the following two steps:

(i) Fixing up the goals.

(ii) Finding out ways and means to achieve those goals.

For any type of teaching, the teacher first of all fixes up the goals. He writes those objectives in a systematic way in behavioural terms. Then he thinks of the methods and techniques to be followed for achieving them.

At this stage, the teacher plans the lesson, how he will introduce the topic, how he will motivate the students, how he will go about teaching the whole lesson. Whether he will teach by using lecture method or demonstration method or some other method, with or without aids. If some aids are to be used, he will check up whether those aids are ready, then at what time during teaching he will use those aids Thus everything about the lesson before its start, is planned.

Inter-active Phase

This is the stage when actual teaching-learning takes place. This is the execution or implementation stage of the planned lesson. Here the teacher and the taught are actually participating in the teaching-learning process. No doubt, the teacher teaches according to his plan but that plan is not followed rigidly. It is rather kept flexible. Wherever the learners find some problems in understanding, the teacher helps them in every way. In case need arises, he may give more examples. Success or failure of this step will reflect the interaction of the teacher and the taught. It consists of three points:

1. Perception
2. Diagnosis
3. Reaction

Perception : Perception means to perceive-it involves perception on the part of the teacher as well as the students. On entering into the class, the teacher tries to perceive the class room climate. He sees within his oneself in comparison with the class. The students also perceive the behaviour, personality and capability of the teacher so as to have desirable interaction in the teaching learning process.

Diagnosis : The teacher tries to assess the mental ability, attitude, interest etc. of his ownself and also of the learners so as to make the phenomenon of teaching-learning easy. The learners also try to form estimate about the teacher and also of themselves. Thus everyone in the class room situation tries to see within his ownself. May be the teacher does more about himself as compared to the students. The simple reason being that a more responsible person shoulders greater responsibility in every situation.

Reaction: It is the actual interaction between the teacher and the taught. The moment the teacher goes in the class room, non verbal reaction starts between him and the students. With his speech, starts the verbal reaction between the two. Through more questions put by the teacher to the students, the reactive process gains momentum. When the students also put the questions to the teacher, it makes teaching all the more learnable for the students. Thus action and reaction makes teaching go on and ultimately makes it a success.

The Post-active Phase

This stage is also known as the evaluation stage. It is related, with both teaching and learning. The teacher analyses and is able to see whether the methods or strategies used by him were successful and if so to what extent. Whether the students grasped the basic thing or not? If 'yes' to what extent, if 'not' why of it and then the remedies. It is a clear cut assessment of the interaction process. It helps the teacher to teach things better in future and also the students to learn things better. The desirable improvement in the teaching-learning can be made on the basis of the assessment made. The teacher is able to decide whether he should proceed to the new contents or he should reteach what has already been taught.

Thus we find that all the three phases of teaching-learning process are important in their own ways. They are all inter-related and inter-dependent. Each one helps in modifying the other so as to make it more meaningful and significant.

Structure of Teaching

"In order to understand the process of teaching, it would be better if we find out its structure and understand it. Anatomy of teaching reveals the following elements:

Signs and Symbols : When we observe a teacher teaching in the class-room, we find that he is frequently using signs and symbols. He uses the signs and symbols at different stages of teaching. i.e. at diagnostic stage, prescriptive stage evaluative stage. In this way, the teacher is able to catch their attention. He is able to communicate well. The students also make use of signs and symbols while expressing themselves. The use of signs and symbols make the whole process of teaching-learning economical and easy.

Teaching - A Linguistic Process : While teaching, the teacher aims at better communication between the teacher and the taught.

He is expected to explain the concepts describe certain things, motivate the students and above all, enhance verbal interaction. All this is possible through the use of a language. So it is language which helps the teacher to have a start in teaching and ultimately makes him successful in the attainment of objectives.

Teaching and Logic : During the process of teaching, the teacher has to ensure his success in the teaching-learning process. He takes the help of logic for this purpose. Whatever he does, whatever he plans and whatever he thinks, logic is the basis guarantees his overall success in the teaching process.

A good teaching means good learning. A good teaching means effective teaching where the teacher as well as his teaching are models and methodology of teaching is quite suitable for the situation as well as for the learners. The teacher as well as the learners have to be face to face with each other, then only there is effective learning. Suppose there is a teaching-learning situation where the class is sitting and the teacher is teaching. In that situation, if the teacher looks upwards and goes on speaking or he is looking at his lecture notes and does not look towards the students continuously, there will not be good learning by the students. In the same way if some learner or learners do not face the teacher while listening to him and instead they are busy with writing in their notebooks or they are gazing at their books or note-books, they may not be able to receive the whole thing fully from the teacher. Their grasp of the subject matter will not be maximum. So the teacher's posture during teaching has to be inter-active with the students who are face to face looking towards the teacher.

Sometimes the teacher is writing on the blackboard. If he goes on speaking while looking towards the blackboard and not towards the students, in this situation also there will be lesser reception of the subject matter by the learners.

No doubt, teaching centres round speaking by the teacher and listening by the students. But other things like habits, attitude, gestures shown by the teacher i.e. punctuality, regularity, honesty, truthfulness, straight forwardness, impartial behaviour etc. also have their impact on the learning by the students. Whatever etiquettes are shown by the teacher in the class-room the same are reflected in the learners through their actions on their behaviour in different situations. Only an honest teacher can produce honest learners in his class-rooms. Therefore, teacher and his teaching ought to be ideal one only then we shall be able to have ideal learners.

Whatever may be the situations, whatever may be the environment favourable or unfavourable, a good teacher succeeds in teaching. He is able to attain the targets of good learning. The teacher has to be educational technologist. His concern is to help an educator to devise the most suitable and efficient strategy within the resource available to optimize students learning.

QUESTIONS

1. What do you understand by teaching? Discuss some suitable definition of teaching.
2. Describe briefly the nature and characteristics of the concept of teaching.
3. What are the different variables of teaching? Discuss their functions briefly.
4. What are the different phases of teaching? Discuss their importance. Which phase do you think is the most important?
5. What is the concept of teaching? Define it and describe the characteristics of teaching task.
6. Explain in details the operations of interactive stage of teaching. How are these operations different from those used during the operative and post-active stages of teaching.
7. Write notes on:
   - (i) Concept of Teaching.
   - (ii) Any Phase of Teaching.
   - (iii) Anyone definition of Teaching.

2

Teaching : Principles and Maxims

It is a complex social and cultural phenomenon. Teaching is not as easy to teach as it appears. While teaching, a teacher has to keep in mind the aims and objectives of his subject, needs, interests of his pupils, the environmental situations suitable for them etc. Success of this profession depends upon good planning and mastery in the subject to be taught. Hence for helping the teacher, some principles have been designed on the basis of general experiences, traditions and researches. These principles provide guidelines to the teacher as to what methods should be adopted in the class room to increase the teaching efficiency.

A good teacher always wants that his teaching should be effective. He wants that all the students of the class should properly attend, listen to him and try to grasp what he teaches in the class. The principles evolved help the teacher to carryon his routine of teaching efficiently. They provide him guidelines and keep him on the right track. They check him from going away. They ensure good achievements for the teacher in the process of teaching.

General Principles of Teaching

A few principles of teaching which are of general nature are explained below :

Principle of Definite Objectives : While teaching anything the teacher should first of all fix up some objectives. Then he can select the material, use the appropriate methods and then ultimately ensure the attainment of those objectives. In the absence of definite objectives, teaching may not remain a purposeful activity. The learners may also deviate and may fail to achieve anything solid.

Objectives may vary from subject and from time to time. Behind teaching English, the objectives usually are listening, speaking, reading and writing. But at present in free India, the objective of reading for comprehension is being emphasized. So in teaching, the objectives should be fixed and then efforts be made to achieve them.

Principle of Model Presentation : The teacher who presents the material while teaching should see that his presentation is really a model one in every way. The personality of the teacher, his behaviour, actions etc. should be model. The learners imitate the teacher to the maximum. So the teacher should present all excellencies of life in him which he ultimately wants the learners to acquire in life. The pronunciation of the language that he uses for teaching should be reasonably good. Through his behaviour he should reflect regularity, punctuality, honesty, truth, sincerity etc. Then only he will be able to make his learners reach the goals of ideal life. That way only his teaching will come out to be worthwhile and profit yielding for that humanity.

Principle of Selection of Material : In teaching whatever material is to be presented by the teacher should be well selected. It should be in accordance with the aims and objectives of teaching. It should also be according to the likings and the mental level of the learners. Then only it will be digested by the students properly. The right selection of material will result into proper teaching and hence desired results will be achieved.

Suppose the teacher wants to teach composition. For this, he selects topics keeping the syllabus in view, the mental level of their teaching ability, their learning ability etc. The type of material will make the teaching efficient.

Principle of Gradation : The material which is selected should be graded properly. By gradation, we mean which item will come at serial No.1 which item after that and which item at the end. While grading the material, easy and simple things will come first and difficult and complicated things win occur afterwards. Thus placement of material in graded tonne will make teaching-learning process more effective.

Suppose the teacher has selected to essays of English for teaching some school class. By gradation, those essays will be numbered as 1,2,3 etc. which means that essay no. 1 will be taught first and essay no.2 will come after No.1 and so on.

Principle of Activity : The traditional methods of filling up the minds of the children with a lot of information are useless now. The learners sitting passive in the class are not considered good students. Teaching-learning is a bipolar process. Both the teacher and the students should remain active. The more the activity of the children, the better is the teaching-learning process.

Every subject, every topic within a subject can be taught through activity method. An intelligent teacher tries to involve the maximum number of students in his teaching. That makes guaranteed learning by the students. Moreover, the students do not feel any type of lethargy or boredom.

Principle or Correlation : Good teaching makes the students feel everything for better life. The learner in the class room feels as if he is being prepared for better life. A good teacher tries to correlate his teaching with life. He also tries to correlate one subject with various other subjects which the student is expected to study.

According to John Dewey "Education and life are two different names for the same phenomenon. Education which does not prepare the student for life is meaningless. Suppose the teacher is teaching arithmetic to the students, he should enable the students to apply that knowledge in his day today life situations. While making purchases in the market, the student can apply the knowledge of mathematics and thus he feels happy and satisfied. The teacher of English should also teach English in such a way that the student fed that he is becoming a better social being by the study of this subject. He should be enabled to speak English with his parents, relatives, teachers or friends. He should also be able to listen to T.V. Programmes telecast in English. It will give him a lot of confidence.

While teaching one subject the teacher should try to correlate that subject with some other subjects which the student studies. It will make his whole studies interesting for him. The child may also get a sort of feelings that the different subjects are preparing him for better life.

Principle of Child Centredness : Teaching should be made child centered as far as possible and it should not be allowed to remain teacher centered as it has been so far. By child centredness we mean interest and liking of the student should be made meaningful for the child. It should be taught to the child as per his liking and in no case it should be thirsted upon him. Thus the child who is not interested in studies should not be compelled to study. He should first of all be mentally prepared for studies. Then only any teaching done for him will be of any use.

Suppose the child wants to study English. In that case, the teacher should teach him that subject and not some other subject which the parents want to teach. An intelligent teacher is able to deal with this type of situations very wisely. In the above situation, he initiates teaching English to the child as per his desire but gradually he makes the child shift to the other subject which the teacher wants to teach.

Principle of Cooperation : Teaching learning is a cooperative venture of all concerned. For best teaching, the teacher, the students, the Head of the institution, the parents and everyone else concerned with it cooperates. Then only there is efficient teaching and good learning by the students. Sometimes the Head of the school does not cooperate with the teachers, the result is poor teaching. Thus, co-operation of the teacher, the taught and the Head of the institution forms the basis of efficient teaching-learning.

Principle of Planning : The principle of planning is the *sine qua-non* of efficient teaching. The teacher comes prepared with everything planned before entering into the class. He tries to foresee the problems and he thinks of their possible solutions. Thus the principle of planning helps him to perform his duty of teaching excellently. A good teacher keep his planning flexible-throughout. He may mould things here or there according to the needs and requirements of the learners in different situations.

Principle of Individual Differences : In any group of students, no two individuals are exactly the same. There are always variations as far as likings and disliking, attitudes and aptitudes are concerned. The teacher teaching the whole group by using one and the same method and dealing with everyone in the same way will fail miserably. A good teacher expects the individual differences among the students. He tries to deal with the students according to their individual differences. He tries to satisfy one and all by using different tactics and strategies of teaching.

Principle of Democracy : In a successful teaching democratic environment is created. In such an atmosphere there are many a characteristic

Characteristics

1. The models are teaching strategies.
2. They are a sort of guidelines.
3. They are of prescriptive type.
4. They help in the accomplishment of instructional goals.
5. They help the teacher in designing instructional activities and environmental facilities.
6. They can be used to shape a curriculum.

Thus, we find that teaching models are of great value and they can work wonders in the hands of teachers. Whatever may be their significance, but they are just like a servant in the hands of an experienced teacher. They are in no way the masters. Under good control, they can be used for the attainment of various useful purposes.

Different Models of Teaching

The different teaching model are enlisted here below :

1.	Against Dogmatism	Alternate Models of teaching,
2.	Concept Attainment	The Basics of Thinking.
3.	Inductive Thinking	Collecting Organising and Manipulating Data.
4.	Inquiry Training	From Facts to Theories
5.	Advance Organizers Lee	Improving the Effectiveness of trues and other Presentations.
6.	Memory Model	Getting the Facts Straight.
7.	Cognitive Growth	Increasing the Capacity to Think.
8.	Biological Science Inquiry Model Researcher's	Approaches Built on the Tools.
9.	Non-Directive Teaching	Counselling Method as a Model.
10.	Syenites	A Model to Develop Creativity.
11.	Awareness Training	A Model to Increase Human Awareness.
12.	Class-room Meeting Model	Mental Health Through Group Process.
13.	Group Investigation	Democratic Process as a Source.

14.	Role Playing	Studying Social Behaviour and values
15.	Jurisprudential Inquiry	Clarifying Public Issues.
16.	Laboratory Training	To Group Model.
17.	Social Simulation	Interactive Games and Other Approaches.
18.	Social Inquiry	A Social Inquiry Model.
19.	Contingency Management	Recognizing Cause and Effect.
20.	Self-Control Through Operant Methods	Managing our own Environment.
21.	Training Model	Design, Demonstrate, Practice and Feedback.
22.	Stress Reduction	A Basic Procedure for reducing Anxiety.
23.	Desensitization	Replacing Anxiety with Relaxation.
24.	Assertiveness Training	Expressing Feelings Honestly and Directly.
25.	A Model for Matching Environment to People	Conceptual System Theory.
26.	Mastery Learning as a Consideration	Making Time Count for the Lamer.
27.	The Conditions of Learning	Focusing Instruction.
28.	Models of Teaching and Educational Objectives	Boosting Learning of various kinds.

Types of Teaching Models

There are a number of teaching models available for use by the teachers. Every model is based on some theory founded by researchers. The teacher has be the right model in accordance with the objectives. Different researchers have tried to put the models to various categories.

In 1975 Hillgard and Bower tried, in 1977 an effort was made by Paterson, and thereafter Dececco and Crawford also suggested. In 1980, Joyce and Weil of Ped the models into the following four major families.

Information Processing Models : In the words of Joyce and Weil (1972) "Information processing refers to the way people handle stimuli from the environment, organise data, sense problems, generate concepts and solutions to problems and employ verbal and non-verbal symbols."

This type of models help the students to develop the methods of processing information from the environment. Models of this category are concerned with the intellectual growth rather than the emotional or social development of the individual. For example: Concept Attainment Model (Jerome Bruner), Inquiry Training Model (Richard Suchman), Development Model (Jean Piaget and Others), Advance Organizer Model (David Ausubel), Inductive Thinking Model (Hilda Taba).

Social Interaction Models : Teaching models of this group help in social interaction. They bring social efficiency in an individual. In the words of Weil and Joyce, "These models give priority to the improvement of democratic processes and the improvement of the society to the improvement of individual's ability." The models of this group lay more and more emphasis on the development of society.

A few examples of this type of models are Social Inquiry Model (Byron, Massialas and Benjamin Cox) Group Investigation Model (Herbert, Thelen and John Dewey) Class-room Meeting Model (William Glaser) etc.

Personal Development Models : This type of models help an individual to develop fully in the environment. One is able to realize the personal goals. A few examples of this type of models are : Non-Directive Model (Car Rogers), Awareness Training Model (Fritz Peris), Synctics Model (William Gordon), Conceptual System Model (David Hunt), etc.

Behaviour Modification Models : These models are related with the behaviour modification theories. Operant conditioning has given birth to most of the models belonging to this group. A few examples of this type of models are : The Training Model, Stress Reduction Model, Desensitization Model etc.

The above classification of models suggested by Joyce alld Weil should not be taken up in water tight compartmentalization. One model may have many objectives and that way it can be considered in the other family or group.

Elements of a Teaching Model

Each Teaching model is of unique importance in the teaching-learning process. The teacher should have a good working knowledge of it. Only then he will be able to use it fruitfully. The fundamental elements of a teaching model are :

Focus : Focus means the central thing of a teaching model. It highlights the main objectives of the teaching model. The objectives in relation to the environment of the learners are given.

Syntax : Syntax means the detailed description of the model in action. Each model has some phases and activities which are arranged in a specified sequence. By knowing the syntax of a teaching model, the job of the teacher becomes easy. He comes to know how he should begin and proceed further to achieve his objectives.

Principles of Reaction : Each model has a few principles of reaction which concern the teacher. The teacher comes to know how he has to react to the responses/activities of the students. For example, during teaching the teacher puts questions to the students in order to elicit their responses. How will the teacher react to the responses of the students? How he is to accept the right responses and how he will reject the wrong responses by least discouragement?

The whole process of teaching has mainly the four stages *i.e.* objectives, entry behaviour of the learners, the instructional process and assessment of the outcomes. These four stages are interconnected and interdependent. In the light of all these the teacher deals with the students. He accepts or rejects their responses.

The teacher has also to see that in the process of teaching by using a model, the learners have to be actively involved. For this, the teacher has to be very careful. Only through proper understanding between the teacher and the taught, active involvement of the learners in a useful way is possible. Besides, the follow-up in the instructional process also is of great value and that is cared for by the teacher.

Social System : A teaching model deals with the relationship between the teacher and the taught. The interactive role between the two are important. The different interactive roles lead to some type of social links and ties which ultimately grow and bring in social efficiency.

In some models, the teacher is the dominating authority and the whole teaching process centres round him. Directly or indirectly he tries to influence the learners. In some other models the learner hold the key position. But in every way, better ties of relationship are encouraged.

Support System : Each model has a support system that contributes towards the success of the model. It generates proper class-room environment for it. The model functions in such a way that it goes on generating climate which supports it further and makes it function better. Thus support system of every model guarantees its success.

Application : In every teaching model, application is an important element. In the absence of this constituent, teaching may not remain effective. This element describes the application aspect of the model the learner is able to apply the learn things in other situations.

Concepts Oblique Elements of A teaching Model : Views of Joyce and Weil :

Joyce and Weil (1985) describe various concept/elements of a teaching model under four major points :

1. Orientation of the Model, Goals, Assumption.
2. Teaching Model in Terms of Four Concepts;

   (i) Syntax (ii) Social System (Hi) Principles of Reaction and (iv) Support System.
3. Application of the Model.
4. Instructional and Nurturant Effects of the Model.

Orientation of the Model :

Following concepts/elements are discussed under this heading:

1. Goals of the model

2. Theoretical assumptions
3. Principles and other relevant major concept of the teaching model.

Teaching Model in Terms of Four Major Concepts/Elements :

(i) Syntax : Syntax describes the model in action i.e. sequence of activities there are three model the syntax of models differs.

(ii) The Social System : The social system describes the roles of the teacher and the students and their interrelationship. The roles of the teacher and the students very depending upon the structure of the model.

(iii) Principles of Reaction : This aspect highlights the reaction of the teacher in relation to nature of the learner, and response of the learner in a given situation. Depending upon the type of the model, teacher may shape the behaviour using reward for certain student activities or may adopt other reaction in line with the nature of specific model.

(iv) Support System : This aspect/concept/element deals with the supporting conditions necessary for its existence. We are to be see here the additional requirements of the model beyond the usual human skills and capacities and technical facilities.

Application : Application aspect of the model provides information about the use of the model in the classroom. Sometimes this information is an illustration of various subject areas, a guide for age-level adaptations or for curriculum design or suggestions for combining the model with other models of teaching.

Instructional and Nurturant Effects : Instructional effects are the direct effects of the learning environment in the model while nurturant effects are the indirect effects of the learning environment.

Concept Attainment Model (C.A.M.)

The Concept Attainment Model belongs to the category of Information Processing Models. In 1956; Jerome Bruner and his associates developed this teaching model. Usually it is named as Bruner's Concept Attainment Model used for teaching concepts 'to the students, It enables them to understand fully the similarities and relationship among various things present in the all around environment.

Concept Attainment Model is Described under four major headings :

1. Goals & Assumptions 2. Model of Teaching 3. Application 4. Instructional and Nurturant Effects.

Goals. & Assumptions : The assumptions on which this model is based are some basic ideas from the works of Bruner which are briefly given below :

1. In our environment, we are surrounded by a large number of diverse things. Those things are ever increasing. It would become impossible for us to adjust if we are not endowed with the capacity to discriminate, to categorize things in groups and to form concepts.

2. Categorizing things into groups reduces the complexities of the surrounding environment.

3. A concept has three elements (a) examples (b) attributes (c) attribute values. Examples are instances of the concept. The examples may be positive or negative. Attributes are the common features of characteristics. They help in placing the examples in the same category. Each attribute has an attribute value. To have clear understanding of these terms, let us take up an illustration. Suppose the concept is 'apple'. Then each fruit is an example. Oranges and 'grapes are negative examples- whereas apples are positive examples. The colour may be an attribute and red or yellow are the attribute values.

4. The different things are put into categories on the basis of attributes. The categorizing activity has two components- the act of category formation (concept-formation) and the act of concept attainment. This concept formation is the first step which leads to concept attainment.

5. In concept attainment, the concept is determined in advance. Then efforts are made to determine the elements of the concept. The concept formation is an act of contrast and invention. It is an act by which new categories are formed.

6. Concept formation and concept attainment differ significantly in terms of thinking processes require different teaching strategies.

On the basis of the above given ideas, Bruner and his associates developed a number of teaching models. Weil and Joyce (1978) have mentioned three teaching models of concept attainment which are enlisted here below :

(a) The Reception Model of Concept Attainment.

(b) The Selection Model of Concept Attainment.

(c) The Model of Unorganized Material.

Each of the three models given above has a slight different sequence of activities (syntax) but they have been developed from a common conceptual base.

The Model of Teaching

The Reception oriented Model

Following are the four major steps according to Joyce and Weil (1985) with specific reference to reception model of teaching :

1. Syntax
2. Social System
3. Principles of Reaction
4. Support System.

Syntax

Phase-I : Presentation of date and identification of concept. Following steps are followed under phase-I.:

1. Teacher presents labelled examples.
2. Students compare attributes in positive and negative examples.
3. Students generate and test hypotheses.
4. Students state a definition according to essential attributes.

Phase 2 : Testing Attainment of the Concept:

1. Students identify additional unlabeled examples as 'yes' or 'no'.

2. Teacher confirms hypothesis names concept and restates definition according to essential attributes.
3. Students general examples.

Phase 3 : Analysis of the Thinking Strategy.

1. Students describe thoughts.
2. Students discuss role of hypothesis and attributes.
3. Students discuss type and number of hypotheses.

Social System: Social system requires following functions on the part of the teacher:

Functions before teaching in the class :

1. Teacher chooses the concept.
2. He selects the examples.
3. He organises the examples into positive and negative examples.
4. He sequences the positive and negatives examples.

Function during teaching in the class:

1. Teacher keeps a track of the hypotheses and the attributes given by students. Thus, the teacher is required to perform the function of a recorder.
2. He is also required to supply the additional examples as clues are prompts as and when needed.
3. He is also required to present additional data as and when needed.

Principles of Reaction: The following principles of reaction/ response should be followed by the teacher during the flaw of the lesson :

1. Teacher should be supporting of the students hypotheses. He should not discourage them but their responses should be recorded and discussion should be held on the various hypotheses.
2. The students should be helped to pay attention to the analysis of hypotheses.

3. Teacher should encourage or support the use of variety of thinking strategies by students.

Support System : Following points should be taken care of regarding support system :

1. The data sources (positive and negative examples) should be known beforehand.
2. The aspects of concept attainment activity should be clear to the learners.
3. The characteristics/attributes as described by students must be recorded in a column on the blackboard.

Application

1. Concept attainment model may be used with all ages and grade levels.
2. Use of the model with kindergarten children has been found very successful. This has been cbserved that children at this stage love the challenge of the inductive thinking.
3. In case of young children, the lesson based upon concepts attainment model must be short and heavily teacher oriented.

   The concept should be simple, the examples selected for the concept should also be simple.
4. The phase-3rd analysis of thinking strategy is not possible with very young children. The upper elementary level students are responsive to analysis of thinking strategy phase.
5. The reception model of concept attainment is comparatively less useful for secondary level students, the selection and unrecognized models of teaching are more useful as compared to the reception model of teaching.
6. Concept attainment model is also useful in evaluation as a tool/device. Student's understanding in the contents taught earlier can be effectivity measured.
7. New inquiries (individual and group) can also be initiated with the help of the model.

8. Teacher can easily follow the model in their routine teaching learning activities.

Instructional and Nurturant Effects

Instructional Effects :

Achievement of Instructional Objectives : Aims and objectives of any teaching subject can be achieved through the use of lesson using concept attainment model. Students develop the understanding of the concepts. Besides understanding of nature of concepts, they undergo practice in inductive reasoning.

Improvement in Concept Building Strategies : Teacher can develop and improve teaching-learning strategies in the light of the nature of the learner.

Nurturant Effects : Following nurturant effects are also observed through the use of concept attainment strategies :

1. Development of alternative perspectives.
2. Development of sensitivity to logical reasoning in communication.
3. Development of tolerance of ambiguity, but appreciation logic.
4. Development of inductive reasoning.

An Example Illustrating Concept Attainment Model : Suppose the teacher wants to teach the concept of 'Proper Noun'. He teaches the concept as detailed below:

1. The teacher says that he has a concept in his mind. He gives one positive example and one negative example of it.

   (i) Delhi Yes
   (ii) Good No

2. The students are asked to think of the possible categories into which the positive example 'Delhi' can fit in.
3. The students form some hypotheses. They are asked to write down these hypotheses.

   (1) Perhaps the teacher wants to teach about the capital of India.

(2) May be the teacher is teaching about big cities of India.

(3) The teacher wants to teach words formed with (DELHI) five letters.

(4) The teacher wants to teach about some places.

4. Now the students are asked to give one positive example and one negative example. One student speaks :

Positive example		Ambala
Negative example		Bad

Another student gives one more example

Say	Chandigarh	Positive example
	Beautiful	Negative example

Another Student

Palika Vihar	Positive example
Going	Negative example

Thus with the help of more examples, some hypotheses will be rejected by the students and some will still remain in their minds.

More examples will be given by the students. A stage will be reached when the students have only one hypothesis in their minds. They are able to confirm it on the basis of numerous positive and negative examples. At this stage, they are able to analyses the whole data (examples already before them) and they are able to generalize and conclude under the guidance and directive of NCERT which are briefly given below:

Concept Attendance Model (CAM)

Title	*Investigation*
1. Effectiveness of CAM (Reception Oriented) with Variations in Demonstration in terms of Specific Teaching Competencies of Pre-service Teacher Trainees.	Dr. KL. Choudhary & Dr. S.A. Katra
2. Effectiveness of Strategy of Training in CAM of Teaching in terms of Specific	Dr. (Mrs.) S. Bhouraskar and

	Title	Investigator
	Training Out-comes of Pre-service Teacher Trainees, their Understanding, Recreation and Willingness to Implement the Model in the Class-room.	Dr. D.N. Sansanwal
3.	Effectiveness of Strategy of Training in CAM of Pre-service Teacher Trainees.	Mrs. Indra Rani and Dr. M.S. Sachdeva
4.	Effectiveness of Training through CAM Using Different Sequences of Demonstrations DO/DI and PPF in terms of Specified Teaching Competencies of Regular B.Ed. Students of Rohelkhand University.	Dr. V.S. Gupta and Dr. J.S. Jha
5.	Effectiveness of Concept Attainment Model in Variation in Demonstration	Dr. M.S. Bawa Dr. S.K. Bhatia
6.	Effectiveness of Concept Attainment Model with Variation in Demonstration and Peer Practice in Terms of Specific Teaching Competencies of Pre-Service Teacher Trainees.	Mr. G.I. Nagpal and Mr. O.P. Chaudhry
7.	Efficiency of Peer Practice Feedback in Pair and in Quadrant for Training in Concept Attainment Model in terms of Specific Teaching Competencies of B.M.Ed. (Bachelor of Mathematics Education) Students of Nagpur University.	Dr. U.G. Murthy

Inquiry Training Model

	Title	*Investigator*
1.	Effectiveness of Inquiry Training Model with Variations in Demonstration and Peer Practice in terms of Specific Teaching Competencies of Pre-Service Teacher Trainees.	Dr. S.P. Malhotra
2.	Effectiveness of Inquiry Training Model with Variation in Peer Practice Stage in terms of and Specific Teaching Competencies	Dr. G.S. Sodhi Dr.H.S. Bajwa

and Reactions' of in service Secondary School Teachers.	
3. Effectiveness of Inquiry Training Model with Variation in Demonstration in terms of Specific Teaching Competencies of Pre-service Teacher Trainees.	Mr. V.B. Dodge and Mr. S.K. Wagh.

Suggestions for Research Workers

Model of teaching is, undoubtedly, a new area which can be tackled by the research minded teachers and research scholars to derive maximum gains. There is need of evolving models of teaching suitable for Indian class-rooms. N.C.E.R.T. in collaboration with some universities have already given a start to research work in this field. Many teacher educators have been trained for this purpose in the workshops organised at places like Indore, Mysore etc. A few studies have been conducted in this field. But there is need of working more enthusiastically on the different models:

For teaching purposes, a few lesson plan formats are given here below :

Lesson Plan Format (LPF)
(For Concept Attainment Model)

Date.................................... Name....................................

Class.................................... Institution....................................

Subject/topic..........................

RECEPTION MODEL OF CONCEPT ATTAINMENT

1. Educational (behavioural) Objectives:
   1.
   2.
   3.
2. Name of Concept.
3. Type of Concept-Conductive/disjunctive/Relational.
4. Medium-Picture/words/statements/any other.

5. Essential attributes of concepts.
   1.
   2.
   3.
6. Non essential attributes
   1.
   2.
   3.
7. Noisy attributes (if any)
   1.
8. Rule

Phase 1 : Representation of data, and identification of the Concept. Purpose and Procedure of the Model.

Sr. No.	*Positive Examples*	*Negative Examples*	*Hypothesis Reason*
1.			
2.			
3.			
4.			
5.			

Phase II : Testing Attainment of the Concept

Unlabelled additional examples and justifications.

Phase III : Analysis of Thinking Strategies.

1. Questions on description of thinking process for hypothesis:
   a.
   b.
   c.
2. Questions on roles of attributes/hypothesis in the thinking strategies.
   a.
   b.

3. Evaluation of the effectiveness of strategies and types of thinking processes.

A Few Model Lesson Plans

FOR CONCEPT ATTAINMENT MODEL

Lesson, Plan No. 1

Roll No..

Name..

Class : VIII

Date..

Subject : English

Institution..

Topic-Comparative Degree..

....

Reception Model of Concept Attainment

Education (Behavioural) Objectives

(a) To help the students to acquire a new concept.

(b) To enable the students to state the essential attributes of the concept.

(c) To help the students to state the concept rule.

Name of the Concept : Comparative Degree.

Type of Concept : Conjunctive or Relational.

Medium : Pictures, flash-cards, words, charts and statements.

Essential Attributes of the Concept :

(a) Use of two things for comparison.

(b) Use of 'than'.

(c) Use of 'er' with an adjective.

Non-essential Attributes of the Concept : Absence of all the essential attributes.

Noisy Attributes : No.

Rule : The comparative degree is used when a comparison "between two persons, two-groups or two things is made. It is generally followed by 'than' and 'er' is used with an adjective.

Phase I : Presentation of data and identification of the concept purpose and procedure of the concept.

The P.T. will say. "Well-students, today, I shall teach you English Grammar through play-way method. It is just like a game. The procedure of the game is like this. I have one concept in my mind. But I shall not tell you the name of having 'Yes' and some negative examples having 'No.' Positive examples are related to my concept but negative examples are not related to my concept. First you compare positive examples with positive examples and find out similarities. Then you compare positive examples, with negative examples and find out dissimilarities. Similarities of the positive examples will help you in forming the concept. The P.T. will proceed like this.

Positive Examples No.		*Negative Examples*	*Hypothesis*	*Reason*
1.	Mohan is looking happier than Sohan.	Mohan and Sohan are looking happy.	Use of two things for	All the essential
2.	Sandeep is shorter than Sanju.	Sandeep is very short.	comparison, than or 'er'	attributes are present
3.	India is a bigger country than Pakistan.	India is a big country.	with an adjective are	in the positive
4.	This copy is smaller than that.	This copy is very small.	present in the positive examples.	

Phase II : Testing Attainment of the Concept.

The P.T. will say, "Dear students I will give you some more examples, but I will declare that whether it is my 'Yes' example or 'No' example. You have to justify your answer. Then you will make your own example.

1. He is taller than his brother.

2. He is fatter than you.

3. This room is bigger than that.

Phase III : Analysis of Thinking Strategies.

The P.T. will ask the students to reflect on the roles of the attributes and concepts in their thinking strategies.

Q. How did you guess my concept?

Q. Did you frame any rule to the concept?

Questions on the roles of the attributes/hypothesis in their thinking process

Q. Did you concentrate on Rule or Essential Attributes?

Evaluation of the Effectiveness of Strategies and Types of Thinking Processes
Majority of the Students were Who Lists.

Lesson Plan No. 2

Date............................ Name............................

Class : VI Insitution.......................

Subject: English

Topic: Use of Indefinite article 'An'

(Reception Model of Concept Attainment)

Education Objectives:

(i) To enable the students to form a concept.
(ii) To enable the students to state the attributes of the concept.
(iii) To help the students to state the concept rule.

Name of Concept : Use of the indefinite article 'An'

Type of the Concept : Conjunctive.

Medium : Statements.

Essential Attributes of the Concept : Words beginning with vowel sound in the singular number.

Non-essential Attributes : Words beginning with consonant sounds.

Noisy Attributes : No

Rule : The indefinite article' An' is used in the numerical sense of one before the words beginning with a vowel sound.

Phase I : Presentation of Data and Identification of the Concept.

Before teaching, the P.T. will say, "Dear students today we shall play a game. We shall learn English grammar through a play way method. I shall write some sentences on the blackboard. Some of them having 'Yes' will be the positive examples of the concept which is in my mind.

All the other examples having 'No' will be the negative examples of the concept. You are to guess the concept by comparing the positive and negative examples.

Phase II : Testing Attainment of the Concept.

The P. T. will present the following unlabelled additional examples and ask the students whether these examples contain the concept or not. She will also ask them to justify their answers.

1. An hour has 60 minutes.
2. A minute has 60 seconds.
3. English is an easy language.
4. We speak many languages.
5. I have an uncle.
6. Ram is a good teacher.
7. We saw an aeroplane.

After it, the P.T. will ask the students to give their own examples and to justify them.

Phase III : Analysis of Thinking Strategies.

The P.T. will ask the following questions from the students:

1. When did you come to know the topic?
2. How did you guess the topic?
3. How many of you concentrated your attention on essential attributes?

Lesson Plan No. 3

Date............................... Name..........................

Class VI Institution....................

Subject; English

Topic : Conjunction "And"

Roll No.........................

Reception Model of Concept Attainment

Educational (Behavioural) Objectives

(i) To enable the students to acquire a new concept.
(ii) To enable the students to state the attributes of the concept.
(iii) To help the study to state the attribute of the rule.

Name of Concept : Conjunction "And"

Type of Concept : Conjunctive

Medium : Statements, sentences etc.

Essential Attributes of the Concept :

(i) Conjunction "And"
(ii) Combination of parts of sentences.
(iii) Addition of two words.

Non-essential Attributes :

(i) Sentence of any kind.
(ii) Verb

Noisy Attributes : No

Rule : Conjunction "And" is a word which joins the words of sentences together.

Phase I : Presentation of data and identification of the concept.

Dear students, I am going to play a game with you. I will teach English Grammar by play way method. I will present some positive examples having 'Yes' and some negative examples having 'No.' Positive examples are related to the concept which I have in my mind. You have to guess the concept on the basis of positive examples.

Purpose and Procedure of the Model :

S. No.	*Positive Examples*	*Negative Examples*	*Hypothesis*	*Reason*
1.	I bought a horse and a cow.	I bought a horse. I bought a cow.	Conjunction	"And" All the "And" is a essential attributes
2.	She can read and write English She can write English examples.	She can read English which positive	word in the	are present
3.	God made the country and man sentences or made the town.	God made the made the town.	joins the country. Man	
4.	She is deaf and dumb. She is dumb.	She is deaf.		
5.	She can sing and dance.	She can sing. She can dance.		

Phase II : Testing Attainment of the Concept. Unlabelled additional examples and justification.

Dear students, I will present some additional examples and you have to justify the answer.

1. She is a woman. She is a wife.
2. She is a woman and a wife.
3. This is a rose. This is a lotus.

Students, now you will supply your own examples and identify the essential attributes in them.

Phase III : Analysis of Thinking Strategies.

Q.1. How did you guess my concept?

Q.2. Did you guess the concept on the basis of first example third example?

Q.3. Did you focus on the essential attributes?

Synectics Model of Teaching (A Model to Increase Creativity)

Orientation of the Model : William J.J. Gordon designed synectics model of teaching with a goal to increase problem-solving capacity, creative expression, empathy, and insight into social relations. This model is based upon certain assumptions about creativity. Firstly, creativity is assumed to be a part of our daily work and leisure time. Secondly, creativity can be increased through training. Thirdly, creative invention is common to all fields (the arts, the sciences, engineering) and is characterized by the same intellectual processes. The fourth assumption of Gordon is that individual and group invention (creative thinking) are very similar. Individuals and groups generate ideas and products in much the same fashion.

Synodic Process : Gordon also based the synectics process on certain assumptions (hypotheses)(i) creative capacity of in and groups can be increased by bringing creative process to conscious and by developing explicit aids to creativity (2) emotional companion more important than the rational creativity is essentially an emotionals because it requires elements of irrationality and emotion to enhancetual process irrationality increases the probability of generating f rough rational and intellectual process of problem solving (3) emotional- irrational elements must be understood in order to increase the probability of success in a problem-solving situation. The elements of irrationality can be understood through the deliberate use of metaphor and analogy.

Metaphoric Activity : Metaphoric activity of the synectics model makes the creativity a conscious process. For example, describe human body as a transport system (metaphor or analogy). Transport system and human body both are different but functional relationship is to be identified. Analogous examples are structurally different but functionally same. Three types of analogies are used as the basis of synectics exercises- (i) personal analogy (ii) direct analogy (iii) compressed conflict.

Personal analogy requires students to empathize with ideas or objects to be compared. For example: (i) in view of the car engine, I feel hot or I feel powerful; the identification of the person can be done with living object; non-living object, idea or emotion.

A distance is created between the person and the analogy. The greater the distance/gap between the person (learner) and analog.

Examples of personal analogies:

* Be a cloud. Where are you? What are you doing?
* How do you feel when the sun comes out and dries you up?
* Pretend you are your favourite book. Describe yourself. What are your three wishes?

Direct analogy deals with a simple comparison of two objects or concepts. The comparison may not cover all the identical aspects the analogy is simply required to transpose the conditions of the real topic or problem situation to another situation in order to present a new view of an idea or problem. This involves identification with a person, plant, animal or non-living thing.

Examples of direct analogies:

* An oral is like what living thing?
* How is a school like a salad?
* How are you definets like frozen yogurt?
* Which is softer- a whisper or a kitten's fur?

Compressed conflict is generally two word description of an object where the words seem to be opposites" or contradict each other. Compressed conflicts provide the broadest insight into a new subject. They reflect the student's ability to incorporate two frames of reference with respect to a single object. The greater the distance between the frames of reference, the greater the mental flexibility. Examples of compressed conflicts are: Tiredly aggressive and friendly foe; life-saving destroyed and nourishing flame;

Examples of compressed conflicts:

* How is a computer shy or aggressive?
* What machine is like a smile and a flown?

The above three types of metaphors form the basis of the sequence of activities in the model of teaching. These types are used separately with groups as stretching exercises for the purpose of warming up to the creative process.

The Model of Teaching : Syntax, Social, System, Principles of Reaction and Support System

Syntax : Two strategies or models are used :

(a) Creating something New (strategy -1)

(b) Making the Strange Familiar (Strategy-2)

The above strategies use three types of analogies but their objectives, syntax and principles of reaction are different.

Strategy-I

Strategy-I helps students to see familiar things in unfamiliar ways by using analogies to create conceptual distance. Except for the final step, in which the students return to that original problem, to make simple comparisons. The objectives of this strategy is to develop a new understanding; to emphasise with a show off or bully; to design a Norway to city; to solve social or international problems. The role of the teacher is to guard against premature analyses and closure.

Syntax for Strategy -1 : Creative Something New

There are six phases in this strategy.

Phase 1 : **Description of Present Condition :** Students in this phase are required describe situation or topic as they see it now.

Phase 2 : **Direct Analogy** : Students suggest direct analogies, select one and explore (describe) it further.

Phase 3 : **Personal Analogy** : Students "become" the analogy they have selected under phase-two.

Phase 4 : **Compressed Conflict** : Students are required to use their descriptions from phases two and three for making suggestions for several compressed conflicts and choose one.

Phase 5 : **Direct Analogy** : Students are required to generate and select another direct analogy based upon the compressed conflict.

Phase 6 : **Reexamination of the Original Task :** Teacher asks students to go back to the original task and use the last analogy and/or the entire synectics experience.

Strategy-II : Making the Strange Familiar

This strategy seeks to increase the students, understanding

and internalization of substantially new or difficult material. In this analogy, metaphor is used for analysis, not for creating conceptual distance as in strategy one.

The seven phases of strategy two are briefly mentioned below:

Phase 1 : **Substantive Input** : Teacher provides information to students on the new topic.

Phase 2 : **Direct Analogy** : Teacher suggests direct analogy and asks students to describe the analogy.

Phase 3 : **Personal Analogy** : Teacher involves "being the familiar" (personalizing) the direct analogy.

Phase 4 : **Comparing Analogies** : Students identify and explain the points of similarity between the new material and the direct analogy.

Phase 5 : **Explaining Differences** : Students explain where the analogy does not fit.

Phase 6 : **Exploration** : Students re-explore the original topic on its own terms.

Phase 7 : **Generating Analogy** : Students provide their own analogy and explore the similarities and differences.

Difference between Strategy-I and Strategy-II

The major difference between the two strategies tries in their use of analogy. In strategy-I, students move through a series of analogies without logical constraints; conceptual distance is increased and imagination is free to wander.

In strategy-II, Students try to connect two ideas and to identify the connections as they move through the analogies.

Social System

* Teacher initiates the sequence band guides the use of the operational mechanisms.
* Teacher helps students to intellectualize their mental processes.
* Students have the freedom in the open-ended discussion during the problem solving metaphoric activity.

* Certain norms are essential for creative problem solving. For example: Cooperation; play of fancy; intellectual and emotional equality.

Principles of Reaction

* The teacher notes the extend to which individuals seem to be tied to regularised patterns of thinking and he/she tries to induce psychological states likely to generate a creative response.

* In addition, the teacher himself or herself unjust display a use of the non-rational to encourage the reluctant student to indulge in irrelevance, fantasy, symbolism, and other devices necessary to break out of set channels of thinking. Because the teacher as exemplar is probably an essential of the method, he or she has to learn to accept the bizarre and the unusual. The teacher must accept all student responses to ensure that students feel no external in judgement on their creative expression. The more difficult the problem is, or seems to be, to solve, the more it is necessary for the teacher to accept far fetched analogies so that individuals develop fresh perspectives on problems.

  In strategy two, the teacher should guard against premature analysis He or she also clarifies and summarizes the progress of the learning activity and hence the students problem solving behaviour.

Support System

The group needs most of all facilitation by a teacher competent in synectics procedures. It also needs, in the case of scientific problems a laboratory in which it can build models and other devices to make problems concrete and to permit practical invention to take place. The class requires a work space of its own an and environment in which creativity will be prized and utilized.

Atypical classroom can 'probably provide these necessities, but classroom sized group maybe too large for many synectic activities, and smaller groups would need to be created.

Application of Synectics Model of Teaching

1. Synectics procedures may be used with students in all areas of the curriculum, the sciences as well as the arts.

2. Synectics procedure can be applied to both teacher-student discussion in the class-room and to teacher- made materials for the students.

3. The products or vehicles of synectics activity need not always be written; they can be oral or they can take the form of role plays, paintings and graphics, or simply changes in behaviour.

4. While taking social or behaviour problems, situational behaviour at the beginning and end of the synectic activity should be recorded to know the changes.

5. Modes of expression may be concrete for an abstract concept as a topic.

6. Synectics model can be used for:

   - Creative writing
   - exploring social problems
   - problem solving
   - creating a design or product
   - for broadening our perspective on abstract concepts.

7. Synectics can be used with all ages though with very young children, it is best to stick to stretching exercises.

8. Attention should be given to points like; work within the experiences of the learners; rich use of concrete materials; alternative pacing; explicit outlining of procedures.

9. Synectics model is more effective for such students who withdraw from more academic learning activities.

10. Synectics model can be used in combination with other models.

Instructional and Nurturant Effects of Synectics Model of Teaching

The effects or values of synectics model can be analysed under two categories:

1. Instructional values or effects.

2. Nurturant values or effects.

Instructional Effects or Values : Two values/effects are there of the synectic model from the instructional point of view:

(a) It helps in increase or develop the general creative power of the student.

(b) It helps in the development of creative responses over a variety of subject matter domains.

Instructional techniques specific in line with above values can be developed within the guidelines of synectic model of teaching.

Nurturant Effects : Besides instructional effects, the models has, following two nurtural effects/values :

(a) Model helps to increase learning or achievement in the subject domain.

(b) Model also enhances group cohesion and the result is productive. Group efforts in the social environment of the synectic activity generates energy which enables every participant to function in an interdependent manner and ultimately the result is productive. Thus, some output or product is there as a result of creative interdependent cohesive group effort.

QUESTIONS

1. What do you mean by the term 'Model of Teaching'. Describe in brief the basic elements of a model.
2. What do you understand by concept attainment? Is it different from concept formation? Describe the structure and characteristics of Bruner's Concept Attainment Model.
3. Discuss briefly the broad classifications of Modern Teaching Models.
4. Discuss with one example either the Synectic model or the Concept Attainment Model.
5. Describe synectics model of teaching with specific reference to views of Joyce and Weil.

3
Audio-Visual Aids

This is the age of science and technology. Almost everything has undergone a change under the impact of science. The teaching learning programmes have also been affected by it. The class room has to have it different shape in times to come. It is to be just like a laboratory where in different hardwares such as projector, tape recorder, record player, over head projector, epidiascope, computer etc. are lying. The process of teaching learning depends upon the different type of equipment available in the classroom. In the absence of audio-visual aids the classrooms will be considered traditional ones or the ones belonging to 19th century or early 20th century. Surely the class room in the 21st century has to be modern from every angle.

Undoubtedly, audio-visual aids are those instructional devices which are used in the class room to encourage learning and thereby make it easier and interesting. The materials like charts, maps, models, concrete objects, film strips, projectors, radio, television etc. which heir—a teacher in a good communication, healthy class room interaction and effective realization of the teaching objectives may be called instrumentional aids in the field of teaching learning. In this regard, Albert Duret rightly said, it is easier to believe what you see than what you hear; but if you both see and hear, then you can understand more readily and retain more lastingly.

The children are able to learn more and more if they are taught interestingly. They should better be given rich experiences of life. Jean Piaget, the famous psychologist said that the more a child has seen and heard, the more he wants to see and hear. In the past, the Greeks and the Romans used to convey their thoughts and information through words, pictures, symbols. etc. But

Rousseau the great educator and naturalist discouraged the use of more words in education. His view was that surroundings of the child were more important. Forebel also advocated the idea of learning by the child from his natural surroundings. A visit to a place or its sight through pictures and chart scan teach the child far more than filling his mind with words delivered by the teacher in the form of lectures.

Meaning of Audio-Visual Aids

Teaching aids which effect or organs of audibility and sight are called "Audio-Visual Aids." 'Good' Dictionary of Education speaks of audio-visual aids as "Anything by means of which learning process may be encouraged or carried on through the sense of learning or sense of sight."

Career V. Good. "Audio-visual aids are those aids which help in completing the triangular process of learning i.e. motivation, classification and stimulation."

According to **Burton,** "Audio-Visual aids are those sensory objects or images which initiate or stimulate and reinforce learning."

Edger Dale, "Audio Visual aids are those devices by the use of which communication of ideas between persons and groups in various teaching and training situations is helped. These are also termed as multi-sensory materials."

According to Gandhiji, "True education of the intellect can only come through a proper exercise and training of bodily organs hands, feet, eyes, ears and nose."

Mckowa and Roberts, In his words, "Audio-visual aids are supplementary devices by which the teacher, through the utilization of more than one sensory channels keeps to clarify, establish and correlate- concepts, interpretations and appreciations."

Concerning audio-visual aids Kothari Education Commission (1964-66) said, "The supply of teaching aids to every pool is essential for the improvement of the quality of teaching. It should indeed bring about an educational revolution in the country."

National Policy on Education (1986) has recommended the use of teaching aids, especially improvised aids, to make teaching learning more effective and realistic.

Types of Aids

The different audio-visual aids have been made depending upon the senses involved. They are of the following three categories:

Visual Aids : The aids which use sense of vision are called visual aids. For example actual objects, models, pictures, charts, maps, flash cards, flannel board, bulletin board, chalk board, pocket board, slides, epidiascope, over head projector etc.

Audio Aids : The aids involving the sense of hearing are called audio aids. For example, radio, tape-recorder, record player, linguaphone etc.

Audio Visual Aids : The aids which involve the sense of vision as well as hearing are called audio-visual aids. For example, Television.

Another Categorization of A.V. Aids is as under :

Projected Aids : Aids which help in their projection on the screen are called projected aids. For example, film strips, slides, film projector, slide projector, epidiascope etc.

Non-Projected Aids : Aids which do not help in their projection on the screen are called non-projected aids for example, chalk-board, charts, actual objects models, radio, tape-recorder etc.

Audio Visual Aids are Educational Media

The Task Force appointed by the Department of Audio-visual Institution of National Education Association of U.S.A. defined the Educational Media "as those things which are manipulated, seen, heard, or talked about, plus the materials which facilitate such activity." Educational Media may be classified as :

Traditional Education Media

Media such as chalk board, models, charts flash cards, flannel board, bulletin boards which have no technological base are called traditional educational media. Most of these can be improvised by the teachers and the students. They do not need any instruments for their use in teaching.

Technological Educational Media

Such media have technological base. For using them, we need sufficient training. If we want to prepare the media, some special type of training will be needed. A few examples of this type of media are film strips, slides, recorded tapes, video tapes etc.

Audio Visual aids are of immense value in the teaching learning process. They make the process lively and interesting and hence make it effective and better. According to Kothari Education Commission, (164-66) "The supply of teaching aids to every school is essential for the improvement of the quality of teaching. It would indeed bring about an educational revolution in the country. Just lectures or verbalism of the teacher make the class room dull and mechanical. Every child is interested in seeing concrete things. He wants to handle, manipulate and the teacher should provide situations so as to satisfy his curiosity of doing things. Learning through senses is better and more permanent than just mechanical learning. Out of the five senses it is through hearing and seeing that 86% knowledge is gained. The audio visual aids, therefore, have great importance both for the teachers and the learners. In this context, Rousseau says, "Give your scholar no verbal lessons, he should be taught by experiences only."

In the words of Edgar Dale : "Because audio visual materials supply concrete bases for conceptual thinking, they give rise to meaningful concepts enriched by meaningful association, hence they offer the best antidote for the disease of verbalism. The great educationist and philosopher Froebel also advises: "Our lessons ought to start from the concrete and end in the abstract."

Comerius said, "The foundation of all learning consists in representing clearly to the sense, sensible objects so that they can be appreciated easily."

Advantages of A.V. Aids

The audio-visual as have many advantages which are explained here below :

1. Helpful creating Interest : The use of different aids by the teacher while teaching make the teaching-learning process more interesting. Sometimes the teacher makes use of charts film strips, epidiascope, film protractor and sometimes he just performs an experiment in the class. All these make the teaching-learning process more interesting.

2. Just Lectures by the teacher is to much of verbalism. But the use of chalks and black board reduces verbalism. The

use of other types of aids further reduces verbalism in the crass. Naturally the learners will find it less loading on their minds. The teacher is also able to save energy.

3. The use of audio-visual aids gives reality to the learning situation. Thus by seeing a film show exhibiting the life of the tundras and learn it more effectively in three hours than by reading many books in months together.

4. It gives vividness to the learning situation. For example, we want to know about the Mughals. The film on it provides vividness parallel to which is difficult by the study of books.

5. It gives clarity to the learning situation. For example, the film show of 'A Tale of Two Cities' gives a clear picture of the French Revolution. Anything equal to this is not possible by the study of books.

6. The aids motivate the child and arouse his feelings of curiosity. Thus motivation keeps the child fully absorbed and he tries to learn more and more.

7. They make the abstract ideas concrete and thus help in making learning more effective. It results into more clarity and better understanding.

8. The different type of aids when used successfully in the class room provide variety in the class room situations. Variety in the instructional procedures help the learners to be more alternative.

9. Meet the Individual Differences Requirements : There are individual differences among the learners. Some are ear minded who are able to learn by listening. Some are able to learn through visual demonstrations while others learn better through doing. The different types of aids, thus, serve in different ways for meeting out the varied requirements of the students.

10. Good Substitute for Direct Experiences : Effective teaching requires direct experiences of the learners. It is always not possible to take the children out for direct experiences. Sometimes the object is too far e.g. Elephant caves. A film ora chart showing those caves will serve the purpose. In other case, it is not possible to bring the object in the class.

In those situations, pictures or charts serve the purpose. For example, elephant, lion jackal etc. cannot be brought in the class room. Their models or pictures or charts can be used for teaching purposes. The aids are good substitutes for the real objects as they make learning equally meaningful.

11. Help in Developing Various Skills : The use of audio-visual aids help in the development of various skills among the students. They learn how to draw a diagram of the topic learn how to handle the apparatus and in case where they face some problems in the conduct of an experiment, they apply their mind to solve the problem.

The teacher should not be over ambitious in the use of aids during teaching. Use of aids just for the sake of aid does not help much. Their usefulness must be determined beforehand. In the words of Mc Known and Roberts : "Audio-visual aids wisely selected and properly used, arouse and develop intense and beneficial interest and so motivate the pupils to learning. And properly motivated learning need improved attitude, permanency of impression and rich experience and ultimately more wholesome living." Thus we find that the different type of aids do serve some good purpose but they are not everything for a successful teaching. In this regard, Francis W. Noe says : Good instruction is foundation of any education programme. Audio visual aids are component part of that foundation."

Characteristics of Good Instructional Aids

A few characteristics of good instructional aids are enlisted here below :

1. They are large enough to be seen by the students for whom they are used.
2. They are meaningful and they always stand to serve a useful purpose.
3. They are upto the mark and uptodate in every respect.
4. They are simple, cheap and may be improvised. They are not very costly.
5. They are handy and easily portable.
6. They are accurate.

7. They are realistic.
8. They are according to the mental level of the learners.
9. Their purpose may be informative but it is not just entertainment.
10. They motivate the learners. They capture the attention of the pupils.
11. They help in the realisation of stipulated learning objectives.
12. They are really very useful and can be used in many lessons and at different class levels.
13. They are useful for supplementing the teaching process but they cannot replace the teacher.

Precautions for Using the Different Instructional Aids

The use of audio visual aids in teaching-learning process has multifarious values. They make the process interesting and effective. The variety of medias now available to the teacher provide him powerful supporting material to enrich teaching and to strengthen learning. But the wrong use of aids will certainly invite adverse criticism. Some precautions which are given below must be used while selecting and using the aids:

1. The students should be fully acquainted with the aids. If possible, their help in the preparation of aids should sought.
2. The aids should be fully checked up before' using them in the class. The aid any way spoiled discourages the students. A spoiled picture, a broken model or a cracked slide not only makes the students disinterested, it rather discourages them.
3. Use of black bóard is good for teaching. But it must be ascertained that whatever is written or sketched on the black board should be correct.
4. Aid should not be used just for the sake of aid.
5. In a lesson, too many aids should not be used;
6. While using some special type of aids like radio, television, the students should be mentally prepared for it. They may be given a brief description of the programme.

7. It should be used at the right time making it meaningful for the subject and the topic.

8. Aid used should be in proper condition, worthy of showing in the class room situation.

9. While giving instructions and showing some aid, the teacher should not stand in front of it.

10. Aids should not be allowed to become masters in the teaching-learning process. They should remain as servants in the hands of the teacher. He should be able to use it as per need and requirement of class room situation.

11. The use of different type of aids in teaching may be obligatory for sometime but ultimately goal of the teacher should be to teach well without the use of any aid.

Principles for the Selection of Audio Visual Aids

Carlton W.H, Erickson gave five basic principles for the selection of audio visual aids which are explained here below :

The Principle of Selection

"Teachers should base their selection of high quality audiovisual materials upon valid teaching purposes (objectives) and upon the unique characteristics of a specific group of learners."

In the process of teaching, selection of suitable audio visual aids is very important. Here objectives of learning are also fully taken care of. The material should help in learning well. Age of the learners and the class in which they study are important things which the teacher should keep in mind while selecting the different type of audio-visual aids.

The Principle of Readiness

"The use of audio-visual instructional materials should be proceeded by the development of adequate learner readiness for effective participation."

In learning, law of readiness is quite important. The learners are able to learn well when they are ready for it. So the teacher should make it sure about their readiness and only then audio visual aids be presented. The teacher is expected to motivate the students first. Teaching-learning becomes more meaningful when the interest of the learners is aroused.

The Physical Control Principle

"Details relating to physical facilities and conditions for using audio-visual materials should be handled or arranged by the teacher in a manner that safeguards the material and equipment and provides for economy of time and optimum learning attention."

The teachers should check the physical conditions and the surroundings where audio-visual aids are to be used. Before actual teaching, the teacher should check up if a nail is needed for hanging the chart or the rolling black board. Anything else which is needed in teaching must be checked properly by the teacher. That way there is no wastage of time.

The Action Principle

"Teachers should guide the learner in the important processes of reacting to and taking appropriate action as a result of audio-visual experience situation."

When the audio visual aids are shown in the process of teaching, reaction to them is but natural. The teacher should see that the learners are able to react meaningfully. The different audiovisual aids provide experiences which are only means for the ends. The aids are never ends in themselves.

The Appraisal Principle

"Teachers should subject to both the audio-visual material and accompanying techniques to continual evaluation."

Appraisal of the audio visual material is important. Many teachers show audio visual aids out of curiosity but they never know how far they have been used successfully. Only right appraisal of A.V. aids will help the teacher to improve them further.

A Few other Principles

The use of different type of audio-visual aids helps the teacher to carry on the instructional programme successfully. The aids are in the hands of the teacher which are used by him as per his convenience and utility in the teaching-learning process. The teacher is in no-way a slave to the aids. He is the master of teaching learning show where the different aids are servants available to him for carrying on his duty of teaching more diligently and effectively. A good teacher keeps in mind certain principles while selecting and using the different aids. A few of those principles are briefly discussed here below:

Principle of Utility

The teacher should not select a teaching aid just for the sake of an aid. He should ensure that the aid chosen for teaching purpose must be of some utility. It should help the teacher to teach the subject matter in some better ways or it should help the learners to learn things in a better way.

Sometimes the teacher feels attracted towards a chart or a picture which he has been able to procure from some source. But he knows that in teaching or learning of some topic, it is of no use. Still he uses it in the class just for the sake of showing it. It is suggested that he should not use it in the class for teaching purpose because it has no utility that way. He may, of course, just show it to the class in an informal way saying that it is a beautifully prepared chart or picture.

Principle of Purpose

The different teaching aids serve some purposes in the classroom situation. Whatever aid is used, the teacher should ensure that it serves some useful purpose. An aid may help the teacher in making the subject matter fully clear to the learns or it may serve the purpose of motivating the learners.

Principle of Uniqueness

An aid is of great value and significance. Its uniqueness must be given due recognition by the users of it. Thus it is bound to catch the attention of the learners. Their curiosity is also satisfied.

Principle of Presentation

Every teaching aid is unique and important in its own way. But more important is way of presentation. It should be presented at that right and in the right way. For example, a well prepared chart does not mean that its effect will be equally good. If it is not show properly, its worth in teaching learning programme will be zeroed.

Principle of Assessment

Every teaching aid should be subject to its final evaluation. Evaluation of the half need be made by some competent authority which may be a sub-committee of experts in the field. The aids should be assessed first and then they should be put to use. That way their purposes will be achieved rightly.

Principle of Appropriateness

The aid used should appropriate to the teaching learning programme. It should be according to the mental level of the learners. It should be used at the right moment and in right way.

Principle of being Handy

The teaching aids being used must be handy. The teacher or the students should be able to handle it well. Then only it can be used to serve a useful purpose.

Principle of Correctness

The aid prepared for use in the classroom situation should be fully correct. It should not be a spoiled one or a broken one. That might discourage the students. It should be a fresh one as far as passible. It should be upto the mark and uptodate in every respect. It must be worthy of showing it to the students.

Principle of Simplicity

As far as possible, the aid should be simple. It should not confuse the mind of the learner. It should inspire the learners and help them in becoming imaginative and creative. A very costly aid which is beyond the reach of majority is generally not found suitable in Indian class room situations.

The different aids have their unique significance when the teacher cares fully for the above given principles. The teacher should play his own role well. In the words of Witched and Scihuller, "In terms of educational significances, by all odds, the most important aspect of the administration of these materials and equipment is their selection. Teachers should have a large part in selecting them, but the ordering, payment, storage, inspection and mechanical maintenance are not functions of teachers."

Projected Aids

The different types of projected aids are described below. Films Advancement in the field of science and technology has placed before the teacher many useful and interesting items which if used rightly in the class rooms, can work wonders. Cinematographer is one of them. The financial difficulties of the schools hinder their maximum use in the schools. Efforts are afoot to provide such facilities in the schools. The films make the concept clear to the learners. Then they are able to learn it realistically and in a much effective way. Films really useful and suitable for the school children have now caught the attention of film manufacturers and producers. The Government is also encouraging them for producing worthwhile films really useful to influence the emotions of the children.

Types of Educational Films

The educational films are mainly of the following types:

Film for the Class Rooms : This type of films are directly related to class room teaching. Thus we have films for teaching change of seasons, circulation of blood etc. There are films for general information which may not be directly related with the curriculum. Then there are films for demonstrating a skill, e.g., the film on how to use a flannel board in the class room? And then there are films which dramatise an event or episode concerning the life of an individual.

Educational films such as 'A Visit to a Big City of India' celebrations of 'Diwali in Amritsar', Mahatma Gandhi, Rabindra Nath Tagore, Ramayana etc. may be shown to the students. Then they are asked comprehension questions or they can be asked to describe something or write as a piece of composition. They can also be asked to speak something for five minutes on the film they have seen. All this will improve the different abilities of the students such as thinking, speaking, explaining, comprehending, reasoning etc. The students may be given home assignments of similar nature. Thus the students can have extra practice when they have got TV's and V.C.R.'s at their homes.

Films Library : In each educational institution, there can be one section where they may have a number of educational films. Educational films can be prepared on the basis of best institutions, best teaching-learning situations, life stories of great men, education of different levels and so on and so forth. Then in one part of the library some cabins can be made with facility of ear head phone in each cabin. There should be library study period for students as per their convenience. During library periods, some students can see educational films by sitting in the cabins without disturbing others.

Thus educational films can serve many useful purposes. Learning by the students will be real and hence/will last for longer. It will modernise the system of education.

Newsreels : They are also produced by the Govt. of India. Some important news of the country are made to reach the masses through such films. It may be on some current event of our own country of some other countries etc. This type of films acquaint the people with the latest happenings.

Documentary Films : The documentary films are also produced by the Govt. of India. Here the Govt. tries to cover a wide variety of subjects. Usually the social themes are the basis of preparing such films,

Method of Showing a Film : Films provide lot of useful information to the learners apart from their recreational value. But they need be shown properly in systematic way. Before showing a film, the teacher himself should know well the contents of that film. He should make preparations for showing it. For this, arrangement of a projector, operator, dark room etc. should be made well in advance. After showing the film, there should be open discussion, where the students should be free to seek clarifications of their doubts, or they may put questions as they like. In this way, the desired aims of teaching through films can be achieved.

Advantages

The different types of films have a number of advantages which are explained below:

1. Education through films adds variety in the methods of teaching.
2. Generally the students love to see a film as compared to listening to somebody. In this way, the films are self-motivating for them.

3. With the help of films, the students are able to see many things which otherwise they would find difficult to see. The reason being that this is comparatively cheaper.

4. The films help in developing the imagination of the students.

5. They also reduce the load of work of the teachers. Surely, the teacher relaxes when the learners are shown some film.

Limitations

1. Showing a film to the students is costly, because there is need of film-projector. And every school may not be able to have it.

2. There is need of technical trained staff. And that is generally not available in the school.

3. When a film is being shown, some students want to put a question but that is not possible. Later on, those very students may find difficult to put the same questions.

4. There may be some site or situation which the students want to see for more time, but that is not possible.

Film Strips : Film Strips are more flexible than cinema and so they are quite useful in many respects. They are available specially for teaching and more directly associated with the classroom. They are used on a slide projector or a film strip projector. They can be successfully used for composition lessons.

These film strips were not popular in Indian schools in the past but now they are gaining popularity.

Opaque Projector (Epidiascope) : This instrument is an improvement upon the Magic Lantern because the preparation of slides reduces the utility of the magic lantern, in epidiascope there is no need of making slides. Any diagram, picture or even opaque object can be directly had on the screen.

It is a very useful type of visual aid. Sometimes the diagram given in the book is rather difficult to draw. Moreover, it takes a few minutes to draw the same diagram on the black board. The diagram so drawn on the black board may not be accurate. In such cases, the opaque projector is of much value. The book is placed in the projector with the page of depicting the diagram so that it is reflected and then projected on to the screen.

The Epidiascope serves two purposes:

(a) When it is used to project any opaque object, it works as an epistle scope. (b) When it is used to project slides (with the help of a lever) in that case it serves as a diascope. Because of these two purposes this instrument is named as epidiascope. The working of this instrument employs the principle of horizontal straight line projection with a lamp, plain mirror and projector sense. In it is fitted a high power bulb whose light falls on the opaque object. Over the object there is plain mirror fixed at 45° angle which reflects the light in such a way that it passes through the projection tense. With the result a magnified image of the object appears on to the screen.

The epidiascope serves many useful purposes in the class room situations. Suppose some student has very good hand-writing on his note-book and the teacher wants to show it to the whole class. If he shows the note-book to the students straight way, it is not properly visible to everyone. He places that note-book with that page of good hand-writing open in the epidiascope, switches the instrument on and that hand writing of the student appears on the screen. All the students sitting in the class can see it properly and they can learn from it many things how they can improve their own hand writing.

Overhead Projector : It is another useful and more convenient way of using black board. In case of black board work, generally it is seen that the teacher stands in front while writing and thus his writing on the black board is obstructed. The students can't see it properly. Moreover, the teacher has to stand as he is writing on the black board. Besides the teacher has to rub it off occasionally. All these drawbacks can be overcome in case of overhead projector. It can also be used successfully in a class having a large number of students. The overhead Projector can be used in any type of room. There is no need of a dark room for this purpose.

Slides or Transparencies : A slide is usually a piece of film in a frame for passing strong light through or to show a picture on a surface. It may be a small piece of thin glass to put an object on for seeing under a microscope. It may be made of cellulose acetate film, translucent paper, glass etc. The slide is mounted individually in a projector and strong light is passed through it. The picture or diagram or image on the slide appears on the screen from where it can be seen by the learners.

The slides serve many useful purposes in the class-room situations. Sometimes a slide is prepared for some difficult diagram or picture appearing in the book. The different type of slides serve many useful purposes. Micro slides are prepared for Biological Sciences. According to Hass and Packer (1954), the following are the advantages of slides:

(i) Attract attention (ii) Arouse interest (iii) Assist lesson development (iv) Test students' understanding (v) Review instruction (vi) Present next lesson or subject (vii) Facilitate student teacher participation.

A few other advantages are:

(a) Details of the subjects or the diagram can be shown very nicely with the help of slides of larger size.

(b) They can be procured easily and at low cost.

(c) Their handling and storing is not difficult.

From where to get slide :

Preparation of a simple slide is not a difficult job. Every teacher should learn how to prepare a slide for himself. Here below is given the outline for preparing a simple slide.

1. At first, the base material for preparing the slide is selected. That basic material can be a plain glass, etched glass or translucent paper.
2. A rough layout is laid down. The basic illustration is sketched and letters or other symbols are marked.
3. The glass or cellulose acetate on which slide is to be prepared is placed over the original sketch or layout. But using a drawing pen or marked pencil, the figure is traced out.
4. For better illustration, colour may be added or some art work may be done.
5. Then the transparent sheet is attached to the back of a card board mount with the help of pressure sensitive tape.

Photographic Slides:

The photographic slides can be produced with the help of a suitable camera where photographs of the objects or the diagrams are taken. In this age of science and technology the photographic slides are ready within a few minutes.

Slide Projector (Magic Lantern)

It is a simple type of hardware aid because its mechanism is very elementary. It is used to project slides. That is why it is also called slide projector. The magic lantern help in showing the magnified image of the transparent object called slide on to the screen. The slide is placed inverted in the slide carrier of the magic lantern and its erect image is projected on the screen.

Suppose the teacher is teaching the students about some diseases, their origin, effects etc. He can prepare slides on T.B., Malaria, Cholera etc. and show the same to the class. Another example: A teacher teaching some groups of learners about Mughal period, he can show slides of Mughal art. It will make teaching more interesting and better learnable for the students.

Points to be kept in mind while using a Magic Lantern (Slide Projector):

In order to use the magic lantern successfully, the following points should be kept in mind :

1. Just showing slides to the students is only visual representation of things. The teacher should give a commentary side by side. It would be better if the teacher tells the students first what they are going to see in the next few minutes. That will make the learners psychologically prepared for the work in hand.
2. Some slides may not be self explanatory type. The teacher should give a running commentary.
3. After showing the slides, the teacher should encourage common discussion. Doubts of the students, if any, can be clarified there. Their problems of any type are also solved.
4. The teacher should not disallow or discourage the students putting questions.

Advantages

1. It is a simple device easy to handle with the help of white

magnified objects may be shown on the screen.

2. Any school can afford to have it as it is not costly.
3. The picture on the screen can be allowed to remain there as lot as the learners wish.
4. There is no wastage of time and energy.
5. It is very handy and can easily be taken to any class room or place where it is to be used.

Disadvantages

Undoubtedly the magic lantern is of immense value for the class room teaching, its shortcomings cannot be ruled out. It has a few limitations which are as under:

1. The glass slides are becoming costlier now. It may not be put to excessive use.
2. Every kind of material cannot be projected by the magic lantern.

Non-projected Aids

The different types of non-projected aid are detailed here below:

(i) Graphics: Graphics are related to writing, drawing, painting, etc. They are vividly descriptive. For example, maps, diagrams, graphs, atlas, charts etc.

(ii) Three dimensional aids are models, globe, specimens etc.

(iii) Display Board: Any type of board on which something can be displayed and the students may consult and be benefited. For example, pocket Board, Flannel Board, Bulletin Board, Magnet Board, Fixo Graph Board,. etc.

(iv) Audio Aids: Those aids which can be heard. For example, Tape Recorder, Record Player etc.

(v) Charts: A chart is another software aid used quite frequently in the instructional process. It is defined as "a visual symbol summarizing or comparing or contrasting or performing other helpful services in planning subject maker." A Chart is a commonly used aid very 'popular with teachers under training though actual class room teachers use it rarely.

According to Mckown & Roberts; Charts are analytical in nature, they depict the sequential arrangements or inter relationships of their various elements."

Haas and Pacher say; Charts are the "spark plugs" of visual training, "they" make dry and often meaningless facts more understandable and interesting."

Charts are of various types. Each one of them meets a specific need. Let us now see the different type of charts and the utility in the teaching-learning process.

(i) Table Chart: Table chart means a chart, on which some table is given. It may have a list of rulers and battles in a chronological order. For example, a table chart may have the minimum and maximum temperature of a City/region for the last 10 days. We can prepare a table chart of tenses for teaching English.

(ii) Tree Chart :. As the name indicates, we have a trunk of the tree and its branches. In the same way, we can have charts showing the growth of a thing. This type of charts are quite useful in the teaching of science and social studies.

(iii) Flow Chart: This type of chart is shown by rectangles, circles, lines, arrows, colours etc. to represent the structure of a big institution. Thus control of education in Haryana State can be depicted as;

Control of Education

|

Minister of Education

|

Education Commissioner

|

Director (Higher Education) | Director (See Education) | Director (Primary Education)

Joint Director | Joint Director

Deputy Director | Deputy Director

ADPI ADPI ADPI AD PI ADPI ADPI

(iv) Comparison or Contrast Chart : Any type of comparison or contrast between two persons, places, countries etc. may be depicted on a chart by using columns. Thus we may have a comparison of illiterate people in different states of India. We may 'have such a chart of comparison showing maximum and minimum temperature of big cities. This type of charts make the process or teaching-learning easy and more effective:

Specimen

Name of City	*Max. Temperature*	*Minimum Temperature*
Delhi	40.6	20.4
Bombay	42.4	21.2
Kolkata	43.3	21.6
Madras	44.4	22.0

(v) Pupil Achievements Chart: This type of charts give a comprehensive and detailed information of a student. A cumulative record card is an example of this type of charts.

(vi) Isotope Charts: In this type of charts, symbols are used for the thing to be represented. 'The symbols are easy and can be understoodly. We can use this type of charts for the younger children who are unable to understand the graphs.

(vii) Pie Charts: In a pie chart, a cirque is drawn which represents the whole. Then the circle is divided into segments were each segment represents a percentage of the whole. Many things can be taught with the help of a pie chart. Thus we can teach the students the percentage of various gases in the atmosphere.

Pictures : Pictures are one of the most common type of visual aids. Here the generally, accepted meaning of picture is readymade or machine are pictures. We fan have these from some old magazine or purchase from the market. According to the old Chinese saying; "A picture is worth ten thousand words." The idea is 'that if we explain something to say 15, or 20 minutes to the students, it can be forgotten. But anything visualized through a picture, has its impact for a longer time.

Through pictures, we can illustrate a story of some accident, an activity, a sight, a place etc. Now the question arises: Can we use a bazaar made picture for teaching a class? Yes. Why not? Our purpose is teaching and for this we can use readymade pictures.

Pictures may be used in the class room situations where actual objects are not available or they are beyond the reach of the teacher due to one reason or the other. While using pictures, the teacher should ensure that they really serve some purpose. Suppose the teacher wants to teach about the Headmaster's office or punishment being given to the students in these cases actual situations or places should be shown. Bringing pictures for these things will not help. It rather dilutes teaching. So pictures for the sake of pictures should not be used.

Atlas and Maps : Atlas is a very useful teaching aid. It is used in teaching social studies. In atlas different maps of countries are given. The map may be on the basis of roads, railways, distt., states, etc. Blank maps are also available alongwith the filled up maps. The students are taught consulting of maps and filling up of blank maps. This type of activities are very interesting for the school children especially while studying social studies.

This type of visual aid has the following advantages:

1. It is an activity which motivates the students and make them learn things interestingly.
2. Whatever is learnt in this way, is retained by the students for a long time.
3. The students associate the material with the different situation of the map. Thus they are able to understand well.

Globe : Globe is a round shaped wooden or plastic model of earth on which different countries of the world are shown. It revolves round a central axle called Dhuri which shows that the earth moves and it moves round the sun.

Globe is used for teaching History and Geography to the students. Many topics of Geography are well taught with the help of a globe. It makes the subject matter fully clear to the students.

The different countries of the world can be shown simultaneously to the students. Thus a better comparison can be made between the different countries.

Diagrams : Diagrams help the teacher in teaching many things clearly. The diagrams can be drawn on the Black board. The diagrams can also be shown on the charts. Diagrams are used for teaching Science, Geometry, Geography etc. Simple type of diagrams help the students learn things in a better way.

An expert black board writing can draw the diagram on the black board and teach thereby. The teacher may also use a chart showing some diagrams. Overhead projector can also be used for showing some diagrams. In that case, the teacher prepares the diagram on a glazed sheet at home. Opaque projector can also be used for showing some diagram straight way from the book.

The diagram should be drawn as simple as possible. They must be according to the mental level of the learners.

Graphs : A graph is an important visual aid. Graphs are used while teaching subjects like Science and Geography. Comparative values can be shown very clearly on a graph paper. When the students see the different graphs, they can at once compare things and pick up the main points easily and very clearly.

Models : A model is usually the miniature structure of the original object. It shows almost all the details of the original thing. It may be of the same size or larger or smaller than the thing it represents. It is a three dimensional recognizable imitation of an object. As compared to a picture or a chart which are two dimensional, the model is three dimensional. It can be seen from different angles and so it is generally more interesting and instructive. They are used as great deal in the teaching of science. They can also be used for teaching other subjects.

According to Edgar Dale: "A model is a recognizable imitation of that real thing with an increase or decrease in size as the chief difference."

Haas and Packer say: "Models include the replicas of significant units used in manufacturing or operation usually copied on a smaller or larger scale."

Mckown and Roberts say: "Models are replicas of objects house, engine, boat, aeroplane bridge etc. These models may be operating a pump; solar system or water wheel or Don operating a simple weapon, animal, tool or table."

The models are of the following types:

(i) **Scale Models :** This type of models represent the things through exactness of scale. In certain learning, situations, we need correct representation of things. For example the students of engineering are to be shown of Bhakra Dam. For them, scale model will be needed.

(ii) **Simplified Models :** This type of models show roughly the external form of object. For example, models of animals, birds etc. are all simplified models. Thus the teacher shows to the small children the models of elephant, parrot, horse etc.

(iii) **Cross Sectional Models or Cutaway Models :** This type of models show the interior side of the object a longwith the exterior side. This type is used for teaching the senior students. For example, model of an aeroplane is shown to the students of military science. Both the exterior and the interior vision of the aeroplane are needed to be shown to these learners'.

(iv) **Mock-ups :** Mock-ups is a special form of model. It may not be similar to the original in appearance. It is an imitation of a thing in certain aspects only. Here some element of original reality is highlighted to make it more meaningful to the students. Thus we can tell the students about trains, aeroplanes, ships etc. by making their mock-ups with card board. In technical institutions, mock-ups are often used for the purpose of training.

Utility in the Teaching-Learning Process

In the class room teaching, many times it is not possible to show to the learners the actual objects. They may be too big, they may be too afar, they may be dangerous etc. So in those situations, their models according to requirements of the learners are brought and show to the learners. For example, the students are to be taught about a dam, it may not be possible to take them to the dam for first hand experience, in that case its model is shown. Second situation Bhilai, it may not be possible to take them 50 far, their models serve the purpose of teaching. Third situation, the students are to be taught about the lion, snake, which are dangerous animals, their models will be used for teaching. Fourth situation, certain things may be invisible for example, the interior parts of an eye. In such cases, outway model is used to make the learners fully understand it.

Flash Card and Flannel Board

Flash Cards : Flash cards are pieces of card board on hand paper on which a word or words are written on some picture is drawn.

They can be shown to the students at any time. Moreover, they can be shown for less or more time depending upon the teacher. They can be successfully used for a number of purposes e.g.

Word Recognition : A flash card bearing a word of a senten may be shown to a group of students or to some individual.

Team Competitions : Class may be divided into two teams. The flash cards may be shown to the groups by one. They will try to read out as quickly as possible.

Training in Speaking : Some questions may be written on the flash cards. The cards are shown to the students one by one. They are asked to speak out the answer.

Teaching Writing : They can also be used in teaching writing. By writing beautifully on them, they can also be used for improving the handwriting of the students.

Match Cards : Flash cards in serve the purpose of match cards. In match cards, we have flash cards in pairs. They are displayed on the flannel board. The students watch them carefully.

Then they are asked to match them rightly e.g., we have different flash cards for the words book, child, watch, woman books, children, watches, women etc. They are mixed up. Then the students are asked to match these flash cards, may be according to the number/plurals or genders etc.

Order Cards : Flash cards may carry words or expressions which mean some sort of order. These flash cards are shown to the students one by one and they may be asked to carry out the orders. For example, we have flash cards with the words or expression- sit stand, go out, come in, come here, go to the black board, bring chalks, call the peon etc. These are shown to the students and they act accordingly.

Flannel-Board (Felt Board) : It is a wooden board on which flannel is fixed. The different flash cards on the back of which flannel is fixed, can be placed on the flannel board. It is really a very useful, versatile and exciting aid.

The flannel board is not just an aid itself. It is, in fact, that type of aid which helps the other aids. A few other aids can be adapted to be used with the flannel board. In the hands of a creative and hard working teacher, it can probably be the most useful and exciting aid available next to black board. It can be used for teaching spellings, reading of English, formation of sentences, picture composition etc.

Bulletin Board

It is aboard of soft wood or cork. It is used for pasting papers, pictures of paintings. It displays announcements, records news items, newspaper cuttings, illustration etc.

This type of board helps in popularising any idea. The board is generally placed at some important place in corridors or in the classroom. The bulletin board is useful not only for teaching learning purposes but it also brightens the look of the school.

Pocket Board : It is wooden board on which pockets are made with about 1½ inch wide cloth wrapped from one corner to the other parallel to the base of the board. The pockets so formed are meant for holding the flash cards. Anything written on the flash cards may be hung in the pocket of the board and then removed by the teacher at any time.

If we want to use flash cards in the pocket there is no need of fixing up flannel at the back of the flash card.

The Magnet Boards

The magnet boards are used by the commercial firms to display something. They are a bit costly. Their use in Indian schools has not started as yet.

The magnet board is a display board made up of a milky glass sheet. There are four magnet strips spread over length-wise. Iron letters form the material to be displayed. If tube lights are fixed at the back of the glass, the material will be visible even at nights.

The Fixo Graph Boards

It is an evenly perforated plywood board or asbestos board painted in black colour. Plastic letters of different sizes are fixed into the perforations to display the matter. The letters may be of red colour or white. Quantitative data may be displayed on them.

Chalk Board

The chalk board is one of the oldest and easily available software aid in the schools. No doubt, a lot of progress has been made in various fields on account of advancement by Science and Technology, it is still a popular aid in the instructional process. If this aid is used properly, it becomes the most valuable device for making instructions concrete and comprehensive. The chalk-boards may be of hanged type, roller type, fixed type etc. Usually we have fixed boards in the class room. In subjects where too much in continuation is to be written roller board is recommended. In ordinary situations, fixed black board is all right. What type of colouring of the chalk board is more suitable? The experiments have proved that the use of white chalks and black surface are more suitable. We may have green boards.

Chalk boards may be of different types; (a) Wall Boards (b) Wooden Boards on Stands (c) Roller Boards (d) Graph Boards (e) Map Boards.

How to Use the Chalk Board

1. While writing on the chalk board, the teacher should start from the top left hand corner and continue writing till the lower end is reached. The systematic and uniform writing captures the attention of the students.
2. Whatever is written on the chalk board, it should be correct.
3. Whenever a new lesson/subject is started, it should be rubbed off and start afresh.
4. Lengthy drawings and sketches should be avoided. That will obstruct teachers' attention to the class for a longer time.
5. While writing the teacher should stand aside on the left. His own standing before the chalk board should not be any obstruction for the learners.
6. Sometimes a part of the chalk board is not visible to the class because of the reflection of light. That should not be used by the teacher.

7. The style of writing on the chalk board should be correct. The writing on the board must be reasonably good.

Advantages of Chalk Board

1. If a teacher goes on speaking in the class finishing up the syllabus, his teaching becomes dull and monotonous.' Many things may not be properly understood by the learners. The use of chalk board adds variety to the teaching on one side and on the other side it makes the lesson more clear to the students.

2. Some sketches or diagrams can be drawn on the chalk board. While teaching science subjects, some diagrams or sketches have to be drawn on the chalk-board.

3. In a language period, spellings of the words when written on the chalk board simplify things.

4. A teacher who is an expert in chalk board work is able to work wonders in teaching. He need not use a chart or picture. He can draw these on a roller chalk board and use the same in teaching. Thus it is economical in many ways.

5. While teaching, the teacher often goes on writing the summary of the lesson on the chalk board. It helps him in quick revision of the whole lesson in hand.

6. It is very flexible type of aid. The teacher man use it any way he likes according to his interest and liking. Sometimes when the teacher is not in a mood to write anything on the chalk board, that does not matter. He can very easily avoid usage. The total control of writing on the chalk board is in the hands of the teacher.

7. The chalk board is the heart and the soul of teaching Mathematics. The teacher as to use if for solving the sums.

Tape Recorder

No doubt, it is a very expensive type of audio aid, but it is quite useful. It is helpful to the teacher in many ways. Now improved models of the tape recorder are in use throughout the world : It comes under the category of Hardware aid.

Advantages

1. The tape recorder is an extension of a lecturer's work. When the teacher feels tired, he can teach vigorously by recording his voice with the help of a tape recorder.
2. It can be used for title improvement of pronunciation. The students can listen to the recorded programmes, speeches and thus improve their own pronunciation. Sounds, stress, intonation etc. can be taught by using a tape recorder.
3. The tape recorder can be used in learning music. The learners can record their performances and then discuss the same with their teacher.
4. It can be used for self-examination, self-criticism and self-education.
5. It can be used for giving a commentary on a slide or film strip.
6. It can be used for giving drills to the students.

Limitations

1. It does not function when electricity supply fails.
2. It needs careful handling as it is very delicate and can be out or order soon.
3. It is an expensive aid. Some schools may not afford to purchase it.

Record Player

Undoubtedly it is an expensive aid but it is of great advantage in the class room situations. Some records are available on which well known speeches are recorded. Listening to this type of records can prepare the students for becoming good speakers. There are gramophone records on which the poem and prose passages are recorded. In the same way these are records for teaching stress, intonation etc. of english language. While teaching english different type of records can be successfully used in the class rooms.

A record player can be used for teaching spellings of english words. For this purpose some records are available on which words alongwith spellings are spoken. These records can be used for that type of students who are ear-minded.

The record player works wonders in the class rooms where music and defacing are taught to the students. The students can learn singing by imitating the records. They can also dance according to the tunes produced on the record player.

Use of Radio, T.V. and Newspaper as Teaching Aids

Radio, T.V. and newspaper are commonly available in almost every home may be a village or a city. They are used for different purposes mainly for entertainment and knowing what is going on all around within the country or outside on this earth. In schools and colleges, their significance is becoming unique. They are very useful teaching aids. In the hands of a good teacher, they contribute handsomely to the class room teaching-learning programme. Even at their homes, the students are able to derive a lot of benefits with their uptodate knowledge in different spheres.

Radio : Radio is a very common type of hardware aid. It is an unparalleled vehicle, for mass communication. It is now recognized as an education medium that reaches millions of interested listeners. Its use for : educational purposes was tested in English in 1924. Later on Canada and Sweden, tried in 1926 followed by the experiments made by Switzerland in 1930 and by India in 1930, with the result many educational institutions of the West started using radio for instruction purposes, though in India, the number of such institutions was limited.

The radio programme for the schools become popular very common now with A.I.R. and B.B.C. Radio programmes for the schools became popular during the period from 1950's to 1970's. A large number of cities and rural schools started using radio in class room teaching. Generally the radio installed in the library or common room of the school and it is under the degree of one of the teachers.

A number of Akashwani stations (about fifty four) broadcast programmes for the school-children. These programmes are for (i) Teachers (ii) Children of Higher Secondary Classes (iii) Children of Primary Classes(iv) General enrichment programmes for young children etc. The themes and topics of the programmes for different type of audiences are planned by the Akashwani stations. They have advisory committees for this purpose whose personnels concerned with education are represented fairly. Mostly the Akashwani stations produce educational programmes for their broadcasts. NCERT, New Delhi, CIEFL, Hyderbad and CIIL, Mysore also produce some educational programmes which are used by Akashwani stations.

Highlighting the importance of the radio George Waston says : "Radio is not an addition to education. Radio is something to be placed on top of education. Rather, radio is education." Commenting upon the use of radio as an instruction aid, R.G. Raynolds writes: "Radio is the most significant medium for education. As a supplement to class room teaching its possibilities are almost unlimited. Its teaching possibilities are not confined to the five or six hours of the school day. It is available from early morning till long after midnight. By utilising the rich educational and cultural offerings of the radio children and adults in communities however remote, have access to the best of the world's stores of knowledge and art. Some day its use as an educational instrument will be as common place as text books and black boards."

Types of Programmes

Many types of radio programmes are broadcast such as children's programmes, Women's programmes, religious, agricultural and commercial programmes, variety show, drama, music, quiz contest programmes etc. Besides, there are educational programmes on various topics in different subjects. Generally there are radio lessons for the following subjects :

Science : There are talks on scientific inventions and interviews with the leading scientists and research scholars. Sometimes new developments in various branches of science are highlighted.

Languages : The learners can improve their pronunciation of english by attending radio programmes broadcast in english medium. Sometimes, we have a lesson on teaching of a poem. Presenting dramas and stories of famous writers is another feature of the radio.

Social Studies : We have dramatization of historical events, acquaintance with the lives of great men etc.

Music : National songs and other interesting musical items can be heard on the radio. This type of programmes arouse feelings of national unity.

A Radio Lesson

The Radio broadcast can be used :

(i) to introduce a new lesson.

(ii) to present a complete lesson.

(iii) to review the previous lesson.

(iv) to solve major problems occurring in a lesson.

Preparation : The teacher should find out beforehand from different sources about the lesson to be broadcast, its timings, any accessories if needed. He should tell the students how they will be benefited by the lesson. Then the different aids needed for the lesson should be got prepared-preferably with the help of the students. Seating arrangements of the students be made in a circle or semi-circle. The radio should be placed facing the students at a nearby distance. The teacher must make sure the working of the radio, the availability of electricity. If possible, provision of a generator should be there.

Before the actual broadcast, everyone should be seated properly. The different aids are displayed as per their utility in the class room situation.

Presentation of Broadcast. The radio lesson being broadcast is presented to the class. The teacher takes down a few points on his piece of paper/or note book side by side. The students may also write down some hints or points in their note-books side by side.

In fact, the students are asked beforehand to take down any query, doubt, question on their note-books for which they can consult the teacher later on.

Discussion : Immediately after the broad cast, the teacher discusses the lesson thoroughly with the students. Their doubts are classified and questions are answered. Whatever problems about the lesson are raised by the students, their solutions are given by the teacher. The outcomes of the lesson are highlighted.

Follow Up : As a follow up, the teacher may give the students some working assignment, hold an oral test to find out their understanding of the lesson.

In cases some suggestions are put forth by anyone from the class attention is paid to the same.

Advantages of Radio Lessons

1. Radio brings subject experts and other great men in the class room. Lectures, talks and addresses of important personalities from any corner of the world can be heard on the A.I.R.
2. A single broadcast can be heard and understood by a large number of students at a time. The cost of per capita of the listeners is very small and is almost negligible.
3. The class room instructions are supplemented by radio programmes. The routine and monotonous type of class room environment is ended.
4. The general knowledge of the pupils is widened. They are able to have extensive knowledge of many things.
5. The radio becomes a very important medium for leisure time activities.
6. The radio lesson helps the students in the improvement of pronunciation, speech and language.
7. It develops critical thinking of the students.
8. The voice of the speaker on the radio is heard by the children and they are attracted towards it. It is really very impressive and life like for them.

To sum up Fredric Wittis says, "Like to think of education by radio as a timely, vital, dramatic thing, a system operating or acquiring more information, a means of widening one's horizon or enriching one's life and breaking down prejudices through inspiration and not prescription, an education by desire and not by discipline; a pattern of slowly changing pictures, events with keen interpretations, not statistics and formulas; a moving panorama of the world in which we live right now, while we are living in it — not a dreary drill of text books and tests. In short, I feel that one of the broadcasting's most useful contribution to education and one of its responsibilities to itself and its listeners is the popularising of education itself."

Limitations

But radio lessons have some limitations also which are as follows :

1. The broadcast is one way communication. The students cannot get the doubts clarified. They cannot put any question. Only the teacher can help and that too after the broadcast is over.
2. Every time, the time of broadcast does not suit the school or the class.
3. No doubt, home assignment can be given by the radio lesson. But correction is not possible. Only the class teacher has to do it.
4. The financial problems are there in the way of the educational use of the radio. The number of receiving sets is inadequate.

Whatever may be the drawbacks of the radio lesson, its utility and extraordinary advantages cannot be ignored. The teacher should try to make fullest use of the radio programmes. Radio is, undoubtedly, a force in education with vast potential. In the words of K.N. Srivastva : "The radio is full of promise for the future of education."

Television : Like radio, television is also a means of mass communication. Its advantage over the radio is that it appeals both to the ear and the eye. It has been described as the queen of audio-visual aids. It combines photo and voice. It is said to be the 'electronic black board of the future.' Of late; its utility in educational process has been recognised. It has now become powerful means of communication of ideas all over the world. For making it really useful, the teacher inculcates among the pupils good viewing habits, critical and attentive listening. He also psychologically prepares them to receive the information from the television. After the lesson also, he plays his role as per needs and, requirements of the learners. The teacher is given a guide sheet for each T.V. lesson. He can, however, deviate from that sheet if he finds it necessary.

Television is being used for educational purposes in our country for the last about 30 years. First it was used in schools of Delhi in 1961. Later the scheme was taken up by Doordarshan

Kendras of Mumbai, Chennai and Srinagar. The first attempt to use T.V. on a mass scale was made by using an American Satellite (ATS-6) in 1975-76 during the Satellite Instructional Television experiment (SITE). The SITE was conducted for about one year in rural areas scattered in twenty districts of six states namely Andhra Pradesh, Bihar, Karnataka, M.P. Orissa and Rajasthan. There was twenty minutes programme every day for the children during school hours. The Satellite was also used for 12 days in order to give orientation programme to primary school teachers in science.

In April 1982, India acquired its own national satellite (INSAT) and since then T.V. is being used on a mass scale for qualitative improvement of elementary education. Its services have been utilized in Andhra Pradesh, Orissa, Maharashtra, Gujarat, U.P. and Bihar. Since 1984, ETV programmes are being relayed by High Power Transmitters (HPTS) and Low Power Transmitters (LPTS). Day by day, more and more efforts are being made to make educational TV reach all corners of the country.

Kinds of Educational T.V.

1. Open Circuit Television : It is the usual type of telecast by commercial or non-commercial stations.
2. Closed Circuit Television : It is the selective telecast which can be tuned in only by specially equipped receivers.

Types of Educational Programmes

The following are the types of educational programmes commonly used on T.V.

(i) *Demonstration Type* : It can be commercial as well as educational. Some outstanding class room activity of a school is made known to others through television.

(ii) *Supplementary Type* : In some subjects, there area few problem areas. The supplementary type of programmes assist the schools in supplementing their knowledge in those specific areas. This is also called enrichment programme.

(iii) *Direct Teaching Programmes* : This type of programmes are telecast for direct teaching in the different type of schools. They are used in elementary schools, high schools and adult schools. It has been done in a few selected cities only.

Advantages

1. With the help of television, a large number of students can be given information at a time.
2. Television helps in improving the pronunciation of the students. Listening, speaking and understanding abilities of the learners can be improved.
3. On the television, mode type of handwriting can be drawn. The students may look at it and they can improve their own hand writing.
4. The students with slow speed of writing may be asked to listen to the news and then they may write it down in their note-books. Thus their speed of writing can be improved.
5. The gifted children can be benefited because they can do some work of advanced nature which is usually not available to them in their class rooms.
6. With the help of television, the ablest and the most capable teachers are brought to the T.V. screen. Thus teaching improves considerably in the class rooms.
7. The use of different types of or T.V. aids by the teachers in their class rooms is expensive. On the T.V. such lessons involving the use of many aids may be telecast. It will reduce the expenditure on teaching.
8. Television is a time saving device. More of syllabus may be covered in less time because everything on the lesson will be carefully planned without any sort of deviations.
9. The students who are not able to attend the class due to some reason can watch the T.V. lesson at their homes.
10. From the television, the students will be able to have uniform type of information. No student can grudge that he/she could not listen properly because of back benches.
11. With the help of television, the students can see many things places, situations etc. which otherwise they may not be able to see due to various reasons.
12. It helps in reducing the load of work of the teacher. When the T.V. lesson is on, the teacher is in the background and he helps the students on the points where his help is sought by them.

13. On the television, lessons of the expert teachers are telecast. Surely it improves the knowledge of the teachers and also helps them to become better teacher.

Limitations

1. It is one way communication. The students cannot put any question nor can they seek any clarification when the T.V. lesson is going on.
2. Individual differences of the learners are not attended to in a T.V. lesson.
3. The time for the T.V. lesson may not suit the teacher or the school. It may cause lot of inconvenience to many persons.
4. It may not be learner-centered approach as mostly the students have to remain passive listeners.
5. A television set is expensive and every school may not be able to have it for teaching purpose.
6. The whole T.V. programme is rigid. Everyone has to watch it. The principle of flexibility is not cared for.

Television is certainly a better and more effective aid as compared to radio because it can present action along with the voice of the speaker. It makes the experiences concrete, real and immediate. On the whole, it helps considerably in making the teaching-learning process more concrete and sound.

Experience of the world shows a good deal of advantages of radio and T.V. in education. The more the children use their senses, the greater is the learning on their part.

Newspapers : Newspapers are mostly used for communication purposes in our country. News of different types pass on to the people with the help of newspapers. The unemployed people see vacancies under the column 'vacancies' or 'situation vacant'. The students community see the results of different examinations from the newspapers. Big business centres send their advertisements and attract customers through newspapers. Besides, some newspapers carry news concerning income tax, court notices. Sunday magazines are there to cater to the needs of the literary persons. Very rarely, a newspaper is used to serve some useful educational purposes in the formal education system.

Types of Newspaper

Everybody is acquainted with daily newspapers such as The Tribune, Punjab Kesri, Hindustan Times etc. There are other newspapers also bi-weekly, weekly, fortnightly monthly, quarterly etc. They are put to use differently in different schools. In some schools, one teacher or one student reads out the main news in the morning assembly. In some schools, in each class room, they have some discussions on news. A large number of schools have a chalk board named 'News' and same teacher or students write the news on that board so that all the students of the school may read these news.

Making formal education more interesting need a different use of newspaper for class room teaching purposes. Some newspapers based on education only be published and made available for the students community. This type of newspaper should contain educational items only which may be used by the students, community for teaching the desired goals of communication. There may be columns concerning primary education vocational, education, teacher training, general knowledge competitive exams. etc. It will benefit all type of students who ever aspire for better careers.

Educational Value of Newspapers

Newspapers have great educational value which is briefly given below :

1. They are a very good source of knowledge. Any and every type of knowledge can be gained out of them. A man of science, arts or technology finds useful knowledge in them.
2. They help the students in supplementing the knowledge they get from the text books.
3. They impart information about the cultural heritage. On the day of religious festivals such as Diwali, Dussehra, Holi, Baisakhi, the newspapers contain lot of information on these aspects. All this adds to the knowledge of the students.
4. The newspapers keep the students busy during their free time. Thus they are able to utilise their leisure time fruitfully.

5. They develop the skill of reading. Reading newspapers in the library makes them library minded. Many students are able to do extensive reading which helps them in their future careers.
6. They develop in the students love for literature. Material of literary type such as stories, poems, pieces of literary taste are presented in the newspapers on week-ends.
7. The newspapers also contain material which have a good deal of recreational value. Tit-bits, jokes, cartoons, etc. recreate the students.
8. They give the students information of national interest. Even in international understanding the students are benefitted.
9. The newspapers motivate the students in preparing better for the different competitions.
10. Newspapers also help the students in preparing better for the different competitions.

Thus we find that newspapers can work wonders in developing the careers of the students. There is need of reading the newspapers for different purposes.

Thus we find that the different types of aids have their marked value in the teaching learning process. This does not mean that the use of one aid or the other is a passport to the success of a lesson. In fact, the success or failure of a lesson depends upon many factors. A bad teacher having a variety of aids cannot come out to be an excellent teacher. On the other hand, a teacher without the assistance of some aids can, come out to be a good teacher. If the aids are to be used at all, the teacher should see that they are used at the right moments and in the right ways.

Should audio visual aids be used by all type of teachers? No. every teacher may not use them. A beginner teacher must use them. A teacher under training is expected to use them. Gradually every teacher should go on decreasing his/her dependence upon different types of aid. Undoubtedly, the variety of audio visual aids make the teaching process reasonably good and effective. In this regard Comenius rightly says, "The foundation of all learning consists in representing clearly to the senses, sensible objects so that they can be appreciated easily."

QUESTIONS

1. What do you understand by the term Audio-Visual aids as used in the field of education? Discuss the importance of these aids.
2. Discuss the educational importance of the following aids: (a) Epidiascope (b) Radio (c) Flash Cards and Flannel Board (d) Television.
3. Discuss the major principles of which effective utilisation of Audio-Visual Aids is based. Write by supporting examples.
4. What do you mean by projective teaching aids? Discuss any three aids of this type.
5. Television has revolutionised the field of instruction. Discuss this statement by giving examples.
6. What is meant by Audio-Visual Aids? What are the principles of selection of these aids? What precautions must be kept in mind for using these aids?
7. Discuss the role of the following in education with special reference to formal education : (a) Television (b) Films (c) Newspapers.

4

Different Devices

The prime focus of teaching is to bring about a desirable change in the behaviour of the learner. It is brought about by the teacher using different types of teaching methods, techniques, devices and teaching aids. The selection of these methods and other teaching tactics, depends upon the nature of task, learning objectives, learner's abilities and student's entering behaviour. With the help of these methods, devices, strategies etc., a teacher can make the process of teaching and learning effective and profitable to the children. Apart from following the broad principles of education, a teacher is to make use of certain devices and techniques in order to overcome the possible hurdles during the act of teaching. The devices make teaching interesting as well as stimulating affair.

Meaning of 'Teaching Device'

The word 'device' is often misconstrued in teaching and learning. Some take it as a technique while others confuse the term with method of teaching. But it is different. A device is a plan, scheme or trick invented for the special purpose of effective teaching and purposeful learning. Raymant defines it "as certain external 'forms or modes which his (teacher's) instructions may from time to time assume." Like a method it is not based on classical theory of organisation. It constitutes an external form.

Difference between Method and Device

Method has a wider scope than device. Method refers to the formal structure of the sequence of acts commonly denoted by instruction. Matter is important for determining a method. It is a style of presentation of contents in the class-room. Method is more general. It includes techniques and devices also. The teaching techniques and devices are ways of implementing a method. Different devices may be employed within one method. Device is an external mode of form which instruction may from time to time assume. Method is a systematised way of doing something for effective control. Method is never something outside the material to which the teacher often resorts from time to time.

Importance of Devices of Teaching

The use of teaching devices in teaching is justified by the following reasons :

1. Teaching-learning process becomes effective and easy by their use in teaching method.
2. Devices help to teach quickly. This results in covering more syllabus in less time.
3. Devices of teaching help to teach more thoroughly so that students may retain the subject matter taught.
4. Devices are very helpful in the success of a method of teaching and teacher himself.
5. These are helpful in bringing something new to children.
6. These are good means of integrating a number of separate pieces of work already learned by other means.
7. A teacher needs to use them in order to foster the development of knowledge and to achieve his proposed objectives.
8. With the help of devices of teaching, the teacher can accelerate the pace of learning and get round the pupils to appreciate certain hidden aspects of subject matter.
9. Devices enter teaching aids to the success of the lesson taught by the teacher through any method-Inductive, Deductive, Problem solving or any other.

Classification of Devices

Teaching devices may be classified under two heads:

1. Formal Teaching Devices
2. Informal Teaching Devices

Formal devices are those which involve special technique in their handling in certain typical activities. By the use of these devices, teaching is conditioned and learning takes place by way of indirect experience. These are more effective in language teaching. These are conversation, discussion, recitation, questioning etc. Audio-visual aids used for special purpose during the process of teaching also fall in this category.

In the second category are those devices by which learning takes place in an incidental way and knowledge comes as a by product of direct experience *e.g.* picnics, excursions, tours etc.

There is one more classification of teaching devices which looks more sound and educative.

1. Teaching Devices

2. Fixing Devices

The teaching devices are those which a teacher is expected to use while conducting the formal lesson for the first time. Fixing Devices are made use of by the teacher after he has once finished his first round of teaching and now he wants to fix the content firmly in the mind of his pupils.

Oral communication devices, use of printing information and various sensory aid are the examples of first type. Drill, Review and Repetitive Practices are fixing Devices.

Here below is given the detailed description of some teaching devices:

Oral Communication

Oral Communication is a very good device used while teaching a language. Listening and speaking of a language depends upon oral communication by the teacher. The teacher having a good control over this device is able to teach the language effectively.

Exposition and Explanation

To expose means to open to exhibit, to display or to disclose. Exposition is giving the pupils new information and later explaining this new information to them. This technique is generally employed at the presentation stage in an informative lesson. The overall purpose of exposition is to enable the pupils to have a clear idea of the subject matter presented to them. Through this device, the students are able to make connection between different sets of related facts.

"Explanation means to explode to clear of ambiguity and to develop understanding. When exposition of a particular topic is in action, the teacher will have recourse to the use of explanation. Explanation forms a kind of bridge between telling and revealing knowledge to the learners. The main object of explanation is to enable the children. To take interest in the proceedings in the class, to grasp the purpose of what is being done and to develop their understanding of how to do it. It is useful in skill and knowledge lesson

Difference between Exposition and Explanation

1. Exposition aims merely at placing facts clearly before the learner, while explanation aims at showing facts in their proper relation to other facts in a system.
2. In pure exposition significant relations may be taken for granted while in explanation, they must be made explicit.
3. Exposition exercises memory, explanation exercises understanding, reasoning and originality.

Practical Suggestions

1. The teacher's exposition should be clear, to the point dealing only with the particular subject. Similarly, explanation should be directed towards a specific aim which must always be kept in mind.
2. There should be a logical sequence in exposition or explanation.
3. The language used by the teacher should be simple, clear and within the easy grasp of the pupils.
4. The teacher should take the help of Blackboard for drawing sketches and figures.
5. There should be free use of illustrations, pictures, maps, charts etc. Comparisons and instances taken from day-to-day life situations should also be used in exposition and explanation.

6. Students should be given ample opportunities during exposition or explanation to able them to ask questions. It should not be a one way traffic. Proper interaction is essential.
7. Exposition and specially explanation should come at the proper time and rounded up when the object is achieved.
8. It is not desirable to make the exposition or explanation rapidly, otherwise, it will leave many gaps in comprehension of the material.
9. Over-loading of the lesson should be avoided.
10. To ascertain whether the students have grasped the material, the teacher may ask some questions from the students at different stages of development.

Narration

It is also an important device for oral communication of knowledge. Narration helps children to learn quickly by making the subject matter interesting and easy to grasp. Narration means telling stories, giving accounts to events or recounting some past incidents of life. It is a very effective device for teaching social sciences, literature and natural sciences. It is used as a means of arousing interest in learning.

Narration is an art. In the words of Panton, "Narration is an art in itself, which aims at pre-ending to the pupils through the medium of speech, clear, vivid, interesting, ordered sequences of events, in such a way that their mind constructs these happenings and they live in imagination through the experiences recounted either as spectators or possibly as participators."

The success of this device depends upon the ability of the narrator, his language and way of narrating. Dramatic narration is very useful for creating interest and enthusiasm in snail work.

Practical Suggestions

1. Narration should be in simple and clear language.
2. Purpose of narration should be clear and direct.
3. Style of presenting should be dramatic and interesting.
4. It should present a vivid picture of the subject.

5. Narration should be well prepared and planned. There should be a continues flow in the sequence of events.
6. The material of narration should be both recreational and informational. In order to avoid monotony, different types of material should be presented at different occasions.
7. It should be in direct speech as far as possible.
8. The stories should be selected on the basis of children's needs and interests.
9. In order to make the narration lively and real, the narrator should use illustrations such as models, charts, maps, graphs, similes, metaphors etc.
10. In order to impress the children, the teacher should make use of action and sense impression whenever they are needed.

Description

Description is somewhat similar to explanation. Dictionary defines description as "the act of representing a thing by words, account of the properties or appearance of something". So description implies the use of words or symbols to represent some objects or events. In it, the learner or listener gets a definite mental picture of certain experiences, generally in the form of visual images. In order to make it successful, a teacher must prepare his word picture carefully and skilfully and make descriptions interesting and arresting.

In description, like narration, the effective use of language is very necessary. The teacher must acquire the art of making word pictures through constant practice. In narration, the story-element of it, binds the child, but here the process is somewhat harder and difficult. A teacher must take this point in his mind while using description as a device of teaching.

Practical Suggestions

1. In description, logical sequence should be observed. The sequence should proceed from the known to unknown. But the known should be selected with very great care.
2. Language used should be clear and simple.

3. We should not rely on words alone. Rather some models, diagrams or pictures should be used.
4. Description should be brief and to the point. The size of it must suit the level of the pupils.
5. Appropriate speed should be observed. More speed creates confusion and lack of understanding while excessive slowness leads to boredom.
6. The description should be purposeful and directed towards a set aim.
7. In order to verify description frequent use of homely illustrations such as metaphors and similes should be used.
8. In order to make the description more interesting and effective, the teacher should employ the dramatic style.
9. Question-answer technique should be used because it keeps the pupils active and attentive.
10. While using description, the teacher should keep in mind that it is a means to an end. It should not be used for the sake.

Illustration

In order to make the meanings clear and help the children acquire proper knowledge, the teacher in his class uses illustrations. It gives meaning to abstract ideas and thoughts. The dictionary definition of illustration is "To make clear, intelligible, comprehensible, to elucidate, explain or exemplify as by means of figures, comparisons and examples". Technically, the art of illustration is not merely the employment of pictures, charts or examples, comparison or analogy, but also consists of various types of apparatus like blackboard, scientific and geographical apparatus or models or diagrams and sketches. In fact, illustration includes anything which makes an appeal to the senses and the imagination of the learner.

Importance of Illustration

1. Illustration as a device of teaching has great importance in classroom teaching. In order to attract pupils' attention, make the lesson interesting and facilitate understanding with the free use of illustrations.

2. They give concrete description to the abstract ideas and thoughts.
3. They are useful for the young children, because they hardly indulge in abstract thinking.

So, illustration is very useful in making some idea or mental picture more clear, definite and precise. It stimulates interest and curiosity of the learner.

Types of Illustrations

Various types of illustrations which are used in the process of teaching can be categorized into the following two primary class:

Verbal Illustration : These are illustrations which influence the mind through the medium of related ideas expressed words. It can be further subdivided into three categories:

(i) Stories, anecdotes and descriptions.

(ii) Analogies and comparisons.

(iii) Similes and words.

Non-verbal or Concrete Illustrations : These directly through the senses. These illustrations are of greater politial value than the verbal illustrations. These can be successfully employed when the verbal illustrations fail to bring home the image of the object to be described. This category includes concrete material such as actual objects and specimens, models, pictures, diagrams, sketches, maps, graphs etc.

Practical Suggestions

1. The illustration used should be simple and comprehensible. It should be common to the experience of the students.
2. It should be self-explanatory and obvious in meaning.
3. Illustration should exact and accurate. It is bad to use an illustration for its own sake.
4. Too many illustrations should not be used in a single lesson. An excessive number of illustrations given in a quick succession, confuse and distract the attention of the students.
5. Illustration used must be interesting and according to the general taste of the children.

6. In verbal illustration, language used by the teacher should be simple and correct. Technical and difficult language should be avoided.
7. Illustration to be used in the class should be prepared in advance. Proper planning is necessary.
8. Concrete illustration should be properly handled and exhibited. Display should be proper and timely.
9. Concrete illustration should remain before the students for sufficient time to enable them to observe, feel and draw out their conclusions.
10. There should be a variety and novelty in the use of illustrations. Constant use of the same or the same type of illustration makes the presentation dull and monotonous.

Assignments

Assignment means the work that has been allotted to the pupil or the class. Its main object is to supplement the class work. It is most frequently used by teachers in teaching higher classes. It provides the situation for the assimilation of the content. It is based on the psychological principles.

Importance

The importance of assignments based on the fact that the desire of the student to learn is more important than the methods of teaching. It is pupil's attitude towards learning that matters and that the well-organized course of instructions.

With its help, the pupil's interest in learning can be directed.

Purpose of Assignment : It serves a number of purposes in the teaching-learning process which are given below.

1. It gives the teacher opportunity to give in directions to the learner's acitivity.
2. It arouses attention and interest of the pupils in thorough and serious learning.
3. It is usd to supplement the class work.
4. It encourages initiative and co-operation among the students.

5. It is the determining factor in the development of effective habits of study.

Principles:

It is based on the following learning principles:

(i) Principle of exercise.

(ii) Principle of interest.

(iii) Principle of learning by doing.

(iv) Principle of individual difference and

(v) Principle of assimilation.

Steps in Assignment Making : A good assignment takes care of the following steps:

1. Reference to previous experiences.
2. Discussions.
3. Proposal of a new activity.
4. Acceptance of the activity after discussion.
5. Explanation and clearing up the difficulties.
6. Outlining the materials to be used.
7. Assigning the tasks to be done.
8. Overseeing the beginning of the work, if possible.

Characteristics of Good Assignment : The assignment can be (i) Recreational; for socialised activity; (ii) for individual study and (iii) for problem solving etc. Recreational assignments are generally light and less exacting and short. The problem type of assignments are interesting and challenging. In the beginning, simple assignments should be given to the children and complex types be given afterwards.

An assignment must have the following characteristics:

1. It should be definite and worthwhile.
2. It should relate the old knowledge to the new one, to give the impression of continuity of learning.
3. It should be clear and interesting.

4. It should motivate the students for advance study.
5. It should stimulate thought and develop insight and understanding for carrying out work.
6. It should recognise individual difference.

Advantages : It has the following advantages in teaching learning process:

1. It develops the reading and study habits.
2. The student learns through his own experiences.
3. It is based on the psychological principles of teaching.
4. Right type of attitude towards study is developed by this technique.
5. It considers the individual differences of the students.

Precautions : The following precautions should be observed while using assignment as device of teaching:

1. It should be used on teaching context or specific topic.
2. The name of the books and references should be given to the students.
3. Language used should be simple and clear.
4. Too many assignments should not be given to the students.
5. Proper evaluation should be done as quickly as possible.
6. The assignment should be according to the mental level of the students.

Home Work

Home work is that which is undertaken outside the normal school day. It is a kind of independent work which the pupil is expected to do at home to supplement instruction, received at school. As a practical teaching device, home work is a step towards self-education. It enables the child to use his own resources and work unsupervised.

Importance of Home Work

1. Homework is necessary to supplement the teaching work done in the school.

2. It develops the power of independent and unaided work in the child.
3. It is a useful activity which keeps the child busy at home.
4. It is a valuable aid in fulfilling the demands of too heavy syllabi for different classes to be completed during the school study hours.
5. It is an effective means of fixing up the subject matter taught in the class.
6. It develops the habit of hard work among the children.
7. It develops the moral and intellectual qualities and self-reliance, self-direction and initiative.
8. Home work serves as a link for parent-teacher co-operation.

There are some educationists who are against the allotment of home work to school children. They say that no home work should be given to the students. According to Bray, "Under normal conditions, a reasonable day's work for a child has been done at the close of the afternoon and home work as it is generally organized does more harm than good."

Others feel that in his anxiety to finish the work assigned, the child is but natural to ignore the work, duties and responsibilities. It is a some of friction between school and home. So, it should be avoided.

Practical Suggestions : In fact, it is not the home work that is objectionable, but it is nature and amount that stands critical examination. While allotting home work to child end, the teacher should bear in mind the following points:

1. Home work should be graded as per individual's interests, needs and abilities and not according to the whim of the teacher.
2. It should not be devoted to topics covered in the class.
3. It should cover not only academic work but also activities like hobbies connected with various school subjects. It will break the monotony of routine and mechanical work.
4. It should not be used as a tool for punishment.

5. It should be definite and limited in scope.
6. Home work should be well thought and well planned in advance.
7. It should be sympathetically checked and encouragingly corrected.
8. The teacher should not be very rigid in asking the children to do the whole of the allotted work.
9. It should encourage library readings.
10. Parents should be consulted from time to time about home work.

Discussion

Discussion is a very useful device used by good teachers in their class room situation. During discussion, the teacher and the students are actively engaged in the process of teaching learning. Every teacher can not come out successful in class room discussion. The teacher who has thorough knowledge and fully clear concepts in his mind prefers to pick up classroom discussion. Such a teacher is able to co-ordinate the discussion well. The different students speak one by one and the teacher keeps everything under his thumb and control. In a good discussion, all the speakers address to the teacher and give their arguments. He does not allow any type of verbal disputes in the class. The teacher ultimately is able to give one shape of different through presented by the students during class room interaction.

Discussion as a device should be used for a limited time only. Prolonged discussion does not server any useful purpose and that also becomes dull and boring for everybody.

Dramatization

Dramatization is a very good teaching device where the teacher starts playing different roles. Every teacher cannot dramatize in the class. Only an experienced and seasoned teacher can use this device in his class room teaching. Thus some teachers teach Shakespearieean drama in such a way that the students sitting in the class feel as if the drama is really being staged before them. Here teaching is all activity based where the main role is played by the teacher.

Dramatization means putting some prose or poetry into living action. Some person plays a role and there we have dramatic view of the situation. Surely a number of scenes in prose can be presented in dramatic form. In so doing, acting, gestures, movements and facial expressions are involved.

Dramatization appeals to the children, the reason being that it involves some action, some activity. It makes teaching activity centered. Thus it is a method of teaching. A good teacher loves to dramatize a prose piece or a poem. In fact, his heart dances to read through the matter and he finds thrill in it which makes him act and play some role. The children by nature like imitation.

Dramatization may be used in any subject. Any topic of science make one fact. In teaching English, one act plays surely make a teacher act and dramatize the scene or situation. Of course some teachers are fond of dramatization and they are able to put life into any literary work. Surely in the class room, dramatization can be incidental or spontaneous.

Advantages of Dramatization

1. It helps the children to form good speech habits which are very essential in the learning of a language.
2. It helps the learners improve their pronunciation.
3. A language for communication is better learn by this.
4. The students learn how to act appropriately in the context of feeling and ideas contained in the matter.
5. They are able to make use of gestures and they can adopt facial expression needed by them.
6. It develops in the students love and appreciation for good literature. They then develop the habit of extra reading.
7. It develops the imagination of the students which is the basis of good teaching learning. Surely thus the students come out as better learners who have some originality. It may lead to making them creative persons one day.
8. When a number of students do actions, they learn how to co-ordinate and how to make their role play real.
9. Good speech habits acquired through dramatization help a lot in winning friends and influencing people.

10. It helps in shedding off stage shyness.
11. There is healthy release of emotional feeling of the children. It helps them in the right development of personality.
12. It puts life and action into the lesson which comes interesting for the students. Then they love to read that lesson without any stress and strain.

Lecturing

Lecturing is speaking by the teacher in class room teaching. During lecturing, the teacher goes on speaking giving an outlet to his feelings and thoughts. It is an important teaching device. Lecturing should be done for some time only. That way it remains a device in the hands of the teacher and it remains full in class room situation. If lecturing is done for long time, it becomes dull and montonous affair. Then it is also tiresome for the teacher and boring for the students. Therefore in the school, the teacher should give lecture as less as possible. But for the seniors, lecturing of a more duration serves useful purpose.

Lecturing has some Advantages

1. The person giving a lecture can cover up a lot of syllabus if he is to cover the syllabus.
2. Through lecturing, the person can give an outlet to his feelings and thoughts till he/she is exhausted.

Lecturing has some demerits also which are as under.

(a) Lecturing is one way speaking only. It is not considered good for class room teaching.

(b) The listener may not like it after sometime.

Therefore, the teacher should use lecturing as a device of teaching and not as a full-fledged method which is continued for a longer duration.

Story Telling

Story telling is a very good device of teaching in the hands of a successful teacher. Some teacher are very fond of teaching by telling stories to the students. In fact, story telling is nothing, but narration of some events spread over a given period of time. This device make teaching very interesting for the students. In story telling, the following points should be well taken care of by the teacher who uses this device in class room teaching:

1. The contents for the story should be according to the mental level of the students.
2. The historical facts should not be distorted because that gives bad impression to the learners.
3. The style of narration should be a joyful activity.
4. The main points of the story may be repeated because generally the students enjoy that type of repetition.
5. The activities and experiences as shown in the story, should be interesting for the students.
6. The whole of the story should be narrated in one sequence.
7. The narration should be done in an interesting way. Nothing should be read from the notes of the book.
8. While telling the story, the teacher should create suitable atmosphere. The purpose of telling the story should be clear to the teacher as well as the students.
9. As far as possible, the story telling should inspire the student.
10. At the end, the students should be given opportunities to react to the whole story.

Surely, story telling is an art which can be acquired by a teacher during the course of teaching. Seeing the wonderful benefits of this device, every teacher should try to be good in story telling. That gives a thrill to the learners for learning and it also gives a lot of satisfaction to the teacher.

Study Habits

In the teaching learning programme, study habits are very important. A casual attendance of the class, does not develop good study habits of the students. The students should be very punctual and regular in attending the class. The teacher's actions should be inspiring and encouraging for the students, Every teaching period should be a thrill giving to the students. This type of class room input is bound to develop good study habits of the students. The leaners need be taught self-dependence and self-reliance. Provision of time for library study should be there in the time table. All this will develop good study habits among the learners.

Good study habits developed in the students have the following advantages :

1. The students learn how to use their leisure time fruitfully. They do not waste their time.
2. The students are independent learners without depending upon the teacher unnecessarily.
3. They are able to explore and discover new things for themselves which become useful to them and to the society in future.
4. Self-study habits make them good thinker.
5. The learners learn how to face different type of problems and solve them through their initiation and self efforts.

Supervised Study

In teaching learning programme, supervised study is a very good innovation. Here some students study of their own or as per the direction of the teacher and all this is carried on under the supervision of the teacher. Supervised study is learner based study and it is not at all teacher oriented teaching. The students study and the supervisor is available to them for consultations and guidance. There is controlled type of environment where the students study with full freedom.

Supervised study centres are becoming popular in big cities. The students are able to do their home work or home assignments given in the school by sitting at a place where the teacher is available as a supervisor and as a guide. The supervision helps them in solving their problems. He paids them as per their needs and requirements. Surely, the supervisor does not poke his nose into the affairs of the students studying there.

The supervised study has the following advantages:

1. A number of students are able to sit together and do their home work assigned by the class teacher in the school.

2. There being informal democratic environment, the students learn how to sit together and how to learn from each other.
3. The students are able to utilize their home work properly and very regularly which ultimately make them good students.
4. The students are able to do their home work properly and very regularly which ultimately make them good students.
5. The students are able do their home-work without bothering their parents or guardians.

Source Method

Source method means the teacher will tell the different sources from where some information can be received or collected. Who can tell the source? Not any and every teacher. Only a capable teacher who has a lot of knowledge can do so. That type of teacher is library minded is a researcher and is always keen to add to his knowledge. Surely a seasoned teacher who has life long experience of teaching knows well the different sources from where the details of things can be had.

Telling the source is a good tool in he hands of a teacher. For example, the teacher has taught the topic lesson planning to B.Ed students. For more information, he suggests to them that they should consult Encyclopedia of Education :—

(i) The students become hard working as they remain busy in knowing more and more from different sources.

(ii) The students become researchers type.

(iii) The learners tend to have deep knowledge of things.

(iv) Naturally they are able to reason our well. They are also able to plead and give arguments.

Observation

Observation is another quite useful device of teaching in the hands of a teacher. This device cannot be used in teaching all the subjects. While teaching science, the teacher gives demonstration by performing some practical. The students observe everything. They carry on their experiments. Another example, for teaching English, the teacher performs a number of actions. The students are asked to observe carefully the different actions and write down all that in their note books. One more example - the teacher displays a model. The students observe the model carefully and then they are asked to speak one by one about the details of the model they have seen.

The device of observation helps the teacher in developing imagination of the students. They also become keen observers who notice every detail of the situation. A keen observer becomes a good thinker.

Fixing Devices of Teaching

Fixing devices are the tools, with the help of which the teacher makes the knowledge once communicated a permanent possession with the student. Through these devices, the teacher concentrates and fixes the mind of the students to teaching and remembering. Also through these devices, the teacher attempt to remove the vague ideas and strengthens their hold and the subject matter taught.

Drill Technique

Drill is the most common and indispensable teaching procedure for fixing the matter already learn. It is not mere repetition. It is a serious work actively taken and leads to improvement in performance, its purpose is to develop skill and reduce knowledge to the level of habit. According to Yuakam and Simpson, "Drill is to be used not merely for purpose of developing knowledge and skill. It is vitally important as a means of maintaining good habits, when they are well established." In other words, drill is essential, in making it a running unit of behaviour.

Suggestions for Conducting Effective and Interesting Drill

(i) Drill work cannot be undertaken haphazardly and without any definite purpose in view. It has to be planned intelligently and tactfully.

(ii) It should not be made monotonous and dull routine.

(iii) Proper motivation is essential.

(iv) Be dynamic, enthusiastic and alert. Permit it errors to achieve the particular end in view.

(v) Do not make it a blind repetition. Make it purposive and direct to achieve the particular end in view.

(vi) Fatigue after should be taken into consideration.

(vii) Take individual differences in view while defining the standards of attainment.

(viii) Give every pupil some opportunities to make responses.

(ix) Encourage pupils to drill themselves during out-of-class hours.

(x) Check the outcomes if not satisfactory, plan remedial drill either in the class or for individuals.

The Review

This teaching device is used to obtain permanence in learning. It is based on the principle of practice. It is quite different from drill. While drill aims at making responses automatic, review is the mental process of going over material already learnt and is a device to repeat, recognize and renew previous impressions. According to N.L. Bossing, "Review is not a mere repetition of the facts to fix them more firmly in mind, but rather a new view of these facts in a different setting that results in new understandings, changed attitudes or different behaviour patterns."

Characteristic of Review

1. It is a mental process.
2. Its broader approach ensures longer retention and much more thoroughness.
3. It presents previous knowledge from a new point of view and in new relationship.
4. Only the essential facts are recalled.
5. The subject matter is recognised and the original pattern is presented in new associations.
6. Its appeal is to one's thought since the associates are logical.
7. It adds new insight and understanding, recalls and gives facts.

The Technique of Review

The review should be carefully planned. Different topics or

problems in different areas require different techniques of review. The type of review that might suit a topic in History would be opted to Mathematics. So the selection of the type of review should be done carefully.

For conducting a review successfully, the following suggestions will help a lot:

1. Use the topical outlines to give the students better idea of the relationship of part to part.
2. Concentrate on the most important items.
3. Use the supplementary aids like references, questions, sensory aids etc.
4. Review should to done through reports, oral and written, through check lists, questions and through small discussion groups. It may also be done by the textbook questions. The importance of review as a teaching device lies in the fact that it helps to integrate the smaller units into a meaningful whole. It is employed to fix in mind, activities or materials already communicated by "going over" the same.

QUESTIONS

1. What to you understand by "Devices of Teaching"? How does a device differ from a method of teaching?
2. Why is it important for a teacher to use various devices?
3. In what way do narration, description and explanation differ from each other? How can they be usefully employed as teaching devices?
4. What is meant by illustration as a teaching device? What types of illustrations are commonly used and to what purpose?
5. What is assignment? What is its importance in teaching?
6. What are the characteristics of a good assignment? How will make it the most important phase of teaching?
7. Discuss the importance of the following in teaching:
   (a) Supervised Study (b) Story Telling (c) Dramatization
8. Write Notes on:
   (i) Study habits (ii) Illustration (iii) Discussion.

5

Teaching by Simulation

Problems, related to behaviour and problems concerning class room managements are handled in a better way through simulated teaching. In 1968 Cruickshank "developed a system which is denoted by several terms such as Role playing, Artificial Teaching, Pilot Training, Laboratory Method, Clinical Method and Inductive Scientific Method." Simulated teaching is a teacher training technique. It is quite significant in teacher education programmes. It is used for bringing about modifications in the behaviour of the teachers. The expression 'Simulated Teaching' comprises two words. Let us try to understand the meaning of the word 'Simulated' first.

Concept of 'Simulation'

According to Longman Dictionary of Contemporary English, 'simulate' means to give the effect of appearance of something else The advanced Learner's Dictionary of Current English by Hornby and others suggest its meaning as 'pretend to be; pretend to have or feel. 'Webster's Dictionary suggests the meaning as 'giving the appearance or effect of.'

Find says: "Simulation is the controlled representation of reality."

According to Thomas and Deemer: "To simulate is to obtain the essence of, without the reality."

In the words of !1arman : "Simulations contain the important parts of, but not all of, reality. Simulations do not have to look the real life counterpart, but they do have to 'act' like the real things."

Tansey's view: "Simulation the all-inclusive term which contains those activities which produce artificial environments or which produce artificial experiences for the participants in the activity."

According to Meggary: "A simulation is a technique of teaching and learning in which the students are presented with selected elements of real life events, processes or conditions with specific roles to play and specific goals to achieve. Use of simulation to effect specific needs and interests can provide great motivation for both the teachers and students."(1989)

The word' Simulated' means something made to look like the real thing. It is 'role play' in order to learn something new. The technique of simulation is as old as the man on this earth. Of course, in a systematised form it became popular after the First World War. The pilots were given training in the office with the help of models, maps etc. They were made to experience actual flying in the office itself. Thus mentally they were fully prepared for the actual situation.

At home, every day the children are seen imitating their parents or teachers or olher persons with whom they come in contact with in daily life routine. Sometimes the children are sitting in a group-one child pretending to be a teacher and making the other children sit as if in a class. In that situation, the children are playing the different roles. Their behaviour, action etc. are similar to what they have seen in the school.

With the popularity of television, the children are exposed to new type of experiences. They are able to visualise many new situations. All this is Reflected when the children try to play the different roles. It is very essential that the children should be exposed to healthy, positive and constructive type of learning situations. Imitating others and thus role play of someone or the other is a natural gift with the youngsters.

The technique of simulation has been used in various fields to achieve certain useful objectives. Soldiers are made to learn war strategies through it. Mock parliament gives some training to the students who wish to become successful leaders of future. The laboratory models are used for giving training to pilots, navigators, drivers etc. Thc doctor works on some animals with the purpose of being to lined better in order to become successful professionals. Before Dussehra, some people are made to play the rolls and thus Ramayana is staged before the public. Really, simulation as a technique is quite useful for different type of learners and trainees.

Simulation gaming is defined as a gestalt communication mode, a future's language which combines a game-specific language and appropriate communication technologies with the multilogue interaction pattern.

Types of Simulation

Horman has given the following types of simulation:

1. Identity Simulation: In identity simulation, the actual system is used as a model.
2. Replication Simulation: In replication simulation, an operational model of the system is used in its usual environment.
3. Laboratory Simlulation: In laboratory simulation, replication is employed in the laboratory with features of the real system represented.
4. Computer Simulation: Computer simulation is an abstract representation of the real system with the use of a computer. Analytical simulation:
5. Analytical Simulation uses mathematical models and attempts to get solution by analytical means.

Simulation in Teaching

Simulation in teaching was introduced recently. It is used at different levels of instruction. Suppose a teacher is trained-taught some theory papers and then he is sent to the school for teaching practice, he may not be able to do justice there. There is need of giving him training in simulated conditions. Let him play the role of a teacher in artificially created classroom environment. Let him learn things there and only after that he should be sent to the school for teaching. In this way, the teacher will be able to deliver goods in a much better way.

Simulated Teaching Defined

Simulated teaching may be defined as a process of learning or training technique aimed to increase the potential of one's own problem solving behaviour through role playing. Simulated teaching or training technique for helping the learner to bring desirable changes in his behaviour through some systematic and organised learning experiences in simulated *i.e.* artificial laboratory like conditions.

Simulation is defined a role-playing in which the process of teaching is enacted in an artificial situation with the objective of developing or practising a specific skill of communication.

According to Stone : "Simulation techniques, for all their artificiality can often be preferable to putting students in the classroom to learn, to teach of their own or to lecturing them about the class-room teaching. Simulated teaching for training would be teachers for teaching under simulated conditions, removes the risk from the first steps of the neophyte and enables them to come to terms with the demands of a complex skill learning without the stress of the real situation. It is preferred to merely telling the student, how to teach or control the class, for which the same reasons, as it is better to allow the beginning pilot to practise operating the dummy controls rather than telling him how to do it when he finds himself in the air."

Through simulated teaching, patterns of teaching behaviour can be taught well. It can be used for pre-service teachers to make them efficient. In simulated teaching, one pupil teacher acts as a teacher and other teacher trainees act as students. The teacher, in this situation, teaches considering the students as school students.

This system of training has been given different names such as Role Playing, Pilot Training, Laboratory Method, Simulated Social Skill Training (SSST).

Characteristics of Simulated Teaching Technique

The simulated teaching technique or simulated social skill has the following characteristics:

1. This technique requires a very systematic planning in advance. Whatever is to go on during the training process is decided well in advance. Right time planning ensures attainment of desired goals.

2. Proper involvement of the students in the training programme of this technique guarantees its success. The participating students are expected to have supportive behaviour and they should be committed to learning by this technique.

3. Feedback plays an important role in simulated teaching. The drawbacks noted in teaching are pointed out and appropriate suggestions are given. The feedback is positive and is of constructive type.

4. The supervisor helps in creating proper environment for the smooth functioning of this technique. By giving a really good demonstration, he ensures that the learners follow it in its true spirit and thus come out successful in achieving the desired goals.

5. The learners are made to face minor really good. Gradually they are made accustomed to serious type of problems. All this makes therein learning really good. Later those learners are ready to face any type of challenges.

6. Simulated teaching is based on system approach. There is full control of the supervisors when this scheme of learning is in progress. Then naturally every body's effort is the attainment of goals.

7. The training is provided in artificial situations. So there is no risk for real situations.Through mock trials, 'the learner is fully trained and equipped to face the real situation without any-type of confusion or problem.

8. There is proper adjustment of time factor in accordance with the difficulty in learning. That way it is a flexible method of teaching. Keeping the objectives in view, time can be increased or decreased as the situation demands it.

Assumptions of Simulated Technique

The simulated technique is based on certain principles which are given below:

(a) The underlying skills of teaching can be described, modified and practised.

(b) Immediate feedback helps for further improvement of communication skills.

(c) Different patterns of teacher behaviours are highlighted because of role perception and role play. That helps the teacher under training to identify the ones that they need most.

It goes without saying that simulation is of great use in teacher training programmes. The most important things in teacher training programme are :

1. Demonstration Lesson
2. Discussion Lesson
3. Teaching Practice

For the above, the teacher training colleges have to depend upon the schools. No doubt, these are possible in simulated conditions. But ultimately for making the teacher successsful, the assistance of the school is a must. In the practices for the above, the following are the obstacles:

1. The teacher training programmes have to take the help of the schools. They have to depend upon the schools. How far the Head of the school welcomes the teaching activities of the teacher trainees is important. Usually the Heads dislike it from the core of their hearts. Some Heads may say outwardly that they like it and welcome it whole heartedly.
2. Teacher training carried out in the school by way of practice in teaching causes injustice to the children. The teachers are trainees, their methodology is also not ripe, it may be off the mark or of poor standard, does not bring any benefit to the student The learners feel it just a wastage of their time.
3. The training for teaching has to be sufficient. But the teaching practice for a limited period of time usually comes out to be a sort of farce. It is not sufficient.

Simulated teaching does help the teacher training programme to some extent. The authorities concerned with the training programmes are able to create artificial situations in their teacher training institutes and they can cover up major part of training therein the college itself without disturbing the school only when they are fully equipped with methodologies and they have no fear of failing in the real classroom situations. .

Procedure of Simulated Training

In the simulation techniques there is development of social

skill of teaching in the teachers' training. According to Cruick Shank there are three important roles:

(i) The Teacher (ii) The Pupil and (iii) The Observer, Then there are three elements in the process of teaching which are as under :

(i) Diagnosing (ii) Prescription and (iii) Evaluation.

All the three elements are important in their own ways in the teaching-learning process. The teacher first of all tries to diagnose about the learners. At this stage he comes to know drawbacks, the attitude, aptitude, likings, dislikings of the students. Accordingly, he prescribes things so as to teach the learners suitably. At this stage, the teacher has to see that the subject matter is relevant and suitable for the learners. Then he adopts suitable methodology for teaching the subject matter to the students. After that the students are evaluated where by the teacher comes to know the success or failure of his teaching and also the success or otherwise of the learners.

Steps in Simulation Techniques

Ned Flanders has recommended the following six steps which are usually followed in simulation training technique:

Step I: Assignment of Roles. The student teachers are assigned the roles of teachers, students and observers, respectively. Every pupil teacher has to play all the three roles one after another. It is done on rotation basis.

Step II: Deciding the Skill to be Practised. A few social skills are discussed which are to be practised by the pupil teachers. At this stage the skill to be practised through simulated techniques, is decided and then planning and preparation for it are made. The topic for each trainee is selected according to his interest and intelligence.

Step III: Preparation of Work Schedule. In order to run the programme of practice successfully, the details of the work schedule are prepared. At this stage it is decided who will teach first and who will observe that lesson. It is also decided how everyone, turn by turn, will be teaching and how everyone turn by turn, will be observing the lesson.

Step IV: Determining the Technique of Observation. The teacher decides the procedure of observing the lesson. How different type of datas are to be observed and how are these to be recorded. The procedure for the interpretation of the data is also decided through discussion at this stage.

Step V: Organising the First Practice Lesson. The first practice lesson is started and its observations are recorded for judging the teaching behaviour. This is followed by discussion leading to feedback and suggestion for the improvement of the lesson.

Step VI: Alteration or Procedure. The whole procedure is changed at this stage. There is change of teacher, change of observer, change of teaching skills and also there is change in the topic to be taught. Every student teacher is given opportunity to play the role of a teacher, a student and an observer.

Advantages of Simulated Teaching

The simulation technique of teacher training has the following advantages:

1. The simulation exercise motivates the learners immensely. They show a lot of interest and excitement in learning activities of the class-room.
2. It is good for experiencing problem situations.
3. In traditional class-room teaching teachers' authority dominates. But simulations are self-monitoring. The participants recognise their own progress by various feedback methods. The teacher just acts as a guide.
4. Situation influences not only the school achievement but it also influences the attitude of the learners. The teachers under training are able to acquire a favourable attitude towards teaching.
5. It increases leaners' ability as decision makers in their problematic situations.
6. The learners are able to learn things deeply through simulation. They get insight into the teaching-learning situation.
7. Simulation as a technique is useful for all type of learners gifted as well as slow learners. The gifted can reach greater

heights and the slow learners are able to learn that much with which they can pull on.

8. It bridges the gulf between the theory and practice of teaching.

9. It helps to build self-confidence in the student teacher.

10. It provides them the reinforcement to develop various teaching skills.

11. To begin with, every pupil teacher has got limited knowledge of the skill but gradually through the process of training, each one of them has better knowledge of those skills. They can modify those skills and equip themselves accordingly. Thus they can have mastery over those skills.

12. In simulated teaching, every pupil teacher gets a chance of observing the lesson turn by turn. It prepares everyone to shoulder the position of responsibility in teaching-learning situations.

Limitations

The following are the drawback of simulated teaching:-

1. When simulated technique of training is used, a few adults play the roles of students. Some of them might feel it badly.

2. The observer who is doing the role play, may make incorrect recordings.

3. Simulation cannot be used in all subjects of the curriculum. While teaching art and painting it cannot be used. Simulation is a sort of play. When simulation technique is used, seriousness of learning is rather reduced.

4. For making this technique a success, use of highly sophisticated Audio Visual aids is a must. But in India we can hardly-afford that type of aids.

5. For beginners, it may be difficult to practice some of the teaching skills. For example questioning.

Type of Activities in Simulation

The following types of activities can be included in simulation technique:

1. Role Playing
2. Society
3. Gaming

Role Playing: Role playing is an act of being someone else. Here one person is asked to play the role of someone else. In fact, it is acting in simulated conditions. This activity helps the learner/ the actor in many ways. It is designed to improve the competency of the actor. The role can be played in artificial situation. Generally the actor is not familiar with the environment of the situation in which he is asked to play some role. The role play activity is quite useful for giving training to the teachers. An untrained teacher can improve his competency of teaching by playing the role of a teacher in some artificial situation. It is called the technique of simulation.

Need and Importance. It is not advisable to give the charge of teaching a class to some untrained teacher. It is better if he is given training by creating artificial situations. Simulated teaching will help them in many ways. The doctor under training first given training by asking him to play the role of a doctor and conduct experiments on animals like frog, mouse etc. Gradually he is asked to act in real life situations and treat the human beings.

The following points show very clearly the need and importance of role playing:

(a) Role play provides a lot of confidence to the person who is later on expected to play the role in real situations.

(b) It improves his competency of doing that work.

(c) Some people feel a lot of hesitation and shyness in the beginning while doing any work. That shyness is shed off through role play.

(d) The person playing the role of someone else gives him chances of improving his imagining ability. The more the imaginative a person is, the more he is fit for doing some work of creative nature.

(e) The attitude of a person also undergoes a change about role play. To a great extent, it becomes favourable.

(f) The teacher under training playing the role of someone else in different situations learns how to speak to the point and fluently.

(g) It makes the person thoughtful and creative. These are good characteristics of a would-be-teacher..

Procedure for Role Playing

Selection of Topic/Situation. Proper situation should be thought of for role play. The situation should be significant for the learner. It should aim at teaching the learner something. In every way, it should be encouraging the learner. Moreover; it should be according to the interests of the learners. It should arouse his feelings. It will be good if the the problem or the situation is taken up with which the learner is expected to have some relation in the near future.

Motivation: The learners who have to play different roles should be motivated in every possible way. The supervisor should explain to them the different situations in which role play is possible. Their ideas and thinking should be developed. Thus, they should be mentally prepared to play different roles in different situations.

Demonstration: The supervisor himself gives some demonstration by playing some role or roles. He may involve someone else also who is ready for it. The demonstration should be given by taking up two or three situations should motivate one and all watching that demonstration.

Assignment of Roles: Different students should be assigned roles according to their interest. Thus one person may play the role of the headmaster and the other person may play the role of the teacher. Out of the students, one student may play the role of a teacher and the other may play the role of class monitor. The supervisor should encourage the students to play as many roles as are possible. Nobody should be compelled to play the role which he or she does not like.

Playing the Different Roles: After assigning the roles, two persons should be asked to play their roles. They should be given full freedom to play their roles. The supervisor should be present there. He should not discourage anybody in any way. He should see that there is natural type of role play. The duration of time for each role play may be fixed up. Surely, role play should be stopped when interest of the actors starts decreasing.

Sufficient practice of role play should be given to the students. The objective behind each role play must be attained. The supervisor should see that role play remains an interesting activity and it is not allowed to become a drudgery of boredom.

Follow-Up and Discussion: After the role play, there should be full discussion. The actors and the observers should be given time to give their views freely. In case revision of role play is needed, the supervisor should allow actors to do so. The attitude of the supervisor must be encouraging.

A Few Examples of Role Playing

(i) Role of the Prime Minister

(ii) Role of the Chief Minister of the State

(iii) Role of Education Minister

(iv) Role of a Doctor and a Patient

(v) Role of a Clerk and a Student

(vi) Role of Inspector or Schools.

(vii) Role of a Peon of the School etc.

Thus we find that role play is a very useful activity for the teachers under training. They can learn how to teach in simulated condition. It will change the attitude of many persons. Surely it will add to the, impotency of persons. It is bound to equip the persons with different skills had capabilities for their better performances the near future.

Limitations

Role Playing has the following drawbacks:

(a) There is need of creative teachers for making this activity successful, but there is dearth of such teachers.

(b) Giving training of role playing consumes a lot of time. Many actors will require more time for protection in this art. In such a situation, lower pupil teacher radio is needed.

That becomes expensive in Indian situations whit we can hardly afford.

(c) Suppose there is a group of 20 persons who are to be given training through role playing. At a time one or two persons will be busy in role playing and others will be sitting here as observer and also waiting for their turn. As observers, they are not able to justice in observing them.

Role playing in simulated conditions can help in remedying the situation. In simulated conditions, let each pupile teacher play different roles *i.e.* the role of a teacher, the role of a student and also the role of the supervisor.

Socio-drama: Socio-drama is an activity in which some people play the role of some others in some social setting. Here some social problem is enacted upon through role playing. The problem may be taken from the real world or it may be fictitious. Here the main aim is to seek a solution to some social problem. It is a sort of free drama in which the purpose type of activity changes the attitude of the people.

An Example : Ram Lila near Diwali days which is staged in many cities of the country is socio-drama. It arouses the feelings of the people, teachers then many good things and above all good moral lessons. Ras Lila at the time of Janam Ashtemi is another example of social drama.

Gaming: Gaming is an activity in the teaching learning programme. In gaming, choice of strategies is involved. Decision making plays an important role in the process of gaming. As a result of gaming, some reward is given to the winner or the loser of the game is deprived of something. There are formal rules of gaming and those are rigidly applied.

Gaming in the process of education is a unique idea. It has been introduced in the teaching learning programme to make the process more effective. Learning through games is not taxing for the students anyway. They are able to play, relax and learn things in a very natural and congenial environment. The different games help the students in having human interaction within a social structure.

An educational game may be defined as "an activity among two or more independent decision makers seeking to achieve their objective in some limiting contest". In other words, in any gaming programme, there are two parties-one opponent to the other, each one is independent and can make its own decision in any type of situation they are in when that activity is in progress.

The students in such situations are able to meet both in a normal and informal manner. That gives rise to more and more of human-interaction within that social phenomenon. The children play with toys and they are able to learn many social etiquettes. Different types of games in education teach the children co-operation, tolerance patience, compromise etc.

Purposes of Gaming

Gaming in education can serve many useful purposes. A few of them are briefly explained below:

1. To make the students more and more inquisitive.
2. To make the learners imaginative.
3. To help the learners understand the various concepts very clearly.
4. To make the students have different types of hypotheses first in their minds and then help them take up one correct hypothesis.
5. To help the students acquire different skills such as under standing, the situation properly, interacting with it rightly and then taking the right decision etc.
6. To help the students in their transfer of learning from one situation to another.
7. To enable the students learn a few important values which are based on their judgement in different practical situations.

A Few Examples of Gaming

1. In real class room situations, the teacher uses activity method for teaching certain things. In the lower classes, the teacher teaches with the help of toys. The small children are able to equate themselves with the toys and they put their heart and soul into that situation and they learn many things. They take that game as enjoyment but

ultimately the teacher is able to teach them many things successfully.

2. The language teacher makes use of the process of gaming for teaching the language interestingly. With the help of word flash cards, the teacher gives practice of recognition of words by showing pictures of those words or the actual things alongwith the word flash cards.

3. By preparing word flash cards, a number of games can be played in the class room situations:

   Ten word flashcards in duplicate are prepared. One set ten flash cards is distributed among ten students of the class. Out of the second set the ten word flash cards are displayed on the. flannel board in front of the ,class. The ten students whom word flash cards have been given, are asked to match their flash cards with the flash cards on the flannel board. Through this matching exercise the students are learning recognition of letters and words. Here the teacher may frame rules of the game. The student who is able to compare his own flash card with the one on the flannel board fit will be given the first prize. That way second and third prize will be given.

4. The Concept Attainment Model of teaching the differerent concepts to the students is another example of gaming. The teacher tells the students that he has a concept in his mind and he asks the students to guess about it. For this, the teacher gives one positive example and one negative example of it. He may give one more positive example and one more negative example of it. Then the students stathinking. They try to give positive and negative example That list is prepared on the black board side by side. After that, it is generalised, and the concept is made clear. The game helps the students learn the different concepts very clearly.

5. Forming of unions through elections on the colleges is other example of gaming. The main idea behind this type of activities is to train the youths fully for a better future. They are trained for living successfully in a democratic set of life. The whole activity is carried on as if very real a

close to the assembly elections. In a democratic country like India, the budding youths of today are to be prepared such a way that they are able to shoulder their responsibilities in a refined and applaudable way. But unfortunately, this game in the hands of inefficient and selfish administrators and teachers is not allowed to go on smoothly. The political parties also poke their nose into the affairs of the colleges and their activities. The result is that smooth functioning of the college is hampered by them and the real purpose behind such educational games is defeated.

Gaming and Role Play

Gaming can go on in real situations and also in artificial situations through role play. Generally educational games are arranged for teaching the students. When the purpose of gaming is direct-teaching, real situation should be created and that helps in learning fully. And some times, the purpose of gaming is indirect type of teaching. In that case, artificial situations can help and role play in those situations could be useful. For example, elections of students union in the colleges aims at teaching them indirectly and it is to prepare them for better democratic set up of life. There let them have role play.

Mock parliament is another activity where the situation is all artificial and the students are asked to play the different roles of the people at Govt. level i.e. whatever they do in the parliament and whatever is allowed to happen there in the parliament. All those activities are enacted in the institution by the students. Thus it is an educational game through which the student are asked to play the different roles in artificial situation. The purpose behind this activity is to make the students understand the educational value of political set up of the country which is democratic.

Steps to Make Gaming More Effective

Gaming involves participation of the students in the activity in different ways. In order to make it all successful, the following points should be fully taken care of:

1. In the game, the students are asked to play different roles. Whatever behaviour is expected from a student during his role play, is explained to him fully so that he is fully successful in that activity.

2. The whole social situation is explained to the students so that their performance may be upto the mark.
3. Before the start of the game, the details of the rules to be followed by everyone are explained. All types of allied issues or conditions related there to are explained.
4. Where ever need is felt. Some demonstration of the role play depicting the specific behaviour should be given by the teacher.

Role of the Teacher in Gaming

The role of the teacher during an educational game is non-directive. He is a consultant and a guide there. In the beginning while the game is being introduced, the role of the teacher is directive. During the actual process of gaming, he goes in the background. His help is sought only when it is absolutely necessary. But again after the game is over, he appears there as the central figure. There is full discussion on the game and the roles of different persons. For all this, the teacher dominates the whole scene of discussion.

Educational games process more effective. Learning through games if played well under the proper guidance of the teacher can serve many useful purposes.

QUESTIONS

1. Discuss the merits and demerits of simulation as a technique of teacher training.
2. Discuss the concept of simulation, highlighting its chief characteristics.
3. What is Role Playing? Discuss its need, importance and the procedure of role playing.
4. What are the main purposes of educational games? Discuss the role of the teacher in the organisation of such games.
5. What do you mean by simulation? Explain briefly how this technique can be used successfully in the field of education.
6. Discuss the programme of gaming by giving suitable example. What are its purpose?

6

Learning by Programme

Always, improvements in the teaching-learning process have been thought of and efforts made to implement the same. Some sort of researches have always been going on in this field with the ulterior motives of all round betterment. The chief drawbacks of the traditional system of class-room teaching are - it does not cater to the needs of all sitting in the class. Some of them are satisfied, some main dissatisfied and some rather curse the situations. Population explosion and hence over crowded classes is another challenge which hinders qualitative improvement. The decreasing number of casualty of teachers continuously add to the problem of deterioration and satisfaction. There has been a thinking about individualised teaching which could be taken as qualitatively good.

In this age of science and technology which may be called the age of computer science, the term programmed has become quite popular. Its meaning is to give instructions in a systematic and quenced manner. Here the instructions have to be clear cut in every way and the material is to be in a sequence. That quickens the need of learning. Its basic principle is "Every part of teaching system is subject to the rule, that whatever fails to do its job should replaced."

Programmed learning does not mean only self-instructional material. Rather it refers to the systematic way of developing structural material and also of designing teaching strategies which combine many different methods in order to optimise learning. The public principles of Programmed Learning is "Every part of teaching term is subject to the rule that whatever fails to do its job should replaced."

From layman point of view Programmed Learning means learning by preparing a programme. Programme is a device to control the students' behaviour and help them to learn without the supervision of a teacher.

Undoubtedly, a programme is the subject to be learnt by the pupil. Programmed learning is the arrangement of materials to be learnt, it graded step of difficulty, in such a sequence and in such a manner of presentation that it will result in the most efficient rate of understanding and retention. According to an American psychologist, it is "…. the first application of laboratory technique utilized in the study of learning process to the practical problems of education."

The art of programming is the art of gathering together many minds, teachers, the subject mater exports, educational technologists and from their interaction producing something which will teach and teach well, in the morning, after lunch, to slow learners, to fast, to white and to coloured.

Programmed learning is highly individualised which is a systematic instructional strategy for class-room as well as self-learning. It works wonderfully in the case of correspondence courses being run in the open universities of country.

The programme may be of several physical forms. It may be a book, may be in the form of tapes or strips of paper, may be series of micro filmed slides, it may be auditory material to be used with a tape recorder. All these forms of programmes can be prepared by the experts and put to use for teaching purposes. They will help any and every type of learner and the results are bound be positive.

Programmed material refers to programme, which consists of "a reproduceable sequence of instructional items designed produce a measurable behaviourable change in the student."

Smith and Moore says, "The field of programmed learning or auto instruction materials, is a rapidly developing, extremely exciting movement towards the further development of an instructional technology based in part, on certain principles of psychology derived from laboratory studies of human and animal learning which serve to confirm, in part, the procedures and techniques used by nearly all truly great teachers of the past."

In this regard Gene. C. Fusco observes: "Proponents a the programmed self instruction maintain that this is not a new method of teaching; the basic procedure is found as far back as the Socrates dialogue. What is new, they say, is the development of a science and technology based on a method employed by the great teacher of the past."

A Few Definitions

(i) Smith and Moore (1962). "Programmed instruction is the process of arranging the material to be learned into a series of sequential steps, usually it moves the student from familiar background into a complex and new set of concepts, principles and understanding."

(ii) Leith (1966). "Programme is a sequence of small steps of instructional material (called frames) most of which require a response to be made by completing a black space in a sentence. To insure that expected responses are given, a system of cueing is applied, and each response is vertified by the provision of immediate knowledge of results. Such a sequence is intended to be worked at the learner's own pace of individual self instruction."

(iii) Jacob and others (1966) write as "Self-instructional programmes are educational materials from which the students learn. These programmes can be used with many types of students and object matter either by themselves, hence, the name 'Self-instruction' or in combination with other instructional techniques.'

(iv) Espich and Williams (1967). "Programmed instruction planned sequence of experiences, leading to proficiency, in terms stimulus response relationship that have been proved to be effective."

(v) Programmed learning is a method of giving individually instruction in which the student is active and proceeds at his pace and is provided with immediate knowledge of results.

(vi) Programmed learning is designing a strategy in which course kinds of intellectual emotions, motor experiences can be divided to the learner in a controlled situation through a variety of prices like a book, machine, teacher, radio, television etc.

(vii) Markle S.M. (1969) defined programmed learning as Method of designing a reproduceable sequence instructional to produce a measurable and consistent effect on the behaviour and every acceptable student.

(viii) In the world of Michael J. Apter, "Programmed action is a method of instruction in which the information is to be broken down into small units which are to be presented to student (usually in written form) in a carefully planned sequence. Each unit or 'frame' contains not only information but is also terminated with a question."

(ix) Programmed Learning is now "an integrated instruction system which may employ programmed books, teaching machines, films in various forms, audio-visual devices, simulators and actual apparatus. The instructor himself, trained in formulating objectives and in diagnostic analysis of his teaching results, is an important part of this system."

(x) Programmed Learning is a "method of self instruction, whereby the learner proceeds through instructional material in short steps at his own pace receiving immediate knowledge of the correctness of his answers."

(xi) Programmed Instruction is a systematically planned, empirically established and effectively controlled self-instructional technique for providing individualized instructions to the learner through logically sequenced small segments of the subject matter by using the principles of operant conditioning and schedules of reinforcement.

Out of the different theories of learning, mainly the theory of conditioning has influenced programmed learning considerably. In this context, the following points are worth considering:

Human beings form habits with the passage of time. Once the habits are formed, they become an integral part of our behaviour. Habits can be changed through efforts. So behaviour can also undergo changes through efforts. A change in behaviour is actually learning. This change is gradual and not sudden. It can be controlled as per needs and requirements.

A Few Characteristics of Programmed Learning

Here below are the distinguishing features of programmed learning:

1. It is highly individualized *i.e.*, one person learns at a time.

2. The device presents material to be learned in minimal increments.
3. Each step in the learning process is followed logically.
4. The students make progress at their own pace. The rate of accomplishment of one student is established by his performance alone.
5. There is provision for checking of student's answers immediately. If the answer is wrong, the student comes to know about the error and why it is so. It is not like traditional learner where the child discovers all at once that he is zero.
6. The students are required to be active at each step.
7. Student's over response is needed at every step. That way they can be readily observed, checked and effectively controlled.
8. It maximises the rate and depth of learning, foster understanding and enhance the motivation of the students.
9. There is emphasis on the interaction between the learner and the programme.
10. It is self administrative.
11. It is very systematic and sequence.

Fundamental Principles of Programmed Learning

Programmed Learning is based on a few principles which are briefly explained here below :

Principle of Small Steps : Each programme presents the material to be learnt in small steps. The students are able to learn better if matter is presented to them in small doses. By using this principle of small steps, the possibility of committing errors is reduced considerably. More correct responses by the student naturally encourage him further and he is able to learn more and more further.

Principle of Active Responding : In programmed learning, the learner remains active throughout. Whatever, matter is presented to him in small steps he goes on responded to it actively.

In this type of learning, the student cannot afford to be lethargic or passive at any step even for a short moment of time.

Principle of Immediate Reinforcement: The student learns better when he comes to know immediately whether his answer is right or wrong. In programmed learning, the moment the student gives the response, its correctness or otherwise is conveyed to him immediately.

Principle of Self-pacing: In programmed learning individual difference of the learners are well recognised. They can work at their own speed, slowly or quickly as they like. The gifted children can learn things at a quicker speed whereas the backward children can go on slowly. Naturally this principle keeps every type of learner fully satisfied as far as his speed of learning is concerned.

Principle of Students Testing: In programmed learning, the student is tested continuously. The student is writing his responses on the sheet. His answers help the programmed writer to prove the programme accordingly. Whenever there are more wrong answers, the programmer is able to detect the reasons and accordingly he tries of modify and improve the programme. Thus there is continuous evaluation of the student's performance as well as of the programme itself. With the better programmed material, better learning is ensured for the other learners who are to learn in due course of time.

G.W. Leytahm in this essay "A Programmed Second Year Course on the Psychology of learning; Part 3: Evaluation and Conclusions" says "Programmed learning by its very nature, can certainly contribute to a student's capacity to work on his own, and if applied along the broad lines suggested in this article, it can also improve his ability to think for himself. Cognitive and effective objectives in higher education are difficult to disentangle, and the experience gained from our course suggests that both can be achieved through the broad application of the principles of programmed learning."

He has given nine Principles of Programmed Learning, which will be relevant for any kind of programmed materials. They are:

1. The aims and objectives of a course of learning should be clearly and explicitly specified in advance, in terms of observable behaviour.

2. The student should be actively involved in the process of learning.
3. Each individual should proceed through the course of learning at his own pace.
4. The material to be learned should be selected with reference to the aims and objectives of the course or learning.
5. The student should receive continual knowledge of how he is progressing through the course of learning.
6. Each student should be introduced to new material at a level of difficulty commensurate with his past experience and current attainments.
7. The material to be learned should be graded in difficulty so that the student makes new mistakes as he proceeds.
8. The student should master each section of its material before continuing with the next.
9. And, the material to be learned should be organised in short, progressive steps, following a logical sequence.

Programmed Instruction and Traditional Teaching - A Comparison

A comparison of programmed instruction with traditional method of teaching will give clear understanding of programmed instruction. Here below are given the main points of comparison.

Programmed Instruction

1. It is based on the fundamental principles of teaching.
2. Here the class-rooms are just like laboratories where the students are learning.
3. It is an individualised technique of instruction.
4. Individual differences of the learners are taken into consideration. Every student is able to learn according to his own speed of learning.
5. It provides immediate feedback to the learners.
6. The objectives of teaching learning are clearly defined.

7. The subject matter is properly organised and is very systematic. It is based on the maxim 'Simple to difficult'.
8. Here the role of the teacher in the class-room situation is that of a guide and helper. The teacher provides guidance wherever the students needs it.
9. It keeps the students actively involved in the lesson throughout. The students have to give responses almost at every step.
10. The subject matter is presented to the students in small bits which they can follow easily.
11. The programmed material is very empirically tried out and it is sure to yield good results.
12. There is an interaction between the student and the subject matter.
13. The teacher acts only as a helper or guide.
14. The teaching-learning environment is quite relaxed.

Traditional Teaching

1. It finds difficulty in applying the fundamental principles while practically teaching in the class-rooms.
2. Here there are crowded class-rooms where large number of students are sitting.
3. It is a group technique.
4. The individual differences of the learners are not cared for.
5. It does not give immediate feedback to the earners.
6. The objectives are not well defined.
7. The subject matter is not well organised.
8. Here the teacher goes on lecturing compulsorily which is the same for everyone.
9. The students remain passive. They are expected not to give any response for quite sometime when the lesson is on.
10. The subject matter is given to the students in big chunks. They may or may not understand it properly.

11. The matter is not empirically tried out.
12. Here the interaction is between the teacher and the student or students.
13. The teacher is dominating in the situations. He mostly acts as a dictator.
14. Here the teaching-learning environment is very tense.

Styles of Programming

The Programmed Learning is making headway at a tremendous speed. The advancement in the field of Sciences and Engineering have affected it in many ways. Various styles of programming have emerged. In 1950's B.F. Skinner developed a style which is known as Linear Programming. It was followed by another model namely 'Branching' given by Normal A. Crowder. In 1960's Robert Mager developed a system of programmed instruction known as 'Learner Controlled Instruction' which is learner controlled because the learner here plays a dominant role and the instructor remains in the background. In 1962 T.F. Gilbert developed a new system of programmed instruction which is known as Mathetics. In 1965. E.Z. Rothkopt used a new term known as 'Mathegenics'. In the same year Lawrence Stolurow tried to revolutionise the field of programmed instruction. He gave the idea of computer Assisted Instruction 'CAI'. He tried to use computer as 'NO' teaching brain where students could interact directly without the assistance of teacher.

A few popular styles of programming are briefly explained below:

(i) Linear or Extrinsic Programming.

(ii) Branching or Intrinsic Programming.

(iii) Mathetics.

Linear Programming

This style of programme is associated with the work of Dr. Skinner and Dr. Holland of Harward University. It is also called single track programme. Here the material is presented in unbroken sequence of steps. The advocates of this style believe that errors hinder learning. Moreover, learning here is bit by bit.

Here all the students read and respond to the same frames. All of them follow the same path. The linear programme is generally response centered. In each frame enough material is presented to the students in order to have their correct responses. There is immediate reinforcement proved for each response.

B.F. Skinner, the Chief Originator of this style, was concerned with the shaping and conditioning of behaviour. His viewpoint was that every creature can be guided to a desired behaviour by means of a series of carefully structured small steps on the condition that each correct step is immediately reinforced by some kind of reward. For complex behaviour, it is desired to teach a stimulus response chain. In this case each response becomes the stimulus for the next response. Such a chain can be quite long in the case of animals. The desired type of behaviours are formed gradually, step by step with suitable reinforcement for each desired response.

In programmed learning, each student is taken through many small stimulus response steps. As every learner thus thinks individually, there is enough scope for self-pacing. Here the elements of programmed learning look like the following:

(a) Information presented in small steps.

(b) There is active responding by the learner at each step.

(c) There is immediate knowledge of results given.

(d) There is self-pacing among different learners.

Linear Programming is called extrinsic because the learner has no choice of his own in following the path or sequence of learning. It is decided by the programmer extrinsically.

The linear programme is structured in such a way that the chances of correct responses are nearly 95 per cent. The linear programmes can be produced in a book form. The following format makes the concept clear:

1	...	...	...	
Response 1	...	...	...	
Correct	2	...	...	...
Answer 1	Response 2	...	...	...
Correct	3	...	...	...

Answer 2	Response 3	...	...	...
Correct	4	...	...	...
Answer 3	Response 4	...	...	...
Correct	5	...	...	...
Answer 4	Response 5	...	...	...

There are some programmes, which have been developed on linear models in which a learner can skip a certain number of frames proved that he can respond correctly to a test item given at a particular frame. Such programme is called the skip-linear programme.

Active responding, minimum errors and knowledge of results are three basic principles of a linear programme, which indicates its assumption.

Examples. The following is an example of a linear programme, which demonstrates the arrangement of different types of frames incorporated into it.

Copying Frame:

1. An adult insect has six legs. An insect has six legs, therefore it is an .... (insect).
2. One way of looking at an insect is to count its....(legs).

Prompting Frame:

3. An insect has.....legs (six).
4. A spider has eight legs. It is/is not an insect.

Fading Frame:

5. Because an ant has......legs, it is classified as a.....(six, insect).

Testing

6. An insect has.......legs (six).

Advantages

The Linear Programming has the following advantages:

1. Series of small steps make the subject matter easy for the learner.

2. The chances of error sin responding are minimised because matter is in properly sequenced small steps.
3. Immediate knowledge of results release tension and anxiety of the learners.
4. Repetition ensures learning which further strengthens the purposes.

Limitations

The Linear Programming suffers from some drawbacks which are enlisted here below:

1. Every learner gives the same response. So there is no development of imagination or creativity on the part of the learners.
2. Every learner has to follow the same track rigidly. There is no flexibility whatsoever may be the situation.
3. After some time, learning by this style becomes dull and monotonous.
4. Good teachers are needed for preparing the programme but there is dearth of such teachers.
5. It can be used in some subjects only and that too for limited topics only.
6. It may encourage guessing and thus may not result in real learning.
7. No remedy is suggested for responses.

Branching of Intrinsic Programming

Norman A. Crowder the American Psychologist is closely associated with this style of programming. This type of programme employs multiple choice response pattern. The student is required to pick up one right answer out of many responses pressed to him. In the presented responses, one response is correct and all others are incorrect. The learners who make a wrong choice are asked to follow another branching which corrects their error. Thus through branching the learner gradually teachers the main track from where he is learning further.

This style is based on traditional tutorial methods. It is very near to the normal tutorial process. In the tutorial process, a privative tutor reaches a student. The teacher proceeds step by step as long as the student is following him. But when the student does not understand or he gives a wrong answer, the tutor explains in a different way. He takes the help of different experiences and tries to teach the student and thus remedies his wrong answer. The same style is followed in the branching style of programming.

This style of programming consists of long frames which appear as pages in an ordinary textbook. The student reads the frame and then gives response by selecting the correct answer out of the multiple choice. Each alternative is associated with page number which directs the student to another frame. If the response of the student is correct, then the frame confirms his response and introduces the new material. In branching programme the pupil-teacher relationship is one of interaction between the pupil and the tutor. This continuous interaction is a sort of feedback which is the life blood of the tutoral process. This type of programming is called intrinsic because the learner himself makes the decision to adapt the instruction according to his needs.

Basic Assumptions

The branching type of programmed learning is based on the following assumptions:

1. It is based on the possibility of detecting and correcting errors.
2. By his ability, the learner controls the exact sequence that he will take from the available tracks in the programme.
3. The learner learns better if matter is presented in totality.
4. Wrong answers do not necessarily hinder the learning of a correct answer.
5. Multiple choice items help more in the learning process.

In this type of programme, the student proceeds in a strength line till he commits an errors. The error takes him to branching frames which serve the purpose of remedial instruction.

At the end of the frame, there are multiple choice questions to test whether the learner has understood the information given in the frame or not. On the basis of his response, he is directed to proceed to the other frames of the programme. The frames in this style of programming are of two types:

One is referred to as home page (HP), which leads the students to extra information and second, wrong answer page (WAP) where the student gets elucidated on the nature of his errors. In the diagram above, frames IC, 2C and 3C are home pages while frames 1a, 1b, 2a, 2b etc. are wrong answer pages.

There are two types of branching programmes: one is called micro-branching model and the other macro-branching model.

The micro-branching model consists mainly of a branching within the individual frame without changing the total frame sequence. In second type of branching sequence, special post-checking frame is introduced into the task sequence. If the student solves that test of the frame well, he simply goes on to the new study material, but if he fails to complete it satisfactorily he gets instead large or smaller repetitional task.

Example:

Page 1. Solar system consists of the sun, the nine planets, thousands of small plaetoids, several flashing comets, satellites and meteors, the sun is the centre around which all these heavenly bodies revolve including our earth, which is one of the nine major planets.

The centre of the solar system is:

A. Earth...
B. Sun...
C. Moon...

WAP :

Your answer is earth, sorry, a very bad guess. Our earth is first one of the nine major planets revolving round the sun.

WAP :

You are wrong. Please go to Page 1 and try to select the correct answer.

H.P. :

Your answer is the sun. Very good. You are right. Now you need further explanation on the topic, given in the following paragraph.

Paragraph on 'Solar System'. Then again multiple choice questions in the end. Again the same process as above and so on....

Advantages

The branching type of programming has the following advantages:

1. Big size of the frame reduces unnecessary repetition and responding. Thus the amount of learning time and fatigue are also reduced.
2. Mistake committed by the student are explained in the remedial frames. The student not only gets the correct response, he also understands why some other response is not correct.
3. The frames being of larger size contain good deal of information. The programme may further enrich his style and expand his ideas.
4. It helps in practising creatively.
5. It gives training in problem solving.

Limitations

The branching style of programming has some drawbacks which are enlisted below:

1. Branching programmes are applicable from year to year basis and from student to student. There is need for reprogramming which is cumbersome as well as costly.
2. Most branching programmes are the project of programmer's imagination. They may not be really very good in the context of real situations.

Mathetics

It is one of the major styles of writing programmes. This style was developed by Thomas F. Gilbert in 1962. The word 'Mathetics' has been derived from the Greek word 'Mathein' which means to learn. 'Mathetics is defined as "the systematic application or reinforcement theory to the analysis and construction of those complex repertories usually known as subject matter mastery, knowledge and skill." No doubt gilbert speaks of reinforcement theory. Mathetics is not directly derived from and particular reinforcement theory. He has used only those aspect of reinforcement theory which he found suitable for building the technique of teaching. His main interest lies in building a system that guarantees effective teaching.

According to Harless, the goal of Mathetics is "to evolve a genuine technology of education by welding together the concepts of behavioural science to the effective practices and procedures that have always been utilised by good teachers."

In Mathetics style, an exercise is the technical unit of learning instead of a frame of a linear style. There is no restriction on the size of the exercise. In fact that size of the exercises is kept according to the needs and requirements of the student.

As a technique of teaching, Mathetics may be applied to any subject, but is more suitable for teaching skills. It is a complete training system that gives the programme:

(a) A guide for determining what to teach.

(b) A basis for making teaching strategy decisions.

(c) A detailed procedure for constructing a programme.

Retrogressive chaining makes it unique among all the programming techniques. The child learns the last step first, then the goes to the next one before it and thus to the introductory part. This procedure where the tasks are connected from the last to the first is called chaining.

$$A \rightarrow B \rightarrow C \rightarrow D \rightarrow E$$

Mathetics is electric in nature, but is unique in application. It analyses the deficiencies and tries to make it up. It is most suited to teaching of skills. The closer the student is to reinforcement when he is being taught, the more effective that reinforcement becomes. The reinforcement here is the completion of the task. Each time the student performs he completes the task.

Principles of Mathetics

The mastery of subject matter is the main focus of mathetics. Then it gives emphasis on prescription, the prescription involves three principles :

(i) Principle of Changing : The chain of stimulus and response is helpful in developing the mastery of content and determining its structure. The element of content is presented in stimulus and response form. The chain is formed by arranging stimuli and responses, when diagrammatically, it can be shown as:

$$S_1 — R_1 — S_2 — R_2 — S_3 — R_3 — S_4 — R_4$$

(ii) Principle of Discrimination : The discrimination situation of learning is generated by providing different stimuli, which have different responses. Every stimulus and response is independent of each other.

$S_1 — R_1$
$S_2 — R_2$
$S_3 — R_3$

Every stimulus has its own response.

(iii) Principle of Generalisation : The generalisation is a critical situation of learning. It helps in achieving higher cognitive objective of learning. In this type of situation, a group of stimuli emits single response.

$S_1]$
$S_2] = R$
$S_3]$

It is known as the process of generalization. It is opposite to discrimination..

The Underlying Rationales of Mathetics Programme

The rationale of Mathetics is that the closer the student is to reinforcement when he is being taught, the more effective the reinforcement becomes. The reinforcement, in this case, is the completion of the task.

An Example of a Mathetics Programme

Programme Page 1

Exercise 1

To find the square of any two digit numbers ending in 5.

A. Multiply the first digit number by the next higher consecutive digit.

B. Write 25 to the right of result (No response required).

Programme Page 2

Exercise 2

To find the square of 35.

A. Multiply the first digit (3) by the next consecutive number (4) = 12.

B. Writer 25 to the right of the result 12 = 1225, (No response required).

Exercise 3

To find the square of 65.

A. Multiply the first digit (6) by the next higher consecutive.

B. Write.... to the.... of the result.

C. The square of 65 is.....

B. Write 25, 7 × 6 = 42

C. The square of 65 is 4225.

Thus there are three steps in designing a mathetic programme which can be seen from the example given above. They are demonstration, prompt, and release.

Drawbacks

Mathetics style of programming has the following drawbacks:

1. This style is very technical and it needs lot of skill, training and hard work on the part of the programmer.
2. It cannot be used for different types of material contained in different subjects.
3. When the student learns the last step first, some of them may be overwhelmed and it may ultimately prove harmful to them.

A Comparison of Linear and Branching Programmes

The two fundamental styles of programmed learning have been compared here on next page:

Linear Programme	*Branching Programme*
1. This style of programme is associated with the work of B.F. Skinner.	1. Its chief propagator was Norman A. Crowder.
2. It is based on the theory of operant conditioning.	2. It is based on the theory of electicism.
3. Here the matter is presented in small steps. Each step is very small.	3. Here the matter is presented in paragraphs. Sometimes the paragraphs may run into a page even.
4. A large number of steps are involved.	4. Here the total number of steps comparatively are far less.
5. The textbook pages occur in normal sequence.	5. Here the pages are not in normal sequence. They are in scrambled book form.
6. Simple teaching machine is used.	6. Complicated teaching machine is used which is rather costly.
7. It does not suggest remedies for incorrect responses of the students.	7. It does suggest remedies for the incorrect responses.
8. It provides the same track of learning to everyone.	8. It provides different tracks depending upon the ability of the learners to understand things. Of course, the main track which is ultimately

	followed by all learners is the same.
9. It is very useful in the lower classes where the students are expected to form concepts.	9. It is useful for the higher classes where the learners are expected to make comparison of the concept acquired by them.
10. Here the possibility of error rate is five per cent.	10. The possibility of error rate generally may go upto twenty percent.
11. It works satisfactorily in the case of average type of students.	11. In has greater utility for the more intelligent and creative type of student.

Developing a Programming

It goes without saying that programmed learning has revolutionized the field of education. But still a very big challenge before everyone is the development of suitable programmer for the students. It is a highly dynamic and time consuming exercise. Every person is not fit for doing this job. A person having good imagination and capability of doing creative work can do it successfully. The process of developing a programme is highly cyclic and it never comes to an end.

Phase of Developing a Programme

The different phases of developing a programme are briefly discussed below:

Preparation

Selection of the Topic. At first the teacher decides about the topic on which a programme is to be prepared. Right selection of the topic is the most important thing because on its utility depends the success of the programmer. While selecting a topic the needs and reinforcement of the learners should be kept in view. Only the subject teacher knows which topic is difficult for the learners and only he can take a decision about the inclusion of a particular topic for developing the programme. And above all, one teacher alone should not take such a decision. Efforts should be made to hold some seminar related to one particular subject where different teachers may speak about the difficult topics and thus a united conclusion about the selection of a topic or topics is made.

Writing Assumptions about the Learners: Before developing the programme, the programmer should know well the various assumptions about the learners for whom the programme is to be prepared. The assumptions include likings or dislinkings, interests, attitude, aptitude or their mental make up. The assumptions about the learners are discussed and then briefly written.

Writing Objectives in Behavioural Terms: The objectives of the programme in behavioural terms should be clearly stated. Here the general objectives and the specific objectives of the programme are stated in written from.

Writing Entry Behaviour of the Learners: The programmer writes about the behaviour of the learners before that individual learns things through programmed material. Here actual situation of the mental make up, knowledge, study etc. of learner as far as that topic is concerned, is studied.

Developing Specific Outline of Content to be Programmed: The Programmer takes up the content portion of the topic and he writes its outline. Here a sort of demarcation is made which portions of the contents pertaining to a particular are to be programmed.

Preparing a Criterion Test: Here a sort of criterion test is prepared which will indicate whether the programmed material worked successfully or not. A sort of standard to test the programme is fixed up. In the light of that, evaluation is made whenever needed.

This steps called preparation is the most important in the development of any programme. Equally good writer to administrator devotes sufficient to this phase of working.

Constructing or Writing the Programme

Keeping in view the different aspects, a scheme of actual writing of the programme is chalked out here. Then writing of the programme is carried under the following heads:

Writing the Draft Frames: The Programmer must have a clear idea of the programme he is supposed to teach. He analyses the subject matter. Then the frames are written in a sequence. Simple frames are placed first and complex frames have their position afterwards.

Editing the Draft Frames: Editing is done by a team of experts, usually the team consists of (i) Subject matter expert (ii) A Programmer (iii) A Skilled Writer. Thus the master of the subject the master of writing programmes and someone who has the skill of writing put their heads together and are able to write the programme.

Try out and Revision

In the writing of a programme, its try out and suitable revision ensure the future success of the programme. It is carried to as under:

(a) A few individual students are taken up and the programmed material is given to them. The reaction of those individual students is seen. The programme writer tries to find out various difficulties for the problems which those individual students face while learning through that programmed material. Accordingly some changes are made in the programmed material.

(b) Then the programmed material is tried on a group of students. This is done at two or three places. Suggestions given by the learners on which experiment is performed, are taken care of accordingly. Some changes or alterations are made in the programme.

(c) And then programme is tried in the field where the sample is large one. The programme material may be administered to 2,000 or 3,000 students. The achievements of the students are noted down.

Validation and Evaluation

In every programme, evaluation of the programmed material is quite significant. Only through evaluation the programmer comes to know the success or failure of the programme. Here the achievements of the students are noted down. The programmer or the evaluator applies 90-90 criterion. In other words, the statements or the frames where 10% or less than that number of students have incorrect responses, are considered to be valid. The statements or the frames in which more than 10% students have wrong answers are deleted. In this way, the programmer is validate against the criterion.

Advantages of Programmed Learning

1. Programmed learning makes the students active and self-reliant.
2. In this type of learning, result is known immediately which motivates the students for further learning.
3. The instruction is individualised in the same that each student is able to proceed this own pace. In branching programme, the learner receives information related to his own needs.
4. It makes learning easy because the learning material is presented in small instalments.
5. It provides feeding material to the self-instruction devices like computer, teaching machines, programmed text etc.
6. It may help the teachers in the reduction of their total load of work. The time thus saved may be utilised by the teacher in some creative activities.
7. The programmed instruction is a better prepared and planned material as compared to traditional teaching. So it is bound to yield good results.
8. It involves both learning and evaluation. It is a good self-learning and self-evaluation.
9. The various steps involved in programmed learning help to do the work in an organised and systematic way.
10. It develops scientific attitude among the learners because they are able to think rationally and logically.
11. It develops creativity among the learners.
12. It is quite useful for correspondence course students who want to continue their higher studies by sitting at homes or continuing studies alongwith the jobs or vocations.
13. In-service teachers can be kept abreast with the latest developments in the field of education through programmed material.

14. In the class-room teaching, a few more intelligent or gifted children can be provided with some more courses through programmed material and thus they can make more progress.
15. The falling standards can be checked and suitable remedial measures given with the help of programmed material.
16. By applying it to really difficult areas of some subjects, a lot of help can be rendered to the learners.

Limitations

No doubt, programmed learning has a large number of advantages. It also has a few shortcomings which are stated below:

1. The orthodox teachers who are indifferent to any change in methodology of teaching will not relish to accept programmed learning material for class-room teaching.
2. Teacher-taught relationship is important but through programmed learning it is not strengthened.
3. Some students who are not habitual of working at their own may not study. A few of them may become lazy and feel sleepy.
4. There is need for preparing suitable programmes for the learners in the Indian situations which is quite expensive.
5. It cannot foster proper attitudes, aesthetic appreciation, moral standards etc.
6. In programmed learning, subject matter is presented to the learners and they give the response. It does not help in the development of their imagination.
7. No flexibility is there because every learner has to follow the same track rigidly.

Self-learning Modules

In programmed learning packages, the teacher prepares learning material in the form of packages. Each package contains programmed material of one subject or the other and it is related to any packet or subject. The package is a complete unit in itself. For preparing that package, the writer may use any style of programming *i.e.* Linear, Branching or Mathetics as per requirement of the students.

Suppose a teacher feels that his students of English language find problems in learning direct and indirect form of Narration, he can prepare a package of Auto Instruction Material for this.

He prepares the whole material which is complete in itself and just like one self sufficient packet. As per their convencience, the learners can go on with their own pace of learning and with full freedom. Naturally this type of packages will help the students wonderfully in the improvement of their typical problems pertaining to different subjects. The programmed learning packages can be used with the help of teaching machines. At the higher levels, the programme learning packages can be translated into the language of the computer and that may become useful type of Computer Assisted Instruction.

Each programme learning package consists of Modules or teaching-Learning units. A module stands for a sub-part or sub-system of the curriculum of constructional programme. As a sub-system, a module is quite complete in itself in matter of providing desirable learning experiences to the learners. According to this plan, the whole curriculum or class-room instructional programmes are divided into some meaning units, which are called self-learning modules because a learner does not want the help of a teacher. These are self-sufficient. In an advanced stage, these are self-instructional materials even though they differ from programmed material. In one module, there are a number of capsules. Learning time is approximately fixed for each capsule.

A variety of instructional modules have been developed in science and technology and are used as effective curricular materials. Every module is a self-contained and self-sufficient unit of instruction for the learner to achieve a set of objectives. That is self-contained in the sense that the expect learning outcomes, the sequential learning activities and the evaluation devices are thoroughly planned for the unit of instruction. Second aspect, i.e. self sufficiency is achieved by providing all the materials needed for learning in the package itself. Its sub-parts called capsules, must be linked together to constitute the main module.

Each module has some pre-determined Expected Behavioural Outcomes (E.B.O's). The instructional module contains all possible approaches to learning some specific conceptual unit of subject matter and the pupils can select, if necessary, with the guidance of the teacher, the instructional method or methods most suitable for each pupil or small group of pupils.

At the end of the each capsule, a self-evaluation test is provided to which the trainee has to respond after studying the capsule. Key for test is given. It provides immediate reinforcement.

For a training programme, there may be more than one training package and in each package there may be a number of self-learning modules and for each module, there may be a number of capsules, depending upon the requirement of the content to be presented and the demands of the training envisaged. There are a number of such like Training Packages developed by the Central Resource Centre, NCERT, New Delhi.

Salient Features of a Module or a Capsule :

In general, module or capsule has the following salient features:

1. In the beginning, the average learner engaged time is given.
2. Some general instructions are given.
3. In the module, at the outset, the Expected Behavioural outcomes are given.
4. Then the text of the module or capsule is given in some sections.
5. Instructions to feedback questions are given.
6. This is followed by feedback questions.
7. Finally, the answer key for the feedback questions is provided.

Modular Scheduling

Modular scheduling is a procedure for organising the school day to provide varied lengths of time for different classes and other activities. Normally, the school day splits up into 8 or 9 periods of 35 to 40 minute time modules about 20 per day. Each pupil is scheduled for participation as a member of a large group, medium sized group or small group for 50 percent of his school day.

The remaining 50 percent is devoted by him to planning his own work at an instructional materials centre, where he does independent or small group questioning through materials (motion, picture, films, film strips, taps, maps etc.), at the same time arranging for participation in other activities as well as seek free time to devote to individual conference and assistance. The teachers also adjust themselves according to these modular scheduling. Sometimes, in relation to learning needs, modules may be longer combining 2 or 3 twenty minutes modules. This type of scheduling school day allows for a good deal of flexibility and this flexibility help for individualizing instructional.

Modules in a Simple Book Format

This is the simplest form of the module. Here a module generally includes the set instructional objectives for the modular unit, the broadlines of the content, the presentation scheme of the student matter and in the end, a evaluation matter. For dividing the curriculum in sub-parts or to break it into modules, a teacher has to take care of the following facts:

(i) It should clearly specify the E.B.O.'s in the beginning.

(ii) It should help in the acquisition of some distinctive and identifiable set of knowledge, skills, interests, attitudes etc.

(iii) It should cater to the needs of all types of pupils-intelligent, medium or weak.

(iv) It should present an effective synthesis of theory with practice. Learning by doing should be the motto of the teaching.

(v) It should have a reasonable length and complexity.

(vi) Knowledge should be presented in a practice and systematic way. There should not be gaps in-between.

(vii) It should cater to the need of auto or self-instruction.

(viii) It must have definite indication and specification for the students how to proceed on their self-instruction through the given module.

(ix) Evaluation scheme just reflects the true assessment of the realisation of the objectives.

(x) It must include suggestions for extra reading bibliography.

Priming and Prompts

Priming : Priming is a technique whereby efforts are made to pour information into the minds of the learners for active responding. Generally it is used in the introductory frames.

Priming is used in the programmed instruction as under:

(a) Copying Frame : In this type of frame, the students just copy and give the response out of the material itself *e.g.*

Noun is the name of a person, thing or place. Names of persons and things are called...(Response: Noun)

(b) Echoing Frame: Here a student repeats some sound. It is used for teaching pronunciation.

(c) Demonstration Frame: Here the students are asked to repeat some experiment of science which has been demonstrated.

Prompts: Prompts are supplementary stimuli provided in the programme frame. They help the students to reach the correct response. They are only the guiding points. They are not sufficient in themselves to produce the response.

In the words of John P. Decceco, "Prompts are cues provided in the programme frame to guide the students to the correct response."

For example:

Prompted Frame 1. The capital of Rajasthan is x.......

Prompted Frame 2. The capital of Rajathan is J........

Prompts can't help here if the students have not heard the name of Jaipur.

Prompts are provided in teaching frames. They are withdrawn in practice frames. In tension frames, they are no longer here.

Basic Purposes of Prompts

(a) They guide the students to give the correct response.

(b) They prevent the students from making unnecessary errors.

Types of Prompts

Prompts are of two types:

I. Formal prompts.

II. The Matic prompts.

Formal Prompts

Here some from of desired response is provided. This type of prompts are useful at the early stage of programmed learning. *e.g.*, I want a ....umbrella (Response: an) Formal prompts are of four types:

(a) Partial Response Prompts
Here a part of the actual response is given.
E.G. The capital of France is P.....(Paris)

(b) Rhyming Prompt

The wording of the stimulus provides a rhyme to actual response. For example: The adjective of book bookish.

The adjectives of fool is 'foolish'.

(c) Literal Prompt

5

5 Five 5 5 Five 5 5 Five5 Five 5 Five

5 5

In the above examples there are several literal prompts, but they evoke a single response. Gradually those literal prompts are withdrawn.

Frame Structural Prompt

Here below is given the frame structure prompt. Dashes are used to indicate the number of letter missing in a word.

5 × 5 : 25

5 × 6 : 30

5 × 7 : 35

5 – 40 (Response 8)

Thematic Prompts

This type of prompts are related with the theme. This type of prompts depend upon the previous association of a word of phrase.

Thematic Prompts are of the following types:

(i) Picture Prompts.

In this type of prompts, a picture or a diagram is given.

(ii) Correct Setting Prompt

Here the given contents help the learner to give the right response. *e.g.,*

Learning of a language means learning of listening........and writing.

(Response Speaking, Reading)

(iii) Synonyms and Antonyms Prompts

Synonyms and antonyms are used to prompt the correct response. *e.g.*

In winter, we sit in the sun; but in summer, we sit in the ..... (Response shade)

(iv) Analogy Prompt:

One or more analogies can be presented in frame and it is followed by an incomplete analogy to which the student responds.

For example:

(a) A meter has 100 centimeters. A dollar has ..... cents. (Response 100)

(b) White: Milk......sky (Response Blue)

(v) Rule Prompt:

A rule can serve as a prompt. The rule is the first line of the frame. The next two lines are incomplete examples of the rule which the student completes by correctly applying the rule.

X × Y = XY

9 × 8 : —

9 × 6 : —

(Responses 72, 54)

(vi) Examples Prompts

Here we have a complete example and that is followed by an incomplete example. *e.g.*

(–9) (+9) : 72

(+6) (–7) : –42

The answer to these multiplications are negative because .... (Response) (–) × (+) = (–)

(vii) Inductive Prompts

Here prompts are provided in such a way that the learner is able to induce the relationship.

e.g. Fahrenheit and centigrade are both units of temperature. Kelvin is also a......(Response unit of temperature).

Thematic prompts are very useful in the programmes which are meant for the seniors or mature persons. There is need of providing them tactfully in the frames. Then there should be fading or vanishing of prompts.

QUESTIONS

1. What is programmed learning? Discuss the uses and •limitations of linear Programme.
2. Make a comparison of Linear and Branching style of programming in respect of theoretical rationale, frame structure and sequencing of frames.
3. Clearly differentiate between linear, branching and mathetics styles of programming bringing out their advantages.
4. What do you mean by Programmed Learning? Discuss its different principles.
5. Discuss the different styles of programming. Which one do you think is more suitable for class room teaching in Indian situations and why?

6. Discuss in the different phases of developing a programme.
7. Discuss in brief the advantages and disadvantages of programmed learning.
8. Compare Linear and Branching Style of Programmed learning.
9. Difference between programmed instruction and programmed learning. Describe the steps for the development of programmed learning material.
10. Compare linear branching and mathetical programming with regard to theory, principles, rational, frame structure, uses, advantages and disadvantages.
11. How will you evaluate a linear programme? Describe the various stages of evaluation and the operations carried out in each stage.
12. What do you mean by Self-Learning Module? What are its special features?

7

Micro Teaching

Various teacher training institutions prepare teachers for the schools. During the training period, the behaviour of the teacher is modified. The usual practice in the training institutes has been to acquaint the teacher with theory and then send him to the school for practice in teaching. The teacher under training is taken to the school where he/she is left in a full class and is required to teach that group for full period i.e. 35 minutes or 40 minutes whatever is the schedule of the school. How far is it correct and justified is worth considering. Rather it becomes an interesting proposition for all concerned with education. Let us see to it. Taking a teacher trainee to a school class-room may be compared with taking a person who has learnt theory of swimming to a river and asking him to swim. Will that person be able to swim and survive? Oh! No. It would rather be pitiable situation both for the person who is trying to learn swimming and the person who giving training in swimming. Taking the person to water for learning swimming is all right. But taking him to deep waters is not advisable at the early stages of learning. The person should be given training bit by bit, in knee deep water, say in water where the depth is 3 feet or so, then to 4 feet, 5 feet, 6 feet and so on.

This type of learning, step by step, will prepare him well and then naturally his performance in deep waters will be all right. In the same way a surgical doctor while under training performs minor operations first, then bigger ones. This type of learning step by step, easy things first and complicated and difficult ones afterwards, will ensure him a bright future with all success. This type of learning will encourage him all through. Things learnt first will become a sort of platform for him on the basis of which he will be learning far better things.

The traditional system of training produces incompetent teachers who are hardly half prepared for the job. The teacher does not understand the errors that are committed. One of the new practices evolved for modifying the behaviour of the teachers is Micro-teaching. Micro-teaching has been exclusively used for giving training to the teachers. It is rather interesting to see the historical development of micro-teaching.

Historical Development

It was Keith Acheson, a research scholar in the Stanford University who discovered that video-tape recorder could be used to provide feedback of a demonstration lesson. He alongwith other students of the Stanford University started using Video tape recorder for modifying the behaviour of teacher trainees. After sometime it was Dwight Allen of Stanford University who coined the term Micro-Teaching. Later many others in the U.S.A., the U.K. and Netherlands did pioneering work in micro-teaching.

Micro-Teaching

Micro-teaching was introduced in India in 1967 with the humble attempt made by D.D. Tiwari of Government Central Padagogical Institute, Allahabad.

In 1970, G.B. Shaw experienced with Micro-teaching at M.S. University, Baroda. Then the Technical Teachers Training Institute, Madras introduced Micro-teaching to train the technical teachers. In 1974, Dr. N.L. Desai used Micro-teaching as a teaching device in Teachers Training Institute, Chandigarh. He also wrote a book namely: 'Modification of Teacher Behaviour through Micro-Teaching'. NCERT and SCERT, in the different states have been propagating this concept.

A Few Definitions of Micro Teaching

(i) D. W. Allen (1966) "Micro-teaching is a scaled down teaching encounter in class-size and class-time."

(ii) Allen and Eve (1968) "Micro-teaching is defined as a system of controlled practice that makes it possible to concentrate on specific teaching behaviour and to practise teaching under controlled conditions."

(iii) Buch (1968) "Micro-teaching is a teacher education technique which allows teachers to apply clearly defined teaching skills to carefully prepared lessons in a planned series of five to ten minutes encounters with a small group of real students, often with an opportunity to observe the result on video tape."

(iv) David B. Young defined Micro-teaching as "a device which provides the novice and experienced teacher alike, a new opportunities to improve teaching."

(v) Mc Alleese and Unwin (1970) "The term Micro-teaching is most often applied to the use of Closed Circuit Television (CCTV) to give immediate feedback of a trainee teacher's performance in an amplified environment."

(vi) Clift and Others (1976) "Micro-teaching is a teacher training procedure which reduces the teaching situation to simpler and more controlled encounter achieved by limiting the practice teaching to a specific skill and reducing teaching time and classes."

(vii) Pass; B.K. (1976) says, "It is a training technique which requires pupil-teachers to teach a single concept using specified teaching skills to a small number of pupils in a short duration of time."

(viii) According to Encyclopaedia of Education (Ed. Deighton) Micro-teaching is a real, constructed, scaled down teaching encounter which is used for teacher trainiag, curriculum development and research."

Characteristics of Micro Teaching

A few characterisitics of micro-teaching are as under :

1. It is a teacher training technique and not a method of class room instruction.
2. It is micro in the sense that it scales down the complexities of real teaching.
   (a) Out of contents, a single concept is taken up at a time.
   (b) Only one skill at a time is practised.
   (c) Size of the class is reduced and thus the number of students is just 5 to 7.
   (d) Duration of each micro lesson is 5 to 7 minutes.

3. Feedback is provided immediately after the completion of the lesson.
4. The use of Video Tape and Closed Circuit Television makes the observation very objective.
5. It is highly individualized training device.
6. There is a high degree of control in practising a skill when this technique is used.
7. Micro-teaching is an analytic approach to training.

   Micro-teaching involves actually teaching a real lesson to real pupils with none of the role-playing of earlier modelled teaching situations.

— Micro-teaching lessons are constructed for the benefit of the teacher and student's learning is incidental.

— Micro-teaching provides a significant way to bring speecific educational problems into manageable focus.

Components of Micro-Teaching

The components of micro teaching are:

(i) a teacher

(ii) the pupils (usually 4 or 5)

(iii) a brief lesson,

(iv) the objectives of the specific micro te ach1ng occsion.

(v) feedback by the supervisor, or by using audio tape recordings, video tape recordings and closed circuit television.

Objectives of Micro-Teaching

The objectives of Micro-teaching are as under :

1. To give practical teaching to the teachers undertraining by lessening the complexities of class room situations.
2. To identify the drawbacks of the teachers and to give immediate feedback for modifying their behaviour.
3. To develop experimental teacher education programmes and encourse research identifying new teaching skills.

4. To improve teaching through more control of instructional process and supervision.

Objectives of Introduction Micro-Teaching in Colleges of Education

Duggal and Sharma (1973) have listed the following objectives of introducing Micro-teaching in Colleges of Education:

1. To initiate the teacher trainees to analyse and develop teacher behaviour under laboratory conditions.
2. To send teachers gradually in the real class room after gaining enough confidence.
3. To impart intensive training in the component skills of teaching.
4. To involve the academic potential of teacher trainees for providing feedback.
5. To lessen the work load of teacher educators with the involvement of peer supervisors.
6. To lessen the burden upon practising schools while having practice of teaching skills under simulation conditions in college of Education.
7. To explore the human resources to maximum and making economy with regard to time, money and materials.

Assumptions of Micro-Teaching

The assumptions on which Micro-teaching is based are as under :—

1. Teaching behaviour of a teacher can be observed in class room situations.
2. Drawbacks in the teaching competency can be traced out and then they can be improved upon.
3. Complexities of normal class room situation can be reduced. The size of the class, the duration of teaching, teaching contents etc. can be reduced for giving training to the beginner teachers.
4. Training of specific skills can be given very well by taking up one skill at a time.

5. Practice of teaching can be controlled by providing regular feedback.
6. Teacher training programme can be highly individualised.
7. In-service teachers can also be better trianed through Micro-teaching technique.
8. Observation of teaching can be done objectively by using video tape and closed circuit television.
9. Feedback to the teacher trainee can be possible immediately. The earlier the feedback to the teacher trainee, the better is his learning the different skills of teaching.

Phases of Micro-Teaching Procedures

According to Clift and Others (1976), Micro-teaching procedure has the following three phases:

Knowledge Acquisition Phase : At this stage, the student teacher tries to get knowledge of the skill to be practised. He reads relevant literature concerning that skill. He is also made to observe a demonstration lesson in which that skill figures prominently. The person who demonstrates the skill is an expert of the subject and the skill. By observing that lesson, the teacher under training gets theoretical as well as practical knowledge of that skill.

Skill Acquisition Phase : The student teacher acquires the skill in hand through a lot of practice. He prepares the micro lesson, teaches it to have practice and then through feedback he evaluates his performance. Then he replans the lesson with modifications and improvement and then reteaches that lesson. Again there is re-feedback in order to enable him to have mastery of the teaching skill. In this way, different skills are learnt by the student teacher one by one.

Transfer Phase : At this stage, teacher integrates the different skills. Instead of artificial situation he teaches in the real class room where the number of students is full class. His lesson is of 30 to 35 minutes duration and there he tries to integrate all the skills for which be made efforts in Phase Nos. I and II.

Procedure Adopted in Micro-Teaching

The following steps are used for conducting a micro lesson successfully:

1. There is general discussion about Micro-teaching. Theory of Micro-teaching with all details is discussed. The teacher under training reads related literature and through discussions, clarifications are sought.

2. Different skills involved in teaching are explained to the pupil teachers.

3. Out of the various skills, one skill for mastery purpose is selected. Full details of that skill are given to the pupil teachers.

4. An expert of the subject gives a demonstration lesson on that particular skill.

5. The demonstration lesson is followed by discussions in which the learner teachers discuss things and seek all type of clarifications.

6. The pupil teacher writes the micro lesson plan on the skill already selected. He does this in consultation with the supervisor.

7. The pupil teacher teaches the lesson to a small group of students (*i.e.* 5 to 10 students). The lesson is observed by the supervisor (the teacher) or by the peers or video tape.

8. Immediately after the lesson, feedback is provided. All types of suggestions are given for the improvement of the lesson.

9. In the light of discussion and suggestions, the pupil teacher replans the lesson. It is done again under the guidance of the supervisor.

10. The lesson replanned is retaught to the small group of students.

11. After the lesson is over, again feedback is given and thus improvement in teaching is made.

Thus we find that through Micro-teaching, the pupil teacher is able to acquire 5 Rs i.e. Recording, Reviewing, Responding, Refining and Redoing.

Micro-Teaching Cycle

The Micro-teaching cycle is based on the following steps:

(i) Writing the Micro Lesson Plan

(ii) Teaching

(iii) Feedback is given

(iv) Re-planning the lesson

(v) Re-teaching the lesson

(vi) Re-feedback is provided.
Plan → teach → Feedback
Re-feedback ← Re-teach 4 ← Re-plan

The above given is the Micro-teaching cycle. The student teacher is required to re-plan, re-teach and re-feedback till he is able to have mastery over the skill in hand.

Principles Underlying Micro-Teaching

Micro-teaching is based on a few sound principles which are briefly explained below:

Principle of One Skill at a Time : In Micro-teaching training of one skill is given till the person has acquired mastery over it. Then the second skill is taken up and so on. Thus we find that micro-teaching is based on the principle of giving training of one skill at a time.

Principle of Limited Contents : In micro-teaching. United contents are taken up and the teacher is required to use those contents only. It helps the beginner' teacher teach that limited material easily and confidently.

Principle of Practice : Micro-teaching is based on the sound principle of practice. Here a lot of practices are given by taking up one skill at a time. Practice makes a man perfect. It helps the pupil teacher in becoming better and better.

Principle of Immediate Feedback : The micro lesson lasts for four or five minutes only. Thereafter, feedback is provided to the pupil teacher. It helps the pupil teacher to know his drawbacks and improve them effectively without any delay.

Principle of Experimentation : A lot of experimentations are involved in Micro-teaching. The experiment consists of objective observation of actions performed under controlled conditions. The pupil teacher and the supervisor conduct experiment on teaching skills under controlled conditions. Variables like time duration of the lesson, contents of the lesson to be taught number of students sitting in the class etc. can be easily controlled.

Principle of Evaluation : In micro-teaching, there is continuous assessment of the performance of the pupil teacher. Evaluation helps the learner know his drawbacks and then he is able to improve it. In micro-teaching each micro lesson is supervised by the supervisor or the peers. Drawbacks in teaching are pointed out and suggestions for improvement are given. Self-evaluation is also possible. Thus evaluation ensures good learning by the pupil teacher.

Principle of Individualised Training : In Micro-teaching each trainee is given training very thoroughly. There is individual attention by the supervisor. The drawbacks in teaching are pointed out suggestions given one by one and thus improvement is brought about.

Principle of Continuity : Learning of different skills of teaching is a continiuous process in Micro-teaching programme. Thc pupil teacher is learning one skill at a the and "learning continues till he has mastered thc skill. For each skill the principle of continuity is implied. It makes the teacher good and effective.

Micro-Teaching and Traditional Teaching—A Comparison : Micro-teaching is a new idea in the field of teacher education. People who have traditional outlook don't want to change their ideclogies. They face problems in acceptng the innovation of Micro-teaching. This type of situation always arises whenever new things will come up. The old nations need be converted into the modern ones because the modern ones are undoubtedly unique. The comparison of the two techniques brings home clearly the viewpoint that Micro-teaching is an improved techinique in every way and is better as compared to the traditional teaching.

Micro-Teaching

1. Teaching is relatively simple.
2. It does not pose a big threat or fear to the teacher.
3. It usually encourages the beginner teacher for better Job performance in future.
4. Here the objectives arc given in behavioural terms.

5. The number of students in a class is less. It is rather a small group of 5 to 10 students.
6. There is provision of immediate feedback. That helps the teacher to know his dr awbacks and improve upon them.
7. Teaching is carried on under fully cantolled situations. The supervisor is there who is determined to improve teaching.
8. The teacher practises one skill at a time. He continues the practice till he is able to have mastery of it.
9. Duration of lime for teachint is 5 to 10 minutes.
10. Patterns or class-room interaction be studied objectively.

Traditional Teaching

1. Teaching as experienced by the teacher is complicated and difficult.
2. It poses a big threat and a challenge to the teacher.
3. It may lead to failure and cause frustration.
4. The objectives are not stated in behavioural terms.
5. It is an over-crowded class where the number of students is 60 to 90.
6. Mediate feedback is not provided.
7. There is no control as such over teaching. There is no supervision.
8. The teacher practices the whole teaching behaviour which consits of many skills.
9. Time duration is 35 to 40 minutes.
10. Patterns of class room interaction cannnot be studied easily.

Merits and Demerits of Micro-Teaching

Merits : Here below are given merits of Micro-teaching:

(1) It is an effective device for modifying the behaviour of the teachers under training.

(2) It is a highly individualized type of teacher-training technique.

(3) It is useful for pre-service and in-service teacher teaching. The teachers can improve their competency of teaching.

(4) Feedback being quick, there is scope for early remedy of drawbacks and hence over all improvement in teaching is possible.

(5) It provides a lot of scope for research work especially of experimental type.

(6) It helps in developing really useful type of curriculum.

(7) Usually class-room teaching is a complex and complicated type of activity, but Micro-teaching simplifies it so as to make it suitable for the beginner teachers.

(8) It helps in acquiring various types of skills which ulitmately form the basis of successful teaching.

(9) In micro lesson, the observation is very objective because different types of audio-tapes, video-tapes or close circuit TV are used. Of course, in Indian situations where the observer is usually a teacher it may not remain fully objective type.

(10) It develops a lot of confidence in the teachers.

(11) It helps in sorting out problems related to class-room teaching. Their proper solutions can be thought of.

(12) Close superivision is possible.

(13) The objectives of micro lesson are given in behavioural terms.

(14) Micro-teaching can be carried on in real class room situations or in simulated conditions.

Demertis : The micro teaching suffers from a few drawbacks which are given below briefly:

(a) It requires competent and fully trained supervisor who are able to differentiate objectively and minutely.

(b) It wastes a lot of time of the students. Each micro lesson goes on for 5 or 7 minutes where the main emphasis is on teaching technique. Meaningful learning by the students is almost ignored.

(c) It kills creativity of the teachers. During teaching, a teacher might evolve something new but he has to stop as the micro lesson ends.

(d) Micro teaching can be carried on successfully in controlled type of environment but the class-room situations prevailing all around are not such. There are fluctuations and flexibilities.

(e) The application of Micro-teaching to new problem and practices in teaching is unlimited

(f) Micro-teaching alone may not be sufficient. There is need of integrating it with other teaching techniques.

(g) The programme of giving training to teachers through Micro-teaching is a costly affair. If observation is made with the help of video films, closed circuit TV that is a very costly affair.

Teaching Skills

Teaching is a complex phenomenon that comprises of various specific teaching skills. Through micro leaching, complexities of class room leaching are reduced. The different skills are identified and then mastery of each skill is acquired. Here two important questions crop up which need consideration. The first one is to know what is a skill. The second one is how many skills are involved in the teaching process.

What is a Teaching Skill?

NL. Gage (1968) says, "Teaching skills are specific instructional activities and procedures that a teacher may use in his classroom. These are related to the various stages of teaching or in the continuous flow of the teacher performance."

How Many Skills?

To know how many skills are involved in the teaching process is rather an interesting study. A few research workers have tried to identify several sets of component teaching skills. Some of them are common with a little different terminology.

Hen and Ryan (1969) of Stanford University put forth the view that fourteen skills are involved. Borg and his associates (1970) increased the number to eighteen.

In India, B.K. Passi (1976) on the basis of work done in CASE, Baroda has given a list of twenty one skills. His associates (1979) gave a list of twenty.

None of the lists suggested by the researchers are exhaustive and final. We can add or subtract from the lists as per need of the situation. The list of skills given by AllcII alld Ryall (J 969) is as under:-

Stimulus Variation : Teaching depends upon the stimulus provided by the teacher during teaching. A good teacher goes on varying the stimulus in order to bring in variety in his teaching. That way he is able to attract the attention of the students. Thus the teachers are trained in movements gestures, focussing interactional styles etc.

Set Induction : Set induction helps the students to induce maximum. The teacher uses their present knowledge and skills and tries to involve them in the lesson.

Closure : It is related with the finishing up of a stage in teaching. It helps the students to relate the new knowledge with the previous one.

Silence and Non-Verbal Cues : During teaching, the teacher provides cues to the students in order to elcourage them. Sometimes he puts a thought provoking question. The students speak on it. The discussion goes on and on when the teacher does not give his personal comments. He rather remains silent. It makes many other students to come forward and speak.

Reinforcement or Student Participation : The pupil teaching everyway tries to encourage students participation in the lesson, As far as possible, he accepts their responses with a smile. Only positive reinforcers are used by him. He makes every effort to avoid the use of negative reinforcers which may result into any type of discouragement for the students.

Fluency in Making Questions : While putting questions to the class, the teacher should have fluency. He tries to have as many questions as possible in the scheduled period of teaching.

Probing Questions : The teacher puts such questions with the help of which he is able to dig out something from the students. With the help of probing questions, the teacher is able to lead the students to correct responses.

Higher Order Questions : In every good lesson, the teacher puts some questions which are of higher order. This type of questions enable the students to form generalizations or to reach some definite principle.

Divergent Questions : Putting divergent questions is another skill which makes the students think creatively.

Recognising Attending Behaviour : Every good teacher has the ability to Judge while teaching how far the students are taking interest in the lesson. The teacher is able to do so through visual cues.

Illustrations and use of Examples : A good teacher has the skill of clear teaching. For this purpose he is able to give good examples. Through illustrations, he is able to capture the attention of all.

Lecturing : The teacher is able to present the material effectively by using the right type of techniques.

Planned Repetition : Sometimes during teaching the teacher repeats things in a planned manner. He does so in order to focus the attention of the students over some important points.

Completeness : Communication of teaching is a two way traffic. Through teaching, the teacher is able to communicate himself fully. He is able to give knowledge, develop attitude and interest of the students.

B.K. Passi (1976) described 13 skills in his book 'Becoming Better Teacher - Micro Teaching Approach.' The different skills are as under:

(i) Writing Instructional Objectives.

(ii) Introducing a Lesson.

(iii) Fluency in Questioning.

(iv) Probing Questions.

(v) Explaining.

(vi) Illustrating with Examples.

(vii) Stimulus Variation.

(viii) Silence and Non-verbal cues.

(ix) Reinforcement.

(x) Increasing Pupil Participation.

(xi) Using Blackboard.

(xii) Achieving Closure.

(xiii) Recognising attending Behaviour.

The Baroda General Teaching Competence has divided teaching skills into three categories:

(a) Pre-instructional Skills.

(b) Presentation Skills.

(c) Closing Evaluation & Managerial Skills.

List of Probable Teaching Skills for Different Stages of a Lesson

Below is given a list of probable teaching skills which are required at different stages of a lesson:

Planning Stage

This stage involves the following skills:

1. Writing Instructional Objectives
2. Selecting the Content.
3. Organising Content.
4. Selection of Audio Visual Aids Material.

Introductory Stage

1. Creating Set Induction.
2. Introducing the Lesson.

Presentation Stage

The Presentation Stage has four sub-stages. Each sub-stage needs different type of teaching skills which are given below:

Questioning Skills

(i) Structuring Class Room Questions.

(ii) Fluency in Asking Questions.

(iii) Probing Questions.

(iv) Question-Delivery and Distribution.

(v) Higher Order Questions.

(vi) Divergent Questions.

(vii) Responses Management.

Presentation Skills

(i) Pacing of the Lesson

(ii) Lecturing

(iii) Explaining Discussing

(iv) Illustration with Examples

(v) Discussing

(vi) Demonstrating.

Aid Using Skills

(i) Using Teaching Aids.

(ii) Using Blackboard.

(iii) Stimulus Variation

(iv) Silence and Non-verbal Cues.

(v) Reinforcement Managerial Skills

Managerial Skills

(i) Promoting Pupil Participation.

(ii) Recognising Attending Behaviour.

(iii) Management of the class.

(iv) Closing Stage.

The stage includes the following skills:

(i) Achieving Closure.

(ii) Planned Repetition.

(iii) Giving Assignments.

(iv) Evaluating the pupils progress.

(v) Diagnosing pupil learning difficulties and remedial measures.

Practising Selected Skills

Every teaching lesson comprises a number of skills. A teacher under training should not be asked to go and teach the full lesson in the school. He should be trained to have practice of a few selected skills. Micro teaching helps him in every way. Let him have practice of different skills one by one. The following few skills are recommended:

(a) Explaining (b) Probing
(c) Questioning (d) Stimulus Variation
(e) Class-room Management (f) Reinforcement

Explaining : In every subject, there are some topics which need less explanation by the teacher and there are a few topics which are rather difficult, require more explanation by the teacher. Thus there are peculiar situations in teaching where he/she is expected to explain well. Suppose the teacher takes up some easy point which the students already know well and goes on explaining it, it does not help the learners any way. Rather they find that type of teaching a drudgery arid boredom for them. A good teacher is able to judge well beforehand the different points and the situations within a lesson where he will be required to explain fully. The teacher naturally goes well prepared and with everything planned. Then he is able to tackle the situation wisely.

The skill of explaning like other skills can be acquired by the teacher gradually. By taking the help of micro teaching, the learner teacher can plan and teach and if the need arises there to, he may re-plan and re-teach. Only practice in different situations will help him have mastery over this skill.

The skill of explaining is an art where the teacher speaks a few statements which are inter-related and thus he makes the students understand or grasp something. It is suggested that the teacher trainee should be asked to take up the skill of explaining at some later stage. In the early stages, the skills such as introducing the lesson, B.B. writing, questioning etc. may be acquired. By then, the P.T. has lot of confidence and he finds it easy to take up any skill.

A Few Situations for the Skill of Explaining

1. A teacher of social studies, gives a point to the students and then he explains the point. In explaining sometimes he uses maps or pictures. That helps him and he might be able to do his job of explaining better. Without the different A.V. aids, his job might be a bit difficult. Single handed, he is expected to be more active and the class just passive listener.

2. A science teacher explains the point say 'Preparation of Oxygen in the laboratory' by showing p.n experiment. It makes his explaining more interesting. The students might find it easy to understand and learn.

3. A langugae teacher explains a line of poetry or a stanza to the class.

For this he plays with the words and is able to make his teaching more and more clear and easy for the students.

The skill of explaining is there in the class-room situations when the teacher teaches some new lesson or topic. It may also be there when the teacher is revising something but one or two students of the class stand and ask the teacher to explain some point again. And sometimes, the teacher while teaching skips over some point and that point is put forth by the student where he/she wants explanation over the point by the teacher. At the outset, it puts the teacher in a difficult situation. Only a good teacher who is skilled can do well there. In case-'a teacher fails to explain,' he should frankly tell that he would think more and explain next time. A good teacher with a frank opinion is able to win over the students.

Merits

1. The 'skill of explaining' acquired by a teacher makes him really a fit-person for the job of teaching. It gives him a lot of confidence.

2. The teacher who is able to explain better is able to win over the students. They then like his teaching and respect him fully;

Demerits

A teacher who fails to acquire well the skill of explaining cuts a sorry figure. Such a teacher fails to be called a successful and effective teacher.

Probing : To probe means to dig out. A teacher is said to be good if the teacher tries to probe during the course of his teaching. Every learner has within his ownself everything. The learner may be compared with a budding flower. The flower has everything within its folds. In the natural course of its existence, it blossoms fully. So is the case with every learner. The teacher tries to dig out from the learner somehow or the other. Some teachers while teaching have reeling that the learners are only empty. They try to rill in the mind of the child with different type of information and knowledge. The good teachers place the learners in such situations and let them grow and develop.

The teacher puts probing questions with the help of which he is able to dig out something from the students. Thus the teacher is able to lead the students to the desired type of responses. A good teacher takes the help of probing questions during his teaching.

Now the question arises is it very essential to put probing questions to the students? It is not easy for the beginner teacher or for teacher under training. Let such teachers learn first the skill of questioning. Only thereafter, they can ask probing type of questions. The skill of probing therefore can be acquired by the teachers gradually.

The skill of probing questions may be defined as the art of response management. It comprises a set of techniques used for going deep into pupil's responses in order to have the desired responses. Here the emphasis is laid on the ways and means of response management. So this skills also named as the skill of Response Management (Jangira and his associates 1979).

The following techniques are used for the skill of probing questions:

(a) The teacher gives him hints or suggestions or some guidelines when the students fail to give the answer or they give a wrong reply. It helps the students to reach the stage of speaking correct answers.

(b) In some situations the response of the students is incomplete or it is partially correct. Then the teacher puts questions like- give some examples how can you make it more 'clear'! Elaborate this point etc.

(c) Sometimes the answer given by a student is correct but the student is not sure about it. In such cases the teacher tries to refocus the attention of that student by putting questions like- can you give an example of it' Can you apply it in real life situations etc. ?

(d) Sometimes, the answer of a responding student is all right but the teacher wants to increase his critical awareness. So he asks questions starting with 'why' or 'how', it places the students in more thinking type of situations.

Merits

(i) Probing skill makes the students understand things automatically.

(ii) Whatever is learnt by the students through probing by the teacher is everlasting.

(iii) It helps the teacher as well as the learners in being fully active in the process of teaching-learning.

(iv) There are more chances of becoming creative persons, Both the teacher and the learners may become creative.

(v) The teacher acts as a self-reliant person. His teaching will make the learners also persons of self-reliance.

Demerits

Probing in the hands of inexperienced and immature teachers may fail to deliver the goods. That way its targets may not be achieved.

Skill of Questioning. Teaching is a bipolar process. It every lesson, questioning is one of the major devices used by a teacher. While teaching, the teacher goes on lecturing or explaining things verbally or with the help of some aids. It is all one sided affair. The teacher, therefore, puts questions to the class in order to involve the students fully in the process of teaching-learning. Through questioning, the teacher is able to provide stimuli to the learner.

In this regard Colvin said. "The efficiency of instruction is measured in a large degree by the nature of the questions that'are asked and the care with which they are framed. No teacher of elementary or secondary subjects can succeed in his instruction who has not a fair mastery of the art of questioning," According io Raymont, "The acquisition of a good style of questioning may be laid down definitely as one of the essential ambitions of younger teacher."

A good teacher must be a good questioner.

Questioning is an integral skill of a good lesson. In the process of questioning, the following things are important:

1. The question should be relevant and meaningful.
2. It should be pin-pointed.
3. It should aim at one answer.
4. The wording of the question should be accurate.
5. It should not suggest answer in any way.

Purpose Behind Questioning

In every classroom situation, the questions are put keeping in view one purpose or the other. Usually the following component behaviours are involved:

1. Prompting.
2. Seeking further information.
3. Refocusing.
4. Redirection.
5. Increasing critical awareness.

Prompting. The teacher puts questions with the purpose of prompting the students for speaking. Here the questions serve the purpose of cues or hints. The question itself works in such a way that the students are able to react to it. The different words that constitute the questions act on the minds of the learners in such a way that they start reacting to it.

Seeking further Information: Here the language of the questions is such which enables the persons to think more and give some more information as compared to what has already been given. The learners have already given some responses but those are considered incomplete. For example the questions are: What else do you say'? How can you make it more clear? etc. In this way, the teacher tries to obtain further information from the pupils.

Refocussing: Here the teacher puts that type of questions whereby he is able to refocus the attention of the students on some key point or some typical situation. Suppose the teacher has taught a topic on compound and mixture. Through some questions, he can test their understanding ability. In his mind, he might think of refocussing the attention of the students on some point. For the purpose, he puts that type of questions which help the students to refocus their attention on some fundamental points.

Redirection: Here the purpose of putting the question is to redirect the attention of the students so as to get the desired response. Suppose a student has given a wrong answer, the teacher puts the question redirecting him to think and speak on the right lines. Here the question makes the student reach a situation which compels him to rethink and speak on the desired lines.

Increasing Critical Awareness: Another purpose of putting questions is to increase the critical awareness of the students. The teacher asks questions starting with 'how' and 'why'. That compels the students to think critically and give. The possible correct answers.

The students have already given a correct response to the questions put by the teacher. But the teacher wants to enhance the critical ability of the students. So he asks further. Why is it so? How can you justify what you have said? All these questions increase the critical awareness of the students.

Questioning is, in fact, a very good skill in the process of teaching. The teacher should acquire this skill through practice. Usually while putting questions, the following points should be kept in mind :

1. The teacher should put the questions to the whole class.
2. After putting the questions, there should be a pause for a while-may be of 3 to 5 seconds. Then only one of the students should be asked to give the answer.

3. The question should be well distributed in the class.
4. The question should be worded in such a way so that it does not suggest any answer.
5. A question should be spoken once as far as possible. It should be repeated, the same wording should be repeated.
6. The teacher should have a helping attitude always. By using encouraging words, he should try to elicit correct answer from the students.
7. The teacher should proceed to the next question only when the answer to the first question has been reached.
8. When a question is responded by the students, the teacher should tell immediately whether it is correct or not.

In case of a wrong answer by the student to students, the teacher should not discourage them by passing sweeping statements. His attitude should be of helping type.

Stimulus Variation : Teaching depends upon the stimulus provided by the teacher during teaching. A good teacher goes on varying the stimulus in order to bring in variety in his teaching. That way he is able to attract the attention of the students. Thus the teachers are trained in movements, gestures, focusing, interactional styles etc.

Every teacher uses some stimulus in order to have a desired type of response from the students. If he continues using the same stimulus for the same students, the desired response will not come up. So there is need of stimulus variation. This skill like the skills of 'explaining' and 'probing' cannot be acquired easily. Of course, acquisition of any skill is a matter of practice. But there are comparatively easy skills like questioning, introducing of a lesson, blackboard writing etc. which can be acquired by the trainee teachers or the beginners without any hardships.

A stimulus is something that evokes functional reaction in tissues. It has a touching effect on the learner. He/she does not feel any type of boredom or drudgery during the process of teaching learning. Thus a good teacher does not stand like a statue in his class room. He makes meaningful movements alongside while teaching. He also uses gestures during his narration or explaining of anything in the class. These things add to his style of teaching and help in making it more effective. The movements of the teacher in the class-room have to be meaningful. For example, the teacher moves at too much in the class. That will be rather bad on his part. It will instead deteriorate the academic climate of the classroom. His movement to the B.B. should be for writing purpose or it may be he wants to draw the attention of the class by pointing again to the B.B. Similarly use of gestures have to be meaningful as per the class-room situations related with teaching learning. Only a controlled type of stimulus variation results into positive results.

Another way is that the teacher changes his voice during teaching-sometimes louder pitch of voice, sometimes low, sometimes more speed of speaking and sometimes less speed. At other times, he brings a change in his style of interacting with the class. Thus sometimes, the teacher puts questions to individual students and sometimes to a group and accepts responses individually and in a group.

The teacher draws attention of the students on some important point and also uses the map for the purpose. Just verbal statements also matter a lot in some situations.

Use of pause here and there by the teacher during the course of his teaching the class helps a lot. If the teacher continues speaking without any pauses, it becomes very cumbersome for the learners. So the pauses of short while make the students learn things conveniently and happily without taxing their minds too much.

Still another way of stimulus variation in this age of science and technology is that the teacher uses audio or visual or both audio and visual aids in his teaching. Naturally it will better attract the attention of the students.

Class-room Management : It is one of the managerial skills which includes promoting pupil participation, recognizing attending behaviour of the learners and overall management of the class-room. He is one of the most important skills which is essential for every teacher. Teacher's main job is to show leadership to the learners in the class room situations and thus imbibe the qualities of leadership in the students. He is for the students and the students are with him for the over all improvement of their personalities through the process of behaviour modifications. The teacher must ensure that both he an his students should be actively involved in the process of teaching-learning. He is expected to promote pupil participation in the process of teaching. He is expected to promote pupil participation in the process of teaching. For this, he should be able to recognise their attending behaviour. A teacher with a psychological bent up of mind knows well about it. The teacher who is inquisitive type and is eager to know about the attending behaviour of the learners succeeds in it. This skill is more or less of instructive type. Presence of the teacher in class-room situations equips him with this skill. The more the experience of the teacher in the classrooms, the more qualified and equipped he comes out with this skill.

A good teacher succeeds in promoting pupil participation in the process of teaching-learning. He is able to devise ways and means and then comes out all successful. Everything in the classroom depends upon the over all management of the teacher there. A visit to a class-room or passing by that way at once speaks about the teacher who teaches there. A disciplined class is the outcome of a disciplined teacher only. Tone of the class room is set not in one or two days only. It requires hard labour of many days on the part of the teacher.

Class-room management is over all control of the class. It includes pupils' initial behaviour, readiness for the modification of behaviours, their sitting in the class-room, setting of the class-room, prevailing healthy environment etc. All this is set up by the teacher gradually with the lapse of time. Orders of the teacher or the administrators do not help much. A really model type of teacher or the administrator is able to have it automatically. In it naturally all that matters, whatever is done of presented by the teacher. A really good teacher is able to have it as per his desires and wishes. Who is a good teacher? And how to be a good teacher? These characteristics are acquired by the teacher through experience by observing others and by coming in contact with persons of high ideals.

Merits

1. It being a managerial skill gives an insight of internal administration to the teacher. The teacher ultimately comes out a better teacher.
2. It sets a tone for the class-room which ultimately improves the over all climate of the institution.

3. A mastery over this skill helps the teacher to acquire other skills easily. When the over all tone of the class-room is good under the impact of the teacher, practice of other skills becomes an easy affair for the teacher.

Demerits

The skill of class-room management has a few drawbacks:

A teacher under training or a beginner teacher finds it difficult if he/she takes up this skill as the first skill of learning.

Reinforcement : Anything that reinforces or strengthens is known as reinforcement. In the process of teaching-learning, a good teacher always tries to encourage his students. As far as possible, he accepts their responses with a smile. Only positive reinforcers are used by him. He makes every effort to avoid the use of negative reinforcers which max result into any type of discouragement for the students. The skill of reinforcement is a must for every teacher. It can be acquired easily by the teacher trainees or the beginner teachers. It ensures far better results if used wisely and judiciously by the teachers.

The skill of reinforcement is an art of learning by the teacher. Here he learns how to use the right type of reinforcers to have desired type of students behaviour. During the process of teaching-learning, there are different type of situations where the teacher is expected to react one way or the other. A good teacher is positive and constructive in his behaviour all through which naturally encourages the learners. The teacher, thus, succeeds in the attainment of desired objectives.

Components of the Reinforcement Skill

Broadly the components of the reinforcement skill can be divided into two types:

I. Positive Reinforcers.

II. Negative Reinforcers.

Positive Reinforcers of this Skill

(a) In the different class-room situations, the teacher uses positive reinforcers when the says- Good! fine! nice! all right! excellent! etc.

(b) He accepts the answer and says, "Please! Repeat it!."

(c) The teacher himself speaks the answer of the student either in the same words, or by modifying a little bit.

(d) The teacher does not speak anything. He only writes the response of the student on the chalk board.

(e) He claps or smiles to have the response from a student.

(f) Sometimes the teacher uses extra verbal reinforcers such as Aha! Ooh! Aaha!

Negative Reinforcers of this Skill

Negative reinforcers of the skill can be visualised in the following:

(a) In different class-room situations, sometimes the teacher uses discouraging words such as No, Wrong, Incorrect etc.

(b) Sometimes he makes discouraging statements such as 'It is a poor answer'. I don't think so. I don't like your answer etc.

(c) Uses some gestures strongly which are discouraging *e.g.* nodding the head, moving the hands to show 'no, no.'

(d) The teacher uses reinforce when not required.

(e) The teacher does not use the reinforcer when it is required. Uses the reinforcers too less or too much.

Every teacher should make efforts to acquire the skill of reinforcement. Once acquired by him will always help him to achieve the desired type of response from the students. As far as possible, the teacher should make it a point not to use negative type of reinforcers in the teaching-learning process.

Integration of Teaching Skills

Integration of teaching skills may be defined as a process of selection, organisation and utilization of different teaching skills to form an effective pattern for realizing the specified instructional objectives in a given teaching-learning situation.

According to Jangira and Ajit Singh : "Integration is the process through which a student teacher acquires the ability to perceive with precision the teaching situation in its entirety, select and organise the teaching skills in the desired sequence to form effective patterns for realising the specified imstructional objectives and use them with easy and fluency."

The teachers under training are given practice in the mastery of the different skills through micro setting situations. Once they have learnt the different skills, then they are sent to the schools in real class-room situations where they are required to teach. A question arises- Should those teachers be given training for the integration of the different skills or not?

There are two groups of opinion which come forward' with their arguments on the above said question. One group is of the opinion that some training for the integration of different skills is a must while the other group of thinkers opine that there is no need. They say that the teachers are able to integrate different skills automatically.

The decided opinion is that the different teaching skills have to be integrated by using a number of strategies which are explained below:

Strategies for Integration of Skills

Vicarious Integration : In this type of Integration, the pupil-teacher is sent from micro teaching setting to real class-room situation directly. In between, no special training for the integration of various skills is given to him. He is able to integrate the different skills in his own way as per his own desires and requirements.

Summative Strategy : After the lesson, teacher has mastered, a few skills of teaching in microteaching he is provided with another micro-teaching setting where he learns the integration of skills already learnt by him. The duration of time is increased for this type of lesson. If the P.T. has learn two skills (SI and S), then he will learn the integration of those two skills. If he has learnt four skills ($S_1+S_2+S_3+S_4$), he will integrate those four skills ($S_1+S_2+S_3+S_4$). The training for the integration of skills is provided in a controlled setting. Increase in the length of the lesson will require increase the duration of time. Each lesson is observed and feedback is provided till the learner teacher is able to have a reasonable mastery in the integration of skills. Thus the pupil-teacher is sent to the real class-room situation in due course of time.

Additive Strategy : In this strategy, the pupil-teacher is given training for the mastery of two skills. Then he learns integration of those two skills. After this, training for the third skill is given and then he learns integration of the third skill into the two already acquired. Thus he goes on adding the newly learnt skill into the Ones already learnt by him. Here the time duration is increased as the length of the lesson increases.

Example : Suppose the pupil-teacher has learnt the skill of questioning and skill of reinforcement. He is then given training for the integration of those two skills. Thereafter, he learns the third skill of stimulus variation and integrates that in the two already learnt.

Cluster Strategy : Cluster means a chunk or a group. The teacher combines together, let us suppose two skills S_1 and S_2 in one lesson. Then he learns in another lesson say three skills S_3, S_4, S_5. After this he combines the above two clusters of five skills (S_1+S_2+S_3+ S_4+S_5) in a single lesson. In this way, he is learning the integration of skills.

In one cluster at a time, he may choose any two or three skills as per his liking. In the second cluster again, he can pick up any skill or any number of skills. Whatever he learns in two clusters, then he combines the two and learns integration.

Diode Strategy : According to diode strategy, the pupil teacher leans the integration of two skills say S_1 and S_2. Then he learns the other two skills say S_3 and S_4. Thus all the skills are learnt in pairs. Then they are integrated. This technique is actually in between the summative type and the additive type.

Mastery over the skills is given in controlled setting. The learner teacher takes up two skills at a time as per his liking and convenience. After learning the skills in pairs, he learns to integrate all the pairs, The teacher is provided with real class-room teaching situation after he has learnt the skills and their integration.

Subsumption Strategy: Teaching a class involves a complex skill. That can be analysed into simpler component skills. The component skills concerning some class are arranged in a hierarchical order according to the levels of their complexity, One main skill and its components are taken up and practice given to reach some level of competency say A. Then the other main skill and its component skills are taken up by arranging them in order of complexity, acquisition of those skills is given so as to reach a level of competency say B and so on.

Subsumption-Additive Strategy: This strategy is electric in approach. It is a combination of strategies Nos. 3 and 6. In strategy number 3, there is horizontal integration of skills whereas in number 6, there is vertical integration of skills, Out of the different skills, Questioning, Motivating, Explaining are functional and they are horizontal while component skills fall in the category of vertical integration.

Micro Teaching—Its Indian Model

Ever since micro-teaching was introduced in India, a number of research projects were undertaken. Efforts made at CASE, Baroda, Department of Teacher Education; NCERT Delhi and at Chandigarh yielded Indian Model of micro teaching. The main features of the model are:

(a) Unlike Western World where Films, Video or Closed Circuit Television are used, in Indian model, presenting the skill and feedback is done through written material supplemented by lectures, demonstration and discussion. As compared to the Western Model, Indian model is of a low technology.

(b) In Indian model, the observers are the living persons *i.e.* peers supervisors.

(c) It is less costly because high priced gadgets are not used.

(d) In Indian model, peers act as students. Real students are not used. Researches conducted on this point (Dass 1979) have shown that simulated micro teaching is as effective as micro teaching with real pupils.

(e) Indian model is flexible and it can be used successfully in any type of situation that prevails in teacher training colleges.

(f) Duration of micro cycle can be varied as per need and requirement of the learners.

Types of Pupils for Micro-Class

In a micro class, there can be real pupils or peers acting as pupils. In the Basic Stanford Model, the micro class consisted of real pupils. In many colleges of education in the U.K., real pupils still constitute a micro class.

With Real Students

Advantages. Situation is more real. Training of skill naturally is more meaningful.

Disadvantages : 1. The school students hardly learn anything.

2. There is disturbance to the setting of the school.

Students continued to compare the effectiveness of micro teaching setting with real pupils and peers reveal that both the settings are equally effective in developing general teaching competence in student teacher (*Das, ef a/1977* and 1979).

In the light of the research studies made, peers are used as pupils in the micro teaching model developed by NCERT. In this model, a pupil-teacher performs three roles turn by turn-a teacher, a supervisor and a student.

In the Indian Model of micro teaching developed by the Deptt. of Teacher Education, NCERT, peers (student teachers) constitute the micro class. Studies have been conducted to determine the value of pupils' feedback. Tuckman and Oliver (1968) compared the relative efficacy of four feedback conditions-pupil feed back, supervisor's feed-back, both pupil and supervisor's feedback, and no feedback. Their findings were that both the treatments involving pupil feedback produced significantly greater change than the other two conditions. Morrison and Me Infyre (1973) however, suggest that pupil feedback can be effective only When the same pupils are involved in micro teaching over considerable period and are trained in the use of rating scales or other instruments." Thus pupils feedback in NCERT model where peers act as pupils is likely to be more effective as they are already trained in observation.

QUESTIONS

1. "Micro teaching is powerful training technique most suitable in the present Indian conditions for training student teachers." Discuss the validity of the advantages of micro teaching over traditional student teaching programme.

2. "Micro teaching is a scaled down encounter." Discuss the statement and enumerate the nature and characteristics of micro teaching.
3. Discuss the nature, characteristics and scope of micro teaching.
4. What do you mean by integration of skills? Discuss the different strategies of integrating the different teaching skills.
5. "Micro teaching is not the real teaching but is used for developing teaching skills among teachers." Discuss this statement.
6. What do you understand by teaching skills? How can these skills be developed in the pupil teachers?
7. Write notes on :

    1. Components of micro teaching.
    2. Micro teaching cycle.
    3. Identification Integration of skills.
    4. Feedback in micro-teaching.

8

Teaching Methods

Since time immemorial, the teaching activity has been going on since times immemorial. Surely traditional teaching was not as well planned as we have it now. It is due to the impact of science and technology with the development of scientific thinking, a good many changes have taken place in the field of methods of teaching.

A few methods of teaching become popular as per the needs and requirements of the time. Here below four methods of teaching are discussed:-

1. Play Way Method
2. Dalton Plan
3. The Project Method
4. Heuristic Method.

Play-Way Method

Play is an activity in which natural urges of the child find spontaneous expression. It contributes to the physical, social and mental development of the child. The child does not experience the strain of the activity. Creative faculties of the child are developed here. The child grows into an adult with a balanced personality.

An activity combined with happiness and satisfaction is the basis of play way. It is an improvement on the activity principle. This term was first introduced by H. Caldwell Cook who experienced difficulty in teaching English grammar and language to his students. He discovered that children took keen interest in the subject when they were required to participate in Shakespearian plays. In dramatization spontaneity, freedom and laughter were associated with the learning process.

Underlying Principles of Play-Way

The following are the underlying principles of play-way method:

Learning by Doing : Learning through some activity is more in line with the fundamental urges of the child. This not only leads to a desirable sensory training but also provides opportunity for the gratification of urges like self-expression, self-assertion and construction.

Related to Life : If we relate the activities in the classroom with the life of the child, the child does not feel that he is living in an artificial atmosphere at school and therefore the tendency to avoid attendance in the school does not arise.

Methods of Teaching : Rigid, formal and bookish methods should be replaced by activities natural to the child. These should be based on the needs and interests of the child.

Sympathetic Attitude : Sympathetic attitude is conducive to efficient learning and the child also does not live under the strain of the artificial atmosphere. Report is established easily and children accept the suggestions of the teacher without much hesitation.

Free Expression : Opportunities should be provided for free expression in any form which may be of interest to the child.

Individual's Importance : The teacher should realize that interests and needs of children are seldom alike. Therefore, while planning education through play-way he should cater to the needs of each child individually.

Advantages of Play-Way

The play-way method has a number of advantages which are given below:

Natural-Motivation : Play-way being the natural urge of the child, he takes keen interest in it. Play gives him happiness and satisfaction and education is a by-product of the activities.

Whole-hearted Response : In play-way there is wholehearted response of the child and he becomes serious about his work.

Balanced Development of Personality : Play-way provides means for the social, emotional and moral development of the child besides giving intellectual training.

Self-discipline : When the child is engaged in an activity of an interest, he does not need any external control. He lives according to the self-imposed regulations. It becomes self-disciplined.

Self-advancement : Play-way ensures self-advancement through self-education.

Training of the Sensory Organs : Training of the sensory organs is not ignored.

Methods of Teaching Based on the Play-Way Principle

1. Kindergarten: In this method children are taught through sound movement. Play-spirit permeates the learning process. Activity centres round gifts which were evolved by Froebel, who was the originator of this method. 2. Montessori Method 3. Project Method. 4. Dalton Plan. 5. Heuristic Method 6. Basic Education 7. Self-government. 8. Extra Curricular activities like scouting, girl guiding, N.C.C., excursions and school functions.

Play-Way in the Teaching of Different Subjects

1. Games may be arranged to give practice in spelling. Dramatizations, debates, discussions, class meetings and school assemblies provide sufficient opportunities for expressing one's ideas and thus help in acquiring control over the use of language in different situations.

2. Arithmetic: Counting and simple calculations can be taught by organising projects like laying a garden, running a shop, managing a post office, having a co-operative store in the school etc. It can also be taught through drawing, needle work, wood work, paper cutting and other such hobbies.

3. History and Geography: These subjects can best be taught through dramatics, pageants (processions with different dresses), puppet shows, albums of pictures, stamp collecting, map drawing, globe making or making charts and models. In the initial stages story telling may be profitably applied for the teaching of this subject.

4. Nature study: Science can be best taught in the form of nature study. Usually children are interested in growing plants, flowering and rearing of pet animals. These

activities help them in observing things at difficult stages of growth.

Play-way spirit in this methods is of unique significance. It relativists the child at once, then it keeps him in the right track of learning. In the learning of any and every subject, play way helps a lot. Therefore, there is need of putting to use this method in the teaching-learning programme. The teacher using this method is bound to come not all successful in the mission of his teaching.

Dalton Plan

Experiments have always been made for the improvement of class room teaching. To break away with the traditional class room teaching, one praiseworthy effort was made by Miss Helen Parkhurst in 1920. She evolved a new technique called Dalton Plan or Laboratory Plan. It was planning and organisation of school work for making the children learn more effectively.

Miss Parkhurst worked as a school teacher and also as a lecturer in the training college. In the school, she was in charge of teaching children of different classes with different ages and also with different achievements. She applied her scheme in the school at Dalton in Massachusetts in U.S.A. So the scheme has been named as Dalton's Plan. Her plan came as a reaction against collective class room teaching. There is no change in the curriculum, the change is only in the teaching procedure.

Underlying Principles

The underlying principles of Dalton Plan are :

Principle of Individual Work : Miss Helen realised that not two children are alike. Therefore, recognition of individual differences is the key-note of Dalton Plan. Every child is allowed to work at at is own place and in accordance with his needs and interests. Every child is assigned work according to his own nature. Quality and quantity depend upon child's nature. There are no time table restrictions. Weak students take more time to finish the assignment than the intelligent ones.

Principle of Freedom : Dalton Plan gives freedom to the children to decide their course of action. There is no set time table no class-room restrictions and no worry of Annual Examination. They can move about freely, consulting books in the library, consulting the teacher or participating in discussions with the colleagues. In the words of Adam, "Dalton Plan is really a crystallisation of a widely prevailing desire for greater freedom for children in their school work."

Principle of Self-effort : Responsibility of education is laid on the shoulder of the students. Spoon-feeding is carefully avoided. Every child is expected to know what he is to learn and how he can learn it? He is to exert himself for his education. Learning through self-efforts leads to better individual development.

Principle of Gestalt View of Work : The child is given the idea of annual work as is whole. Although it is divided into monthly assignments yet he is expected to adjust the work according to his own plan. He himself thinks as to how much work he can do in a particular time.

Principle of Co-operation : Teacher cannot be expected to attend to each child. Therefore, students generally take the help of their class-mates and this fosters the spirit of co-operation among them.

Main Features of Dalton Plan

Assignments or Contracts : In the beginning of the session each subject teacher prepares a draft syllabus for the whole year. It is split up into monthly units. While making this plan, he keeps in view the number of working days or the actual time available for carrying out the plan. Monthly units are further divided into assignments. Each assignment is printed and it contains hints and a list of reference books which students have to consult to complete the assignment. Each child is expected to sign a contract form promising that he will finish the month's assignments in due time. The Pupils are not given new assignments unless they finish the previous assignments in all the subjects. The students are expected to work on assignments in different subjects simultaneously. They may complete assignment in one subject and then proceed with work in other subjects. Thus a child can devote more time to a subject in which he is weak.

Subject Rooms : The school which is organized according to Dalton Plan, does not have class-rooms. There are subject rooms or subject laboratories. Each room is furnished with required apparatus, instruments and books on the subject and is under the charge of the subject teacher. School library is thus divided according to the subjects and is distributed among the subject laboratories. Children are free to work in any room for any length of lime.

Subject Teachers : The Subject teachers are specialists in their own subject. They supervise the work of each child who comes to study that subject. Each teacher prepares assignments, checks work of the students, gives them suggestions whenever necessary, helps them in overcoming difficulties during the assignments and guides them in every way. The teacher makes sure that the time of the student does not go waste any way.

Records : Record of achievement and progress of children in each subject is kept in the form of cards-called Progress Cards. The progress of each child is kept in monthly units. At any time, achievements of the child can be directly read from the Progress-Card. There is another card which bears progress of the child in all the subjects. Subject teachers record the progress of children in the form of graphs. The graph serves as a link between the child and the teacher and facilitates the work of the teacher in checking the progress of all the students. Cards always remain with the students and remind them of their promises and make them aware of the progress being made.

Conferences: Sometimes a teacher feels the need of oral lessons in his own subject. Such oral lessons are arranged after the recess. This time is spent in group discussions under the guidance of the teacher and these are called conferences. These conferences are generally held four times a week, but the number of conferences may be increased or decreased depending upon the needs of a class at any time. The teacher removes common difficulties through the conferences.

Role of Teacher in Dalton Plan

1. The teacher must be a specialist in his subject so that he is able to guide his students individually.
2. He should have Training in teaching according to this method.
3. He should be able to pay individual attention to each child and should know the progress of each child.

4. He has to provide facilities to every child in the subject room and tell the use of the material. He should also guide regarding the use of reference books in the school library.

5. He should have full knowledge of the books and apparatuses available in the room. While issuing books, he should take care that every child gets books whenever he needs them.

6. He should be sincere about his work because unless he corrects the assignments of the students properly, he cannot know their real progress.

7. He should not be in the habit of postponing things. Children are likely to suffer if he does not maintain up-to-date records.

8. His attitude towards the students should be sympathetic and friendly. The children should not hesitate from coming to him for help and guidance.

Merits of Dalton Plan

Here below are given the merits of Dalton Plan:

1. Individual differences are recognised : An intelligent child may progress at his own speed and the less intelligent may devote more time to each item in the curriculum. Neither slow learners develop inferiority complex nor the brilliant students have the feeling that school-work is too below their potentialities.

2. Children learn by self-efforts : They learn to use material, consult reference books and acquire knowledge and skills without direct instructions from the teacher. The students become resourceful and acquire the quality of initiative.

3. If any child remains absent from the school due to ill-health or any other reason, his work does not suffer. He can continue with his work as per his sweet will.

4. The contract makes the activities of the child purposeful. The contract takes the form of a project and every child tries his best to finish it in time.

5. There are no failures according to this plan and therefore, no frustrations. Every child has success and sense of achievement.

6. Children develop the habit of shouldering responsibility and self-help. This training is very good for later life.

7. Home-work is not necessary. The children are relieved of this undesirable feature of the traditional method of teaching. Home-work is seldom accepted willingly, generally it is taken as a burden and is done under fear of punishment.

8. Individual work avoids discipline problem in the classroom and outside : Nothing is imposed on the child. Everything that he does is to fulfil his promises in the contract. He feels his responsibility. Self-discipline is inculcated in an atmosphere of freedom.

9. There is close contact between the teacher and the taught. The children learn many things from this contact. No part of the curriculum remains vague in the mind of the child.

10. The progress of each child is keenly observed and carefully recorded. The child is always aware of his progress. He has the correct idea of what he has to do as yet. It makes him work seriously and regularly.

Demerits of Dalton Plan

1. The plan may be very useful for the intelligent and hardworking students but this is not suitable for those who are in the habit of postponing things and are otherwise dull. Such students cannot pick up knowledge without formal lessons. In such cases, this plan may be suitable for revision lessons only.

2. Oral work is neglected totally in this method, but oral work is an important part of language teaching.

3. For efficient working of this plan subject laboratories should be well-equipped. All the material and books should be available in these rooms. There should be many sets of each material so that if many students are in need of them, they may not wait for their turn. For middle and high classes there should be simple and illustrated books. The

equipment needed in this method is rarely available in Indian Schools.

4. This plan needs many roomed building. The hard fact is that the schools have shortage of space.
5. Preparation of assignments needs fully skilled and competent teachers but (there is shortage of such teachers.)
6. This method is not suitable for the teaching of subjects like physical training, music, poetry and oral language because these subjects cannot be learnt individually.
7. Too much is expected from the teachers. They have to prepare assignments, pay individual attention to every child and give him every facility and help whenever he needs it. They have also to do correction work carefully.
8. This plan may develop individualistic tendencies. The learners lack social habits of co-operation, tolerance and fellow-feeling.

Suggestions for Introducing it in Indian Schools : Dalton Plan emphasises that opportunities should be provided for self-study and individual work. The following suggestions may be kept in mind to achieve this end:

Children should be divided into small groups according to their interests and abilities. They should be able to study some special topic or discuss some common problems and take help from each other. Such groups should be small consisting of 3 to 6 individuals. Such a system combines the advantages of group methods of teaching with individual work. Children develop according to their potentialities in social environment and they do not lack the desired qualities of co-operation, healthy competition and social consideration.

(a) Differences between average I.O. of different groups should be constant, e.g. 90, 100, 110 etc.

(b) The teacher should see that every child takes part in the group activity.

(c) The Children should always know well the purpose of each activity.

(d) Size of the group may be varied according to the nature of the subject, but it should never be too large to be handled efficiently.

(e) The teacher should not ignore the group when it has started its work. Everything should be done under his supervision. Group spirit should not lead to unhealthy rivalry and competition.

(f) There should not be any rigidity about the functioning of these groups. If in co-curricular activities students of one group like to participate in the activities of the other groups, they should be allowed to do so.

Records should be maintained for each child in all the schools. With these slight changes and modifications, Dalton Plan may be adopted in Indian Schools to achieve satisfactory results.

Project Method

Project Method is based on John Dewey's philosophy of pragmatism, or experimentalism or instrumentalism. John Dewey was of the opinion that education should be not only for life but throughout life. To him life is a continuous series of experiments with material as well as non-material instruments. He believed that everything is instrumental in achieving some goal. The process of education is no exception. John Dewey keenly felt the gap between the life in the school and life in the society. He insisted that in efficient educational system, this gap should be bridged up. School should be a continuation of society and the students should learn through life itself. Project method is an attempt to bring society into the school. The students should learn Engineering through actual workshop practice.

Kilpatrick was the originator of this method and J.A. Stevenson implemented it.

This method makes use of child-centred curriculum. Everything is looked upon from child's angle-his purpose, interest and utility. Here emphasis is not on teaching but on learning and learning can be effective if it is not only through doing but through living. The children should be trained to live. Learning should be by product of purposeful activity. Subjects should not be taught in isolation but there must be natural correlation between different items of studies.

A Few Definitions. According to Stevenson, "A project is problematic act carried to completion in its natural setting."

Kilpatrick says, "A project is a whole-hearted purposeful activity proceeding in a social environment.

In the words of Ballard, " Project is a bit of real life that has been imparted into the school.

From the above definitions we understand that:

(a) A project is related to real life.

(b) Real life consists of problems and their solutions.

(c) These problems arise and are solved in social environment.

Principles Underlying Project Method

The underlying principles of Project Methods are:

Principle of Purpose : Learning should be based on some activity. That activity should be related to life and should have a clear-cut purpose. This purpose should be known to the students. Moreover, it should preferably be related to some fundamental urge in the child. Success of a project depends upon the extent to which children identify themselves with the purpose of the project. Purpose combines life with learning and improves its quality.

Principle of Activity : More knowledge of the purpose and academic interest in it are not enough. We should provide opportunity to the children to be active to achieve the purpose of the project. They should survey the situation and make plans for realizing the purpose which is generally the solution of a problem in hand. Through action, the children learn to shoulder responsibilities to think independently and to co-operate with others according to their ability and intelligence. In no case, the activity should be imposed on the children.

Principle of Reality : In project method, we should create real life situations in the school where the children may exercise their powers. Very intimate relation with life in a project, ensures that learning will not be a dull and boring task.

Principle of Freedom : There should be freedom at all stages in a project. The children should choose plan and execute the project without the interference of anybody. Project should be the outcome of spontaneous activity on the part of children. In such an atmosphere the children express themselves freely. All this leads to the development of a well adjusted personality.

Principle of Utility : Knowledge gained by children should have some immediate practical significance. Buried past or vague future have very little attraction for the children. The children always love to live in the present. Therefore, unless the project helps the child in resolving some immediate difficulty, he will not show much interest in the project. Utility and reality go side by side. Any knowledge which does not find application in life is not a real knowledge according to the pragmatic thinkers.

Project is a very systematic activity. It passes through the following stages:

Steps of the Project Method

Providing a Situation : Project is not imposed by the teacher on the students. The teacher provides such opportunities to the children that they feel difficulty in meeting the situation. It becomes a problem for them to overcome that difficulty. All the children feel the need of resolving it. Overcoming the difficulty or solving the problem becomes a project for them.

The teacher has to be cautious in discovering the interest of the students in the class. From this analysis, he judges as to what the students would like to do. Then he creates situations accordingly. The situations are presented by discussing with the class. These discussions should centre round the experiences that the teachers and the students might have had during vacation and holidays. Sometimes a new item may become the base of controversy. The job of the teacher is to discuss things in such a manner that the students willingly accept to undertake the activity. It may be excursion to a place of scientific, historical or geographical interest. It may be staging a drama or celebrating some festival in the school or running a co-operative store in the school.

Choosing the Topic for the Project : According to Kilpatrick, purposing is practically the whole thing in a project. Success of a project depends upon the purposing done by the pupils or the teacher. The teacher's job ends with providing a number of situations. He should leave it to the students to select and plan the project individually or collectively. It is wrong on the part of the teacher to choose a project of his own interest and make the class accept it, because the aim of project method is to enable the children to choose the project, to think independently and to carry out the project. So the teacher should act as a guide in selecting the project. Whenever the teacher feels that the choice of the students is wrong he should make the students realize the shortcomings in their choice.

Project should not cover too many new points. It should be based upon very narrow and concise topic. Project should be such that the students may get the necessary apparatus and money which may be needed in the execution of the project without difficulty.

Planning the Project : At this step, the children should be encouraged to draw their own plans. The teacher should keep in mind two or three good plans so that he is able to help the children whenever they need his help. He should make the students realize that it is easy to carry out a good plan. An incomplete plan leads to difficulties when it is put into action.

While planning, at first there should be oral discussions followed by writing of proposals. Proposals may be written on the black-board. After considering all the pros and cons a good plan should be agreed upon. Every detail of project should be thoroughly discussed and responsibilities may be assigned to the different students. The teacher should see that all the resources needed to carry out the project are available.

Carrying O ut the Project : This step is the core of project method. Real learning takes place at this stage. Duties having been assigned according to the interest and ability of the students each student undertakes his own activity. The teacher should be patient to see the activities of children at different levels of accomplishment. The children commit mistakes and learn from self-experience. He should guide them only when he feels that they are committing blunders. He should allow the students sufficient time for the completion of the project.

A single project consists of many activities like reading books, visiting different places, getting information form different persons, calculating prices or enquiring rates from the market. The teacher has to recommend books and persons where from students can receive the required information. The teacher should see that all the students contribute towards the successful completion of the project. Teacher should also make the students appreciate that plan is their servant and not their master and hence plan can be changed or modified if such a necessity arises during execution.

Evaluating the Project : On the completion of the project the students should assess its outcome. They should see whether the work has been done according to the plan and if not what were the reasons for not following it. What were the difficulties that came in the way? How far the choice and the plan were correct? What are the experiences that they have got and what are the new things that they have learnt through the project? In this step, the students should get training in self-criticism.

Recording : The children should keep a record of the whole procedure in the project. There should be a project note-book and details of all the five steps should be recorded in it. They should also keep record of the sources of information like books and individuals contacted during the course of the project.

Example of a Project : Setting up a school shop.

In a school, the students felt difficulty in purchasing things from the market. After a good deal of discussion, the class decided to open a school shop. The students had to write an application to the head of the institution. Application had to be written in ink. Many students did not have ink, so preparation of ink was taken up as a side activity. The class also had lessons on correct technique of writing application.

After obtaining permission from the head of the institution money was collected, things were obtained and their prices were fixed. Students learnt about profit and loss, cash memo, stock registers, oral Arithmetic and many more things through this single project.

Criteria of a Good Project

Utility : The project must be socially useful. The knowledge that they acquire may be useful in a number of ways. Project should fulfil some fundamental need of the children and through it they should be able to learn many subjects.

Activities : A good project should provide opportunities for maximum number of activities. These activities should be according to age and mental development of children. Activities should provide sufficient number of situations where the children may be required to think and carry out work for themselves.

Economy : A good project does not waste too much energy of children. If provides for maximum education in the shortest possible time. Economy of wealth is also considered as a quality of an efficient project.

Experiences : A good project leads to valuable experiences and the child learns to work in co-operation with others. Character training is a by-product of the social activities which form a part of the project.

A practical Project is one for which resources are readily available and for which the teacher can give expert guidance at all stages.

Role of the Teacher : The teacher should have the following qualities for efficient practice of project method :

1. He must be a psychologist so that he understands the needs and interests of the children and suggest projects accordingly.
2. He should have emotional maturity. He should only guide the students and not dictate them in any way.
3. He should have patience to watch the activities of the students and give help only when it is clearly required by the students.
4. He should be tactful so that he may direct the activities of children along right lines without letting them feel that they are being dictated by the teacher.
5. He should think himself as a member of the group. He should not have feelings of superiority and should not expect the students to accept all his suggestions.
6. He should be a man of wide knowledge and experience so that he may guide the students in varied situations.
7. He should pay individual attention to the students and see that each one of them is discharging the responsibilities assigned to him.
8. He should be aware of tastes and interest of all the students.
9. He should be trained to teach many subjects by correlating them with the project in hand and he should take care that maximum subjects are learnt by the students. He should fill in gaps left in students knowledge during the execution of the project.

Merits of Project Method : The project method is based upon sound psychological principles. The following points deserve consideration:

Based on the Laws of Learning.

(i) Law of Readiness : Learning takes place when the learner is in a receptive mood. When an individual is working with a definite purpose, the action gives him satisfaction. When one is not ready to act, the action leads to dissatisfaction. Project method tries to present a strong purpose before the children and thereby create readiness in them for the activity.

(ii) Law of Effect : If an activity leads to satisfaction and pleasure, it is better learnt. Successful completion of the project leads to satisfaction because the activity is self-planned.

(iii) Law of Exercise : Those responses which are practised are retained for a longer time. In project method it is not only learning by doing, it is learning through purposeful living. Children learn by practising real things under real situations.

The Children Learn well in Real Situations : These projects should be selected which are in accordance with the needs and interests of children. Whatever is taught is taught with a view to give the child something useful. For example, Hygiene is taught to develop healthy habits, Arithmetic for business, History for creating an awareness of one's own country etc.

Co-operation : Through social activities of a project, the children learn to work in co-operation with others. They choose things and act together and this contributes to their social development.

Dignity of Labour : In project method, the students work with their own hands and develop a sense of dignity of labour.

Self Reliance : The children form the habits of shouldering responsibilities, taking initiative and arriving at an independent decision.

Democratic Citizenship : Through projects, the children develop habits necessary for good citizenship, e.g., perseverance working whole-heartedly for a common cause, tolerance, consideration for other and self-help.

Correlation : Many subjects are taught through one project. There is no division of knowledge into water-tight compartments. All the subjects are properly connected with each other through purposeful activities.

Economy : According to this method, the children learn much more and much better. There is economy both in teaching and learning and the children learn without any worry and strain.

Learning by Insight : This method is based upon learning through problem solving. Cramming does not find any place in this method. The teacher does not give ready-made plans to the students. He provides sufficient opportunities of thinking and reasoning to the children. He aims at providing training in scientific method of enquiry.

Limitations

Learning not Continuous : When children are taught by project method, gaps are likely to remain in their knowledge. Experiences in a project are not organised to maintain continuity of the subject. In his later life when child comes to know of these gaps he feels that he should have learnt these things in school days. Teachers may try to fill these gaps in an unnatural manner by exceeding the project beyond limits. It is better to realize that all the topics cannot be taught through project method. Learning by project method should be supplemented by systematic study of the subject.

Unnatural Learning : In project method attempt is made to connect every subject with the project. Many a time this link is not the natural outcome of the execution of the project. It may be very difficult for children to understand such items of knowledge which are not involved in the execution of the project, but which are indispensable for understanding the principles, involved in its execution. For example, knowledge of multiplication and division may be acquired in the project. But these Arithmetical operations cannot be understood without knowing addition and subtraction.

Expensive : A lot of material is needed to carry out a project any a time this material is not available. Ordinary school cannot afford the expenses of the material required in the project. In the beginning, projects may be related to the surroundings but to give wide knowledge and better understanding to the students, we cannot dispense with expensive projects.

Too Many Expectations from the Teacher : The teacher is expected to give lesson not by preparing a topic but in the process of completing the project. He has to tackle problems when they arise. These problems are not known beforehand. Thus he has to think quickly. He should be able and tactful to give wise guidance at every stage.

Too much Emphasis on Perceptual Knowledge : Learning by doing is the keynote of project method. Through direct experience, the children acquired knowledge at the perceptual level and understanding of concepts is generally ignored. In project method, emphasis is laid upon applying generalizations and no attempt is made to arrive at them. A stage comes when the pupils lose interest in the project and want to have more intellectual knowledge.

Makes Teaching Disorganized and Irregular : There is no set time-table or curriculum. Everything has to be evolved on the spot. Thus it is very difficult to maintain uniformity in the educational structure. This method presumes that sufficient number of intelligent and conscientious teachers will always be available to manage the projects.

No Uniform Standards of Achievement : Generally more intelligent children take lead at all the stages of a project. They take up all the repsonsibilities. Thus, retarded children get little opportunity of gaining experience and first-hand knowledge. There are many specialised jobs in each project and by repetition of similar jobs, children tend to be experts in limited sphere and their learning remains lopsided.

Unsuitable for Young Children : Too young children are not in a position to either choose a project or to draw plan for its execution.

Neglecting Literary Aspects : Too much emphasis on learning through project method leads to disregard for literary subjects. Handwork is likely to become all important.

Suggestions

In India, we are still following traditional methods and therefore, the real aims of education are not being achieved. There is an urgent need that we introduce new methods of teaching. Project method is one of the most suitable methods that may be adopted. Basic system of education is nothing but project method with emphasis on certain crafts as the only project method. Alongwith crafts, projects may be derived from social and physical environment. The following suggestions may be kept in mind while adopting project method in the class-room so as to get the best possible results.

1. Project should be supplemented by the class-room teaching. The school day may be divided into two part, the first half being devoted to class-room teaching and the second half to carrying out the project.
2. Wherever children do not acquire systematic knowledge of any subject, direct instructions by the teacher should fill in the gaps.
3. To reduce expenses on Project Method such projects should be taken up which may be productive and thus become the source of income at some stage. Gardening, fruit preservation, bee keeping, wood-work are the examples of such projects.
4. Projects should be group activities as far as possible and not individual activities like painting, needle-work or some literary work.

Thus we find that project method is of great utility in making the students learn well. No doubt, it has some demerits also but these can be overcome with the help of suggestions enlisted above.

Heuristic Method

Heuristic method was developed by Prof. Armstrong for teaching Science subjects. His experiment came out to be successful and later on this method was tried for teaching other subjects as well.

The term 'Heuristic' is derived from the Greek work "Heurisco" which means "I find out". In this method, the children find out things for themselves. They are left to their own resources and intelligence. The hard fact about this method is that the children are put in the position of discoverers and they arrive at scientific theories and facts like original discoverers. They do not learn anything by listening to the lectures of teachers. On the other hand, they learn by self-efforts, first hand experience and experimentations.

Psychological Basis of this Method : According to John Dewey, "Mind is not a blotting-paper that absorbs and retains automatically. It is rather a living organism that has to search for this food that selects and rejects according to his present conditions and needs and that retains only what it digests and transmits into a part of energy of its own being". Real knowledge comes through the discovery of principles by first-hand experience.

This method successfully exploits fundamental urges of curiosity, self-assertion and construction. As learning proceeds through exploration of new situation there is no need for artificial motives. Law of readiness and exercise are properly applied in this method.

Aim : This method does not aim at providing, ready-made information to the pupils. Rather its attempt is to develop scientific attitude in the children. They are trained not to accept things without experience. According to one educationist, "Heuristic method is to make pupils more exact, more truthful, observant, thoughtful and dexterous; to lay these solid foundations for future self-education and to encourage the growth of a spirit of enquiry and research. Children are given training in the method of obtaining facts, systematising them and formulating generalization on their basis."

Procedure of the Method : In this method, the problems are presented to the students. One problem may be given to the whole class but each child is expected to find out something for himself. Every child makes enquiry, performs experiments, puts questions, discusses things in the class, consults books and uses some apparatus if necessary. The child is allowed to ask questions without hesitation. When questions arise in child's mind we can be sure that mental activity has begun. Sometimes the children may arrive at understanding of new facts and principles through questioning. This may be the first stage in Heuristic method. In the beginning, the teacher may be required to give proper start to the student but after some practice, the students can dispense with too much reliance on the teacher.

Role of the Teacher

In this method, the role of the teacher is very important. A really capable teacher with all good qualities of head and heart can come out successful by using this method. Such a teacher should have the following qualities:

1. He should be a great reader, interested in getting information and keeping his knowledge up-to-date.
2. He should have much curiosity, observation and spirit of scientific investigation. Unless he has these qualities he cannot inculcate them in his students.
3. He has to suggest different sources of information to his students and he should cultivate in them good habits of reading books.
4. He should be expert in the art of asking questions which may encourage mental activity in the children.
5. He should encourage the students to ask questions and should have friendly attitude towards them. He is not only to give them instructions but he is to act as a guide and friend to them.
6. He should maintain atmosphere of freedom in the classroom which may be conductive to self-development, spontaneity and self-expression.
7. He should be able to devise problems for investigation by pupils of different ages and having different interests and abilities.
8. He should be patient enough to observe activity of children and appreciate that he is not to tell what children can find out themselves. Panton said, "The greatest tribute which the pupils can pay to the teacher is to do without him."

Suitability for Different Subjects:

lthough this method was evolved for teaching science :ts, but wherever we have to teach some generalizations, this method can be profitably applied. Thus it is equally suitable to teach rules of grammar, to teach principles of History and Geography, formulas in Arithmetic and Algebra and propositions in Geometry.

Merits of Heuristic Method

The following are the merits of this method:

1. It is based on sound psychological principle-exploitation of fundamental urges and application of laws of learning.
2. It leads to development of scientific attitude in the children, makes them keen observers and careful experimenters.
3. It inculcates the habit of hardworking in the students and teachers because both *of* them have to study a great deal to keep their knowledge up-to-date.
4. It develops valuable qualities of self-reliance, independent outlook and initiative among the students.
5. Discovery of principle is a source of great pleasure to the students. They get sense of achievement and develop self-confidence.
6. Whatever is learnt is learnt efficiently. It is retained by the students for a longer time. They can apply the principles in new situations with confidence. New knowledge is thoroughly assimilated. The teacher pays individual attention and modifies the method according to the abilities of different pupils.
7. There is no problem of home-work because the students have to work sufficiently hard and think vigorously in the class.

Demerits of Heuristic Method

1. It is unsuitable for younger children because they are too immature to be real discoverers. They need guidance at every step and unless it is available they are likely to be disappointed and develop hatred for studies.
2. Every child cannot be a discoverer and original thinker. Many things have to be explained and learnt before they can make any significant discovery.
3. This method is too slow and under present limitations of time-table, syllabus and examinations, it is very difficult to adopt this method.
4. This method over strains the teacher because there are no text books written according to this method. This burden is likely to destroy enthusiasm for extra study.

5. For successfully applying this method, the teacher should have much experience and training. Moreover, he may expect too much from the students and may be discouraged by their low achievement. It is also possible that he may expect too little from them and may set questions which do not give the students sufficient opportunity to think. The teacher should be expert in the art of asking questions which stimulate thinking. Inexperienced teacher is likely to attach more importance to correct answers than solution. Thus the process of investigation may remain ignored.
6. This method is not applicable to the teaching of all topics indifferent school subjects.

Thus we find that Heuristic method has its merits and demerits. In the teaching-learning programme, Heuristic attitude is needed. The teacher should tell the students as little as possible. He should give them maximum opportunities to think independently.

QUESTIONS

1. What are the essential features of the Project Method? Discuss the various steps in carrying out a project.
2. Discuss the merits and demerits of the' Project Method'.
3. What do you understand by the Heuristic Method? How far can this method be used in our schools?
4. What do you understand by the Play way Method of teaching? Discuss the advantages and disadvantages of using this method in the schools.
5. Critically examine the merits and limitations of Daltón Plan for its use in the schools. How would you overcome the limitations?
6. Name any three methods of teaching. Which method out of those is more suitable for Indian class room situations and why?

9

Educational Objectives and Taxonomy

Usually, the process of instructions usually goes on in a limited type of environment. The giver of instructions and the receivers of instructions keep some objectives in mind while doing so. The person who gives instructions may not necessarily formulate objectives as per his own likings and whims. Generally the objectives are formulated by those persons who determine the contents of subject matter. It lies in the hands of subject of English at high school level. The framers of the syllabi formulate objectives of teaching this subject. According the text books are prescribed and other relevant materials of study are earmarked. Usually for the study of English, the following are the objectives :

(i) To make the students understand English when spoken.

(ii) To make the students speak English and thus they should be able to express themselves in English as correctly as possible.

(iii) To enable the learners comprehend the material written in English to the best of their knowledge, capabilities and capacities.

(iv) To help the learners express themselves in written English as best as possible.

Thus there are different objectives of teaching different subjects to students at various stages of their studies. The objectives of a subject for primary class children will be different from the ones for secondary school children or the collegiates. Let us ponder over what we mean by objectives. How far are aims and goals different or similar to teach other? Are objectives goals same or they are different?

Aims or Goals

Aims or goals are the same thing. They are of unique importance in every walk of life. Without fixing up aims, the work that we take up remains dull and cheerless. Aims, in fact, make the process lively. They also provide satisfaction at the end. Without fixing up aims, our efforts may not be of right type and they may also not be in the right direction. So aims virtually provide a sort of guidelines and thus efforts do not become futile. Aims or goals are the ends in themselves. What ever means are applied, they certainly lead towards the attainment of those goals.

Aims, goals or targets are synonymous. When we say educational goals, we are concerned with broad educational purposes. They are surely lofty ideals we speak of. They may or may not be attained. In fact, only perfect conditions can help in the realisation of those goals. So they are more or less vague and indefinite.

Objectives

Objectives are comparatively narrow. They are specific, definite and also functional. When are say teaching-learning objectives, we are speaking precisely of practical type of things which can be achieved through class room teaching. They are immediate class room goals which may be termed as instructional objectives. They are the desired teaching-learning outcomes always stated in terms of expected pupil's behaviour.

Educational Objectives fall mid way between educational goals and teaching-learning objectives. They are more specific and definite than educational aims but less specific than teaching objectives. They differ from society to society and from nation to nation.

Taxonomy of Educational Objectives

Taxonomy means classification of objectives as does Dewey's Decimal system indicate classification of library books. The objectives are related to with all the three aspects of an individual's behaviour-cognitive (knowing), affective (feeling) and psychomotor (doing). The taxonomy of educational objectives have been considered to be belonging to the three domains. The first one related to cognitive domain has been presented by B.S. Bloom (B loom, et al. 1956), the second related to affective domain by Krath Wohl and others (Krath Wolh, et. al. 1964) and the one related to psychomotor domain by Harrow (1972).

Cognitive Domain

It includes objectives which deal with the recall and recognition of knowledge and the development of intellectual abilities and skills.

Affective Domain

It includes objectives which describe changes in interest, attitudes and values and development of appreciation and adequate adjustments.

Psycho-motor Domain

It includes manipulation or motor-skill area.

The teaching objectives are achieved in terms of change of behaviour of learners. These are specific, direct and practical in nature. Therefore, these are most useful for the teacher. The teaching objectives are related to learning outcomes or change of behaviour of the learners.

The taxonomy arrange the objectives in the domains into six categories :

Cognitive Domain	Here the teacher is interested in what will the students do.
Affective Domain	The teacher is additionally concerned with what does he do to it or with it.
Psychomotor Domain	It concerns with how does he do it.

The following chart shows the taxonomic categories of each domain :

Cognitive Domain	Affective Domain	Psychomotor Domain
6. Evaluation	5,6 Organisation and Characterization	6. Habit formation

4,5 Analysis and Synthesis	4. Conceptualisation	4,5 Co-ordination & Control
3. Application	3. Valuing	3. Manipulation
2. Comprehension	2. Responding	2. Imitation
1. Knowledge	1. Receiving	1. Impulsion

Each domain consists of six categories. These categories are in a hierarchical order. The first is the pre-requisite of the second and the first five categories are the pre-requisite of the last category.

Taxonomy of Educational Objectives in the Cognitive Domain

B.S. Bloom (1956) has written a handbook of taxonomy formulated to stimulate and systematize the assessment of objectives in cognitive domain. The cognitive domain of the taxonomy consists of six broad categories of cognitive learning arranged in an order to increase complexity-Knowledge, Comprehension, Application, Analysis, Synthesis and Evaluation. For each of these broad categories of cognitive learning, the taxonomy identifies specific learning outcomes in behavioural terms and each of these educational objectives may be evaluated.

Outline of the Major Categories in the Three Domains

I Cognitive Domain

Level	Category
Low Level	1. **Knowledge** (Remembering the material) (a) Knowledge of Specifics (i) Knowledge of Terminology. (ii) Knowledge of Specific Facts (b) Knowledge of ways and means of dealing with specifics (i) Knowledge of Conventions (ii) Knowledge of Trends and Sequences. (iii) Knowledge of Classifications and Categories. (iv) Knowledge of Criteria (v) Knowledge of Methodology

Level	Category
	(c) Knowledge of Universals and Abstractions in a Field. (i) Knowledge of Principles and Generalization. (ii) Knowledge of Theories and Structures.
	2. Comprehension (Ability to grasp the meaning of materials) (a) Translation (b) Interpretation (c) Extrapolation
	3. Application (Ability to Use the Material in New Situations)
Medium Level	**4. Analysis** (Ability to break down material into its component parts for understanding) (a) Analysis of Elements (b) Analysis of Relationships (c) Analysis of Organisational Principles
	5. Synthesis (Ability to put parts together to form the whole) (a) Production of a Unique Communication (b) Production of a Plan or Proposed set of Operations (c) Derivation of Set of Abstract Relations.
High Level	**6. Evaluation** (Ability to judge the value of material for a given purpose) (a) Judgement in terms of Internal Evidence. (b) Judgement in terms of External Criteria.

II. Affective Domain

Level	Category
Low Level	1. **Receiving** (Pay attention) (a) Awareness (b) Willingness to Receive. (c) Controlled or Selected Attention. 2. **Responding** (Re-action on the part of the student) (a) Acquiescence in Responding (b) Willingness to Respond (c) Satisfaction to Response 3. **Valuing** (Concerned with the worth or value student attaches to something.) (a) Acceptance of Value (b) Preference for a Value (c) Commitment 4. **Organization** (Concerned with bringing together different values, resolving conflicts) (a) Conceptualization of a Value (b) Organization of a Value System 5. **Characterization by a value or value complex** (Acceptance of value system) (a) Generalized Set (b) Characterization

Writing Objectives in Behavioural Terms

Bloom's Taxonomy is a solid contribution to the process of teaching-learning. But its main drawback is that it does not state the objectives in behavioural terms. In other words, it does not indicate how the behaviour of the learners would be modified through the task of teaching-learning.

Advantage of Writing Objectives in Behavioural Terms

Scafold states the following advantages of the behavioural objectives :

(a) Specification of Objectives.

(b) Selection of Items for Preparing a Test.

(c) Teaching can be Related to Learning.

(d) Integration between Learning Experiences and change of behaviour, and

(e) Selection of Appropriate Teaching Strategies, Tactics and Teaching aids.

Methods of Writing Objectives in Behavioural Terms

Popular approaches of writing objectives in behavioural terms are :

1. Robert Mager's Approach
2. Robert Miller's Approach
3. RCEM Approach

Robert Mager's Approach. Robert Mager is of the view that the objectives should be written in the following way :—

(i) Identify the terminal behaviour and name it.

(ii) Important conditions under which the behaviour will be expected to occur be described.

(iii) Criteria be finalised with which the learner's terminal behaviour will be compared.

Mager sought the help of the associated action verbs for stating the different objectives. These verbs help in describing the terminal behaviour of the learner in a well defined way. Here below is given the list of action verbs :

Cognitive Objectives and Associated Action Verbs

Objectives (Based on Bloom's Taxonomy)	**Associated Action Verbs**
1. Knowledge	Define, List, Label, Measure, Name, Recal, Recognise, Reproduce, Select, State, Write, Underline.

2. Comprehension	Change, Classify, Distinguish, Explain, Formulate, Identify, Illustrate, Indicate, Interpret, Justify, Judge, Name, Represent, Select, Summarize, Transform, Translate.
3. Application	Assess, Change, Choose, Conduct, Construct, Compute, Demonstrate, Discover, Explain, Establish, Find, Generate, Illustrate, Modify, Predict, Perform, Select, Solve, Use.
4. Analysis	Analysis, Associate, Compare, Conclude, Contrast, Criticise, Differentiate, Identify, Justify, Point out, Resolve, Select, Separate etc.
5. Synthesis	Argue, Conclude, Combine, Derive, Discuss, Generalize, Integrate, Organise, Precise, Prove, Relate, Restate, Select, Summarize, Synthesize.
6. Evaluation	Associate, choose, Compare, Criticise, Conclude, Defend, Determine, Evaluate, Judge, Identify, Recognize, Relate, Select, Summarise, Support, Verify.

Affective Objectives and Associated Action Verbs

Objectives	**Action Verbs**
(Based on Blooms Taxonomy)	
1. Receiving	Ask, Accept, Attend, Beware, Catch, Discover, Experiment, Identify, Favour, Follow, Observe, Prefer, Perceive, Receive, Select.
2. Responding	Answer, Assist, Complete, Derive, Discuss, Develop, Help, List, Label, Name, Obey, Present, Practice, Record, Select, State, Write.
3. Valuing	Accept, Attain, Complete, Choose, Decided, Demonstrate, Discriminate, Develop, Increase, Indicate, Influences, Participate, Prefer, Recognise.
4. Organizing	Add, Associate, Change, Compare, Complete, Co-ordinate, Correlate, Determine, Find, Form, Generalize, Integrate, Judge,

	Project, Prepare, Relate, Select, Synthesize, Organise.
5. Characterizing	Accept, Change, Characterize, Decide, Discriminate, Demonstrate, Develop, Experiment, Face, Identify, Judge, Prove, Revise, Serve, Solve, Verify.

The objectives can be written in behavioural terms by combining the action verbs with the element of content. A few example are :

Example 1	**Subject : Mathematics**
	Topic : Area of Rectangle
Instructional Objectives (Cognitive Domain)	Objectives in Behavioural Terms
Knowledge	The learners are able to reproduce the formula for finding out the area of a rectangle.
Comprehension	The learners are able to explain for prove the formula for finding out the area of rectangle.
Application	The learners are able to a apply the area of rectangle in some other situation.
Example 2	Suppose in a College of Education, pupil-teachers are being given training:
	Subject : Education
	Topic : Duties of a Pupil-Teacher
Instructional Objectives (Affective Domain)	Objectives in Behavioural Terms
Receiving	The learners accept their duties as pupil teachers.
Responding	The learners are able to state the duties of pupil teacher.
Valuing	The learners are able to indicate the duties of a pupil teacher.

Drawbacks of Robert Mager's Approach

Robert Mager's approach has the following drawbacks :

1. It is a behavioural approach in which all learning is explained in terms of S&R relationship. All human learning cannot be confined to it.
2. Here the main emphasis is on cognitive and affective domains only. The psychomotor domain is completely neglected.
3. It lays emphasis on action verbs and not on mental process or mental abilities which are involved in the performing of actions.
4. It can be used for writing the lower level teaching objectives. Higher level objectives can't be written clearly.
5. The list of action verbs in different categories of cognitive and affective domains show overlapping of action verbs. It creates confusion in the minds.
6. The list of action verbs is too lengthy. It is very difficult to use them rightly.

Robert Miller's Approach

Robert Miller's approach (19632) is used for writing psychomotor objectives in behavioural terms. Miller put forward his scheme based on skill analysis. He also gave a list of associated action verbs for the psychomotor objectives which is based on the classification of psychomotor objectives pointed out by Harrow (1972).

Associated Action Verbs for Psychomotor Objectives

Associated Action Verbs

(Based on Harrow's Classification)

1. Reflex Movements	Bite, Harden, Jerk, Lengthen, Loosen, Make, Small Relax, Stop, Straighten, Stretch.
2. Basic Fundamental	Befall, Catch, Creep, Drink, Hold Movement Jump, Kneel, Move, Reach, Run, Walk.
3. Physical Abilities	Begin, Bear, Bend, Conduct, Increase, Lean, Reform, Smash, Start, Stop.

4. Perceptual Abilities	Balance, Bend, Catch, Discovery, Eat, Explore, Feed, Identification by touching, seeing, smelling or hearing. Memory, Tracing, small, Throw, Write.
5. Skilled Movements	Dance, Dig, Dive, Drive, Knit, Play the musical organs, Row, Skate, Shoot, Swim, Type.
6. Non-Discussion	Mimic, Pose, Sit, Sketch, Smile, Communication Stand, Tease.

RCEM Approach

Mager' approach and Miller's approach of writing instructional objectives in behavioural terms were not successful. Mager's approach ignored psychomotor domain whereas Miller's approach neglected cognitive and affective domains. Moreover, both the approaches laid stress on list of action verbs which being to many and also overlapping confused the learners. So (RCEM) Regional College of Education, Mysore developed a new approach for writing the objectives in behavioural terms.

In RCEM approach, Bloom's Taxonomy of educational objectives has been modified. In cognitive domain, Bloom gave six categories. RCEM approach covered six categories into four only. The last three categories of Bloom's approach have been denoted by one category. Thus analysis, synthesis and evaluation are denoted by creativity'. The category of comprehension has been changed to understanding. Further the categories given by RCEM approach have been divided into seventeen mental abilities or processes which are used for writing the objectives of all the three domains in behavioural terms.

Taxonomy of Educational Objectives in RCEM Approach

Bloom's Taxonomy of Objectives	*RCEM Taxonomy of Objectives*	*Mental Process or Abilities*
1. Knowledge	1. Knowledge	1.1 Recall 1.2 Recognize
2. Comprehension	2. Understanding	2.1 Seeing Relationship 2.2 Cite Example 2.3 Discriminate

		2.4 classify 2.5 Interpret 2.6 Verify 2.7 Generalize
3. Application	3. Application	3.1 Reason out 3.2 Formulate Hypotheses 3.3 Establish Hypotheses 3.4 Infer 3.5 Predict
4. Analysis 5. Synthesis 6. Evaluation	4. Creativity	4.1 Analyse 4.2 Synthesize 4.3 Evaluate

Thus we find that in RCEM approach, there are two mental processes or abilities for knowledge, seven or understanding, five for application and three for creativity.

Writing Objectives in Behavioural Form (RCEM Approach)

(a) Entry behaviour of the learner is noted.

(b) Topic or content is kept in mind.

(c) Teaching learning objectives are seen.

(d) Keeping the entry behaviour, content and objectives, appropriate mental process or ability is selected.

(e) Keeping the entry behaviour of the learner and the learning experiences given to him, blanks are filled in.

The outline of 17 mental processes/abilities is as under :

1. Knowledge Objectives

    1.1 The learner is able to recognize..........
    1.2 The learner is able to recall..........

2. Understanding Objectives

    2.1 The learner is able to see relationships between..........
    2.2 The learner is able to cite example of..........
    2.3 The learner is able to discriminate between.....and..........
    2.4 The learner is able to clarify..........

2.5 The learner is able to interpret..........
2.6 The learner is able to verify..........
2.7 The learner is able to generalize..........

3. Application Objectives

3.1 The learner is able to reason out..........
3.2 The learner is able to formulate hypothesis for..........
3.3 The learner is able to establish hypothesis for.........
3.4 The learner is able to inform about..........
3.5 The learner is able to predict about..........

4. Creativity Objectives

4.1 The learner is able to analyse..........
4.2 The learner is able to synthesize..........
4.3 The learner is able to evaluate..........

The objectives of any school subject can be written with the help of 17 statements given above. At first, the objective is identified. Then the element of the context is placed in the blank space of the statement which gives the behavioural form of the objectives.

Advantages of RCEM Approach

Writing objectives is behavioural terms as advocated by RCEM has the following advantages :

1. Unlike Miller's and Mager's approaches, RCEM approach is applicable for cognitive, affective and psychomotor objectives of teaching and training.
2. It is very easy and useful for Indian schools as it has been developed in Indian situation.
3. This method explains human learning in terms of mental processes or abilities. Thus there is shifting of emphasis from the product of processes.
4. When objectives are rightly written, it is easy to make efforts in the right directions RCEM approach provides frames or statements with the help of which objectives of all school subjects can be written conveniently.
5. It does not leave any doubt in the preparation of criterion test items.

Limitations

RCEM approach has the following limitations :

1. All the behavioural objectives can be written with the help of 17 mental process or abilities only. Are there only 17 mental abilities? According to Guilford, the number of such abilities is 120.
2. It is difficult to write objectives of subjects which lay emphasis on skills, attitude, interest and appreciation.
3. It is rather difficult to compare exactly the elements of contents with the mental processes.
4. The number of mental abilities is too less for objectives like knowledge and creativity. Comparatively speaking, there is no proper balance.
5. In 'creativity' objectives, there are three mental abilities whereas Torrence and others have given a list of five type of activities.

QUESTIONS

1. What do you mean by 'objectives'? How are education objectives different from teaching objectives? Write fully by giving examples.
2. Why is there need of writing objectives in behavioural terms? Differences between Mager's and Miller's approaches.
3. Discuss in details RCEM approach of writing objectives. What are its merits and demerits?
4. Discuss the Taxonomy of educational objectives of cognitive, affective and psychomotor as given by B.S. Bloom and his associates.
5. Discuss the taxonomy of educational objectives of Cognitive, a Domains given by B.S. Bloom.

10

Planning the Lesson

What is planning ? Planning means thinking about something before hand. Here the planner tries to see to all the details and makes himself/herself ready for it in every way. Naturally planning has its importance in every walk of life. The success of a work is ensured if its work is properly planned. Without planning, we shall be loitering about aimlessly, applying means without aiming at the achievement of ends. Planning in fact, systematises the whole thing and makes a person act in the right direction so as to achieve the ends already fixed up. Thus it is bound to provide a lot of satisfaction to the person who plans the work.

The lesson plan is therefore, an effective tool in the hands of the teacher. Teaching-learning is a complex task. It needs the preparation of a plan or blue print. The teacher needs a full plan showing the different steps to be followed by him logically at the right moment in various situations. He has to prepare the different visual or audio aids that he needs for teaching. He also thinks of different questions and their answers, the difficulties that he might face and their solutions etc.

Planning is Teaching-L earning

Planning is of great importance in the teaching-learning process. Unless the teacher plans well, he won't be able to do justice in the class. In the same way, the learner has also to plan things. Then only, he can learn better and can use the learnt material in a good way. We know that teaching is organised in three phases-preactive, interactive and post-active. Before entering the class room whatever activities a teacher plans, may be put in pre-phase of teaching. Lesson planning is virtually the pre-active phase of teaching.

Every teacher in the school has to teach a number of periods every day. In every period, lesson of one subject or the other has to be delivered by him. The topic that he has to teach in the class prepared in written form or at cognitive level is known as a lesson plan.

Education does not consist merely in giving out information to the young minds, nor does it constitute in keeping the people, acquire a particular skill. It should touch every aspect of the child's personality. Each lesson delivered must contribute something to the total personality of the child. A successful lesson demands much more than mere teaching by the teacher. Teaching situations have to be created, co-operation of the students has to be sought. All these indicate that planning must be done in advance.

The work of preparing a lesson plan originated from Gestalt Psychology. Gestalt in this theory of learning emphasized the importance of unit teaching. A unit, thus plays an important rôle in understanding the whole concept. The whole is perceived by a part. Many parts together make a whole. Thus teaching bit by bit ensures better teaching of the whole.

A Few Definitions of a Lesson Plan

Different educationist have defined a lesson plan in different ways. A few definitions are given below :

Bining and Bining Say : "Daily lesson planning involves defining the objectives, selecting and arranging the subject matter and determining the method and procedure." N. L. Bossing in his Progressive Methods of Teaching in secondary Schools states, "Lesson plan is the title given to statement of the achievement to be realized and the specific means by which these are to be attained as a result of the activities engaged in during the period the class spends with the teacher."

In the words of Lester B. Stands : "A lesson plan is actually a plan of action. It, therefore, includes the working philosophy of the teacher, his knowledge of philosophy, his information about and understanding of his knowledge of material to be taught, and his ability to utilize effective methods."

Some others define a lesson plan as a blue print, a guide map for action in the near future; a creative piece of work, a comprehensive chart of class room teaching, a systematic, elastic approach for the development of concepts, skills, understanding etc. "It is the teacher's mental and emotional visualisation of the class room experience a she plans it to occur."

Need and Importance

A lesson plan is the core and the heart of effective teaching. Thorough preparation of the lesson on the part of the teacher is very essential irrespective of the fact whether he is to teach a lower class or higher class. Even if the teacher has many years of experience to his credit, he must go well prepared in the class. Then only he will enjoy a better status, a good reputation and would be liked by one and all there. I.K. Davies is perfectly right when he says: "Lesson must be prepared for there is nothing so fatal to a teacher's progress as unpreparedness."

Through planning, every teacher is able to make use of his experience of the past. In this regard Ryburn says, "To teach we must use experience already gained as starting point of our work." Suppose a teacher has to teach the same lesson of a book to some school class for five years. He/she should not prepare the lesson plan only once and then use the same all the five years. Every year, he should plan afresh on the basis of his past experience. Addition of experience in his life should help him plan new, afresh and better.

Way to Plan?

It is a very important question whether we should plan for our teaching or we can do without it. The obvious answer to this is that planning is important everywhere. It is important not only in the class room teaching, but also at home where the student is to learn anything or he is to do some other work. Planning actually smoothness the work because a person is able to foresee the hurdles that he may possibly face in times to come.

Importance of Daily Lesson Plans

N.L. Bossing lists the following values of daily lesson plan.

(i) Lesson planning ensures a definite objective for the lesson.

(ii) It ensures a proper connection of the new with the previous lesson.

(iii) It ensures some scheme of selection and organisation of subject matter, materials and activities.

(iv) It directs the teacher's attention to the type of teaching procedure and desirable.

(v) It provides for adequate summaries of the lesson.

(vi) It provides for an adequate checking of the outcomes of instruction.

(vii) It stimulates the teacher to provide pivotal questions and illustrations.

(viii) It ensures some unity in lesson development.

(ix) It ensures a definite assignment.

(x) It makes possible adequate adaptation to individual differences in pupils.

(xi) It tends to ensure availability of materials to be used in lessons when needed.

(xii) It creates assurance on the part of the teacher, and greater freedom in teaching.

Let us see what would happen if the teacher does not prepare lesson notes and goes to his class room without any type of preparation:

1. The entry behaviour of the teacher will fail to impress the students. An unprepared teacher does not enjoy full confidence and every moment that he/she is present in the class weighs him heavily. He is there like an aimless wanderer who has facial depressions, fear of his ownself which go on killing him virtually.

2. Mostly such a teacher tries to while away the period somehow or the other. The learners, however, immature and innocent they may be, are ultimately able to feel the pulse of the teacher. Naturally they may decry him in any way. Surely this type of situations lower the prestigious image of the teacher in the eyes of the learners.

3. The teacher might omit many important things in his teaching: A few of them may be repeated by the teacher knowingly or unknowingly.

4. The whole teaching may come out to be a drudgery on account of the teacher himself.

5. Teaching may remain just one sided affair where the teacher himself pretends to be busy. The learners might be left out from the main stream.

6. The students may remain unmotivated and uninvolved in the process of teaching-learning.

7. The whole teaching will remain unsystematic and ill-planned leading the learners nowhere and just making them confused.

Planning a lesson, therefore, is a fundamental thing for the success of any teaching process. It works as a staircase for the teacher which makes him reach higher and higher in his teaching career. Let every teacher avow firmly to prepare lesson plans before he/she proceeds to the class room. That will improve the all around deterioration in the class room environment. A full satisfaction of the learners in the class is bound to make them-self-disciplined pupils.

Lesson planning has some advantages which are enumerated here below:

Advantages of Lesson Planning

1. By planning, the teacher is able to emphasize the different aspects of the lesson equally, otherwise it is just possible that one aspect may be over-emphasized and some other aspects may be just touched upon and another one may be completely ignored.

2. It enables the teacher to do full justice to the different portions of the syllabus. He is able to maintain interest of the learner throughout. He is also to teach everything systematically.

3. There is no at once rush of finishing the work and hence there is nothing to burden the minds of the learners.

4. It gives sufficient time and ample opportunities to the teacher for the preparation of the lesson before-hand. The teacher knows what he is to teach at what time and so he prepares himself accordingly and goes to the class well prepared.

5. It develops confidence and self-reliance in the teacher which is of great value for successful teaching.

6. Through proper planning, the teacher knows well what has been taught and what has not been covered so far. So he can proceed further without any sort of duplicacy or confusion.

7. A good teacher maintains a diary or record of the work-done. Through planning, he is able to have permanent record of the work finished or the work which remains to be completed. Naturally then he enjoys full confidence both inside the class room and outside the classroom.

8. Once the habit of planning is formed by the teacher, then he gets a lot of time for preparation. He can easily think of the ways and means for making the lesson better and more interesting with the passage of time.

9. Through daily plans, the teacher knows that in every class room period, he is to do a limited work. Naturally he will be able to concentrate more and do more justice to his work.

10. It brings economy in the teaching-learning process because it keeps the teachers and the students on the right track and there is no wastage of time and energy.

11. Through lesson planning, the teacher is able to integrate and correlate his teaching. That helps the students to have better grasp of the subject matter and then they are able to retain it in their minds for a longer time.

12. Lesson planning develops in the teacher the ability to imagine which makes the teacher better and effective ultimately.

13. It helps the teacher to make use of the various skills of teaching which help him in the realization of educational objectives.

14. The different steps involved in the preparation of a lesson plan, helps the teacher to teach, revise and evaluate his teaching. That naturally helps the learners in fixing up the subject matter in their minds.

15. It helps the teacher to fix up the right objectives and then make efforts rightly to attain the desired objectives.

Lesson planning is, therefore, of immense value in the teaching learning process. It serves as a torch for the beginner teacher who using it comes out all successful. Planning has to be kept as a servant in the habit of the teacher and in no case it should become his master. A good teacher uses it as per his requirements, the needs of the learners and teaching-learning situations. The best lesson plan is taken as a guideline and is not followed by the teacher blindly.

Let us now see what constitutes a good lesson plan.

A Good Lesson Plan

A good lesson plan is like a clock. From the lesson plan, we can guess many things about the teacher, his method of teaching, the strategies, the language etc. provided the lesson plan is prepared the teacher himself. A good lesson plan has the following characteristics:

1. General and specific objectives of teaching a lesson are revealed in it. The specific objectives are realistic and achievable.

2. It gives an idea of the A.V. aids. The teacher is capable of preparing and using them for solving the problems confronted in the teaching-learning process.

3. There is fulfilment of the aims and objectives fixed up at the beginning of the lesson plan.

4. It reveals the reference books consulted by the teacher of the lesson plan.

5. It remains as a tool in the hands of the teacher and he is free to modify it as per needs and requirements of the teaching learning situation.

6. A good lesson plan speaks clearly about the teacher's mastery of subject matter.

7. It includes relevant subject matter which is uptodate and is according to the mental level of he learners.
8. It is student centred, contains effective learning activities and is able to evoke active pupil participation.
9. There is provision for the individual difference of the pupils.
10. It is flexible both for the teacher and the learners.
11. A good lesson plan indicates the type and nature of activities that are to be introduced in the class room.

N.L. Bossing gives in a summary form certain characteristics which should be embodied in the different parts of a lesson plan: (a) Well founded aim, good assignment, provision for individual differences, inclusion of pivotal questions, inclusion of important illustrations, review, content materials, motivation techniques, evaluation techniques, rough allocation of time to each phase of the lesson and attention to apperceptive learning-new related to the old.

Types of Lessons

Every lesson plan aims at providing different learning objectives. Thus they can be classified into three main categories:

I Knowledge Lesson
II Skill Lesson.
III Appreciation Lesson

Knowledge Lesson : From teaching-learning point of view, some of the subjects may be called knowledge subjects. While dealing with those subjects, the teacher aims at providing the factual information regarding the contents of those subjects. The main objectives of this type of lessons are knowledge, comprehension, application, analysis and synthesis. So in this type of lessons, all emphasis is laid on the presentation of content.

Lesson plans of subjects like Science, Social Studies, History, Geography, Economics, Civics etc. fall under this category of lesson plans.

Skill Lesson : Teaching-learning of any language is called a skill subject. We may take up any language, the different skills involved in its study are listening, speaking, reading and writing. In the skill lesson, the purpose of the teacher is to develop certain skills of the learners. Apart from languages, subjects like drawing, music crafts etc. also aim at the development of certain skills in the learners.

A skill lesson involves a lot of practice on the part of the teacher and the learners both.

Appreciation Lesson : Some of the subjects are meant for appreciation. While teaching those subjects, the teacher makes efforts so that the learners may learn how to appreciate certain things. Naturally this type of lessons help in developing the attitudes of the learners. Some type of feelings are aroused in them. Inculcation of some values among the students is done through this type of lessons.

Teaching poetry of any language say English, Hindi, Punjabi, Sanskrit etc. involves the feelings of the learners.

Details of different type of lessons are as under:

Knowledge Lesson. The aim of a knowledge lesson is to provide information in a systematic way. For the assimilation of information, it is essential that the new facts are linked with the facts already known and also the facts that are related with the experiences of life. The impressions that remain in our mind are termed as apperceptive mass. This plays an important role in the new lesson. The new facts have to be organised alongwith the facts already known into a systematic whole. These aim can be achieved by following Herbartian steps in a slightly modified form.

Preparation (Introduction) : It does not mean preparation on the part of the teacher. It is preparing the children mentally to receive whatever is to be presented in the lesson. This step may also be termed as motivation or creating a 'will to learn'. This can be achieved in a number of ways but questioning is the most handy device. Suitable questions may and a few more questions may be asked to create interest in the new lesson. These questions may be related to life or with some demonstrations that may be performed in the class. Telling stories, showing of pictures, charts and models or some activity on the part of children may be the other forms of motivation. Thus questions and activities should lead to some problematic situation.

Statement or the Aim : It is the natural outcome of the first step. It gives the right perspective of the Lesson to the students. It should be brief and clearly worded. In certain methods, it is rather preferable not to disclose the aim of the lesson. Aim should never include solution of the problem. Statement of the theory or proposition which we want to prove during the lesson, is also not desirable because to some extent it satisfies the urge to know about goal of the lesson. Whenever a statement of the aim is made, it should be made in simple and clear terms.

Presentation : It consumes most of the time in a lesson. In this step attempts are made to realize the aims of the lesson. Mere statement of new facts by the teacher is not enough. Activity on the part of students is the only way of learning. Therefore, the teacher should see that the pupils learn the new material by their own efforts. He should try to deduce everything from the students. His guiding principle should be to tell only when it has been proved and that students are not in a position to discover whatever he has planned to teach. In this step the teacher should prepare the ground for generalization by asking the pupils to compare the facts before them with the facts already known.

Generalization : The student should be encouraged to draw inference from comparison of facts. It does not matter if generalizations are incomplete or not properly worded. Proper understanding always results from mental activity leading to the "statement of principle or a general law. Generalization may be regarding some definition in grammar, a formula in Mathematics or a rule in science. The more we emphasize discovery by the students the more we encourage and develop insight for learning, the better we achieve the goal of all educational efforts.

Application : Knowledge is not virtue in itself. It becomes so only when we put it to use. Whatever they learn in the course of lesson, should find some application in real life situations.

The generalization may be applied to explain some facts already known to the students for example after a Mathematics lesson on profit and loss, the students may work out, some problems on profit to the bookseller or to the canteen manager.

It may not be always possible to have a good generalization in some lessons, especially in History. In that case, application will mean revision or recapitulation of the facts made clear during the lesson. It may be written or oral. The function of this step in such situations is to know whether the students have properly grasped the material presented to them. Home work is given at this stage, so that the pupils are able to apply the knowledge gained :

Gloverian Approach : here below is a brief mention of the scheme given by A.H.T. glover which is an alternative scheme to Herbartian system.

Questioning : The successful teacher must be an expert in the art of asking questions. Questions in the beginning of the lesson are asked with the idea of testing previous knowledge, to stimulate mental activity in the children, to create an interest among the pupils for the new lesson and to lead them to a problematic situation. The teacher should not reserve this privilege of asking questions to himself only. The students should also be encouraged to ask questions.

Discussion : Preliminary questioning may lead to a point where differences of opinion are possible. Such controversial matters should be discussed in the class under the guidance of the teacher. The teacher should try to develop the desire to know the truth among the students. Discussion should remove all doubts and the students should be clear about the field of investigation. During the conduct of discussion, the teacher should encourage the students in every possible way.

Investigation : In this step, the students make attempts individually or collectively to find solutions of the problems which arise during the discussion. For this purpose they may take help from the library, laboratory, or the teacher.

Expression : Every lesson should be taught in such a way that the students are able to make use of the learnt things in different ways. The learner should be able to express himself fully. That is possible if the teacher provides him opportunities for expression. All type of encouragement by the teacher helps the student to express himself in multiple ways. A few examples of expression are writing something, speaking something, creating something which may be visual or concrete. Glover classifies activities of expressions into four categories (a) Passive (b) Active (c) Artistics (d) Organizational.

A Skill Lesson

Children are active by nature, therefore, they can be very easily motivated for skill lessons. The following points should be kept in mind while organizing skill lesson so as to ensure success.

1. There should be some purpose for acquiring the skill. The pupils should know clearly as to why they should learn and practise the skill.
2. The skill should be neither too difficult nor too easy for the students of the given age group. Too difficult skills are likely to result in frustration. Too easy items of work do not challenge the capacity of the child and therefore do not motivate him to take part in it.
3. The task should not take so much time that the interest of pupils may decrease or disappear before the completion of the task.
4. The standard of achievement expected of the pupils should be within the reach of an average child of that group.

Steps in a Skill Lesson

Preparation (Introduction or Motivation) : Before starting the activity, it is necessary to create interest among the students. This may take the form of presenting finished products of the work done by others and suggesting the pupils to create things of the same type. For example in a reading lesson, the teacher may present model reading before asking the students to read. Children may also be motivated by placing them in such a situation that they cannot do without learning the skill that we wish them to acquire, e.g. many skills have to be learnt for the successful execution of certain projects.

Statement of Aim : By clear statement of the aim, the teacher not only gives purpose of activity but also tries to seek cooperation of the students in the performance of the task in hand.

Presentation : It generally consists of two parts. Firstly, demonstration of the work already done and secondly explaining each step in the performance of the skill with black-board diagram and summary, if necessary. It is always preferable if the teacher himself gives demonstration of the skill, drawing attention of the children to the details and intricacies of the procedure.

Formulation of Steps or Rules : In a skill lesson, this step should be very brief. It is easier to formulate rules in simpler types of skills. Whereas in higher skills it is neither possible to formulate the rules nor it is helpful. Rule should be cautiously applied. Undue emphasis on rules may curb originality and initiative among the students. In creative activities, rules should be taken as temporary aids and freedom should be allowed to the pupils with talent and promise.

Practice : "Practice makes a man perfect". Mastery of the skill comes only through sufficient practice. The teacher should carefully observe performance of the pupils and correct their errors so that faulty performance may not develop into a wrong habit. The teacher should not correct the pupils directly. Chances should be given to the pupils to detect their mistakes by comparing their performance with the model of the demonstration given in the beginning of the lesson. For example, in a reading lesson after the model reading, the teacher should explain the points to be kept in mind while reading and then ask the pupil to read slowly. Other students should be asked to carefully observe while one pupil is reading and correct him wherever he commits a mistake. During the practice period in a skill lesson, the teacher should watch the different stages of practice. In the beginning, there is initial spurt i.e. the pupils on account of motivation and curiosity, gain greater speed and efficiency. At the second stage, the speed of progress is rather slow. At the third stage, consolidation of what has been already learnt takes place. After the period of consolidation, new skill is acquired and thus the rotation goes on.

Application : No lesson can be considered to be complete without the application of the acquired skill in some real life situation or in the solution of some practical problem.

Education is defined as process of transmission of cultural heritage, its conservation and enrichment by the next generation. Skills revolved by human society during the past history of thousands of years form a very important part of the cultural heritage. Many of these skills may be transmitted and conserved through the process of imitation. But this is not enough, we have to enrich the heritage by our own experience and effort. Therefore, we should not be satisfied by imitation in learning and teaching of skills. The pupil should be given insight into various aspects and they should be encouraged to make experiments and thereby revolve new techniques. Originality and initiative should find free expression in skill lessons. Due emphasis should be laid on creativity because it is this quality which had been responsible for evolution to present level of culture and civilization.

The Application Lesson : Application lesson deals with the feeling aspect of human behaviour; whereas knowledge lesson deals with truth; skill lesson may deal with goodness; appreciation lesson deals with beauty. The function of an appreciation lesson is to enable the children to enjoy beauty through form, sound or colour, i.e., painting, sculpture, poetry, drama. Training of appreciation is mainly based upon the exploitation of tendencies of sympathy and suggestions. Gradually emotional tone of the pupil is raised to such a high pitch that they identify themselves with the object of beauty and enjoy its subtleties. Steps in appreciation lesson are as follows;

Steps in an appreciation lesson have to be modified according to the subject, the topic and the situation.

Preparation : Success in appreciation lesson wholly depends upon the atmosphere in the class. Therefore, the function of preparation step is to create appropriate atmosphere. It should suggest the topic and arouse feelings which may raise the mind to such state that one can enjoy beauty. The environment should be calm and quiet and free from all interruptions. Real enjoyment can come when mind comprehends object of beauty with full concentration.

The teacher should be very cautious in the selection of topic. Theme of a poetry lesson should favourably correspond with the weather outside. Lessons on natural beauty are likely to prove failure if these are delivered within the four-walls of the class room. In a poetry lesson, it is desirable that the language difficulties are removed before the commencement of an appreciation lesson.

Presentation : It requires considerable skill on the part of the teacher to present an appreciation lesson. He has to create feelings of the author in the minds of his students. Success of presentation depends upon the degree of identification that the teacher can achieve with the poet. If the teacher is really moved by the feelings expressed in the poem, he can very easily influence the class and pupils can also enjoy it by the mechanism of sympathy.

Contemplation : It is a brief pause given to the students to feel and think about the object of beauty. Analysis should be avoided. It helps the pupils in locating the points of beauty.

Expression : The pupils are asked to express their opinions regarding the points in the lesson which they enjoyed the most. They may also be required to evaluate the whole poem or music or story or drama. The class is gradually led to critically appreciate the work art. At this stage the pupils experience such feelings conscious which they had unconsciously at the contemplation stage.

Repetition : These aspects of the situation such as most beautiful stanzas or passages are repeated to fix the joyful experience in the minds of the students. After this the poem or music or drama is repeated as a whole so that the pupils may enjoy the work of art as a complete unit.

Attempt should also be made to encourage the students to create articles of beauty in the form of painting, poetry or music. Attempts of the children may prove to be below standard but these things have great educational significance. Comparison between two works of art of the same nature may also prove helpful in better appreciation of the lesson.

Requirements of an Appreciation Lesson.

Success of the appreciation lesson depends upon the fulfilment of the following requirements:

Real Interest of the Teacher : Because sympathy plays an important role in an appreciation lesson, therefore it is essential that the teacher really enjoys and is thrilled by the object of beauty. The degree of emotional enjoyment of the class depends upon the emotions experienced by the teacher.

Proper Atmosphere : The teacher should be capable of handling the work of art in such a manner that proper atmosphere is created for its appreciation. For example, the teacher should be able to read poetry with expression or create a peace of art with brush or pencil in the class.

Proper Material : Material for appreciation should be understandable to the pupils i.e., it should be selected according to the age and interests of the pupils.

External Conditions : These should help in maintaining calm atmosphere throughout the lesson so that enjoyment of art continues without break.

Suggestions and Sympathy : The teacher should be an expert in the art of using suggestions and sympathy as tools during the lesson.

The lessons must not be difficult ones.

The beauty to be appreciated must be of social value. Vulgar or antisocial appreciation is prohibited.

Styles of Writing Lesson Plans

Ever since lesson planning found its place in the teaching learning process, the different styles of writing lesson plan by the teacher which have been popular from time to time is a study worthy of good discussion. Of course, one thing is definite that before Herbort-the so called originator of writing lesson plan systematically, lesson plans as such did not exist. As insignificant thing, they might have been in vogue from times immemorial. So it was during the 19th century only when lesson plan was established by Herbort and then propagated by his school and his followers gained ground with the passage of time.

The different styles or approaches used in the writing of lesson plans are:

1. Herbartian Approach
2. Morrison's Approach or Unit Approach.
3. Evaluation Approach or Bloom's Approach.
4. RCEM Approach.
5. Electic Approach.

Herbartian Approach or Herbartians Five Step Approach : John Fredrik Herbart was a great European educationist and philosopher of nineteenth century. He advocated that teaching should be planned actively if we intend to make it efficient. He applied the knowledge of psychology regarding the learning process.

The Herbartian approach is based on Apperceptive mass theory of learning. The main thing in that theory is that the learner is like a clean state and all the knowledge is given to him from outside. If new knowledge is imparted by linking it with the old knowledge of the student, it is acquired easily and is retained for a longer period. The contents should be presented into units and those units should be arranged in a logical sequence.

For the writing of a lesson plan, he suggested the following five steps:

(i) Preparation
(ii) Presentation
(iii) Comparison and Association
(iv) Generalization
(v) Application.

Preparation: In the teaching of any lesson, preparation stage is the basis. Here the learners are prepared for receiving the new knowledge. The teacher tries to motivate the learners through various means. Once they are mentally prepared, then they are able to receive the subject matter easily. The teacher is also able to achieve the desired ends. George H. Green says in his book 'Planning the Lesson. "In the preparation step the teacher brings well into the pupils mind the knowledge that will be required as a foundation for the new knowledge to be gained in the course of the lesson. In the preparation step nothing new is learned: the relevant old knowledge is marshalled, and the pupil is made ready to receive the new."

This stage is also called introductory stage. Here the teacher tests the previous knowledge of the students, introduces the lesson by taking care of the general or specific aims of the lesson.

These days in the teacher training programme, this step has been modified. A few activities now included in this step are;

(i) About the pupil teacher- his Roll No., Class that he is to teach, subject, topic average age of the students, period, duration of the period etc.

(ii) General and specific aims of the lesson.

(iii) Aids to be used.

(iv) Previous knowledge assumed.

(v) Previous knowledge testing.

(vi) Announcement of the topic.

Presentation: At this step the teacher presents the learning material before the students he tries to do as best as possible by making use of different strategies. Sometimes he use ,narration, question-answer method, exposition, explanation, verbal illustrations, maps, pictures, diagrams or drawings on the black board — all these how that the learners are able to grasp it. Throughout his lesson he takes care of the maxims like-proceed from simple to complex, easy to difficult, concrete things first and abstract things afterwards, Nearer things first and farther things later on etc. Thus he makes special efforts so that teaching should not remain just one sided affair. The learners are engaged fully in the lesson, they are kept active and ultimately the teacher comes out successful in that teaching-learning situation.

While presenting the subject matter, the teacher makes sure that his teaching remains an interesting activity. He applies all type of strategies to makes his teaching-learning process a really meaningful affair. He also tries to make adjustment with the environment being created in different situations.

Usually a good teacher makes sure that his teaching remains an interesting activity. He applies all types of strategies to make his teaching-learning process a really meaningful affair. He also tries to make adjustment with the environment being created in different situations.

Usually a good teacher takes care of the following things at this step:

(i) The material is presented step by step depending upon the capabilities and capacities of the learners.

(ii) He tries to sustain interest of the learners throughout the lesson.

(iii) He makes sure that he is able to involve the learners actively in the lesson. He never allows the teaching process to become just one sided affair as is seen often in many cases at this stage.

(iv) He tries to keep his planning of this stage flexible as far as possible.

(v) He makes use of the strategies suitable to teaching as well as apt to the learners.

Comparison and Association : The teacher here tries to compare the newly learnt matter with the one already learnt. Association is, in fact, the main contribution of Herbart to educational theory. The newly acquired things are no doubt learnt once but soon after they vanish from the mind. Through association they are then retained in the mind for a longer time. When comparison and association is made between the two subject matters, then no doubts and confusion are left in the minds of the students. The teachers should, therefore, try to teach by the method of comparison and association.

This step is related with the task of strengthening the acquisition of newly learnt subject matter. It is based on the assumption that a child grows in knowledge through comparison and association. Accordingly the teacher is required to compare, contrast and associate every new knowledge acquired by the students with the one already with them.

Generalization : Generalization means arriving at some formula, principles or laws. As far as possible the teacher should teach the students in such a way that they themselves should be able to draw out conclusions the teacher should try to remain in the background for providing only necessary guidance and correction. Sometimes the generalizations made by the students may be incomplete and wrong. The teacher should help them to complete and correct these. The important thing here is that the pupils should clearly understand the laws that they have discovered. This step involves reflective thinking because the knowledge acquired in presentation is systematised and that leads to generalisation rules etc.

Application : The knowledge acquired is applied to different situations and thus more knowledge is provided to the learners. If knowledge is not applied in the discovery of further facts, it might lose half of its value. The laws arrived at in the generalization step are applied to the solution of particular examples in application step. Thus application serves the purpose of revision and recapitulation of the matter learnt. The more the application of subject matter, the greater is the learning. Thus we can say that practice, recapitulation, prĕvious knowledge testing and home assignments are all ways of application.

For application purpose, both familiar and unfamiliar situations should be provided to the learners. This step tests the validity of the generalization arrived at by the pupils. Thus the new knowledge gained by the pupils is well fixed up in their minds.

Herbartian Scheme of lesson planning is a significant land mark in the field of teaching. Its merits are as under:

Merits

1. It helps in making teaching systematic. The teacher proceeds on well thought of and definite lines and does nothing haphazardly.
2. It is useful for achieving the cognitive objective of teaching.
3. It helps in avoiding needless repetition in teaching.
4. It employs the previous knowledge of the students for imparting new knowledge.
5. It employs the inductive and deductive methods of teaching.
6. It provides a frame work to the beginner teachers. They can make their teaching success by following these steps. They are also to gain confidence and self-reliance.

Herbart's Scheme of teaching significantly influenced educational theory and practice. But it is not free from some defects which are given here below:

Demerits

1. It is highly dominated by the teachers.
2. Specific objectives are not written in behavioural terms.
3. It does not work well in the case of appreciation lesson and skill lesson.
4. There is more emphasis on teaching than on learning.
5. It provides less opportunities to the learners for their initiation, originality and creativity.
6. It confines teaching to memory level only.
7. It is suitable for the average students only. The gifted and below average are not benefited.

8. It is highly structured. Almost all the activities are controlled.

9. This type of approach does not succeed in the hands of ordinary teachers.

10. Sometimes the teachers find it difficult to fit their lesson notes into the set pattern.

Morrison's Approach or Unit Approach

As the name suggests, this approach was developed by Professor Henry C. Morrison, (1871-1945) of the University of Chicago. The main objective of this method was to teach the children in small units till they are able to have mastery over the subject matter. This approach is the result of fine blending of the Herbartian method of instruction. It is based on Gestalt's psychology. In this approach the lesson is divided into units and further these units are divided into sub-units. The units are divided in such a way that they are meaningful and complete in themselves. The units are made homogeneous and coherent. One kind of matter is placed in one unit. All the units are properly linked so as to present a coherent piece of knowledge in proper sequence. The teacher teaches one unit till the learners have mastery over it. Thereafter he proceeds to the next unit and so on.

Major Steps or Unit- Approach

(i) Exploration

(ii) Presentation

(iii) Assimilation

(iv) Organisation.

(v) Recitation.

Exploration : This step stands parallel to the Introduction step of Herbartian approach. Here the teacher explores the initial learning of the students by putting some questions. He also tries to find out the interests, aptitude and general abilities of the students. He plans about the strategies that he would use in accordance with the environment and the situations prevailing there.

Presentation : Here the teacher presents the material in small sub-units. Then he tries to find out how much the learners have been able to grasp. He repeats the presentation of contents till they are able to have mastery over the subject matter. The teacher keeps in his mind the fundamental principle. Teach and test, re-teach and re-test.

Assimilation : At this stage, the students try to assimilate the knowledge acquired in step 2 above. It leads to intensive learning and deep understanding by the students. The learners have their individualised study. They may study in the library or at a place convenient to them for their self study. Then there is a test to see how much the learners have been able to grasp. If their performance in the test is not satisfactory, they are asked for more assimilation.

Organisation : The students reproduce the matter in their note book without consulting their notes or books. Here they are able to learn how to organise the matter and put it in a systematic way. Virtually this step helps the learners to have complete understanding of the subject matter.

In the case of more contents and extra practice, this step is of great value.

Recitation : The students present the learnt matter orally in the class before the teacher. In fact, the oral expression of the students reveals clearly their grasping ability. Here they are allowed to take the help of black board summary or the written material, equipment etc. as per their needs.

Advantages of Unit Approach

1. Since the matter is divided into small units, it ensures mastery over the subject matter.
2. It involves active participation of both the teacher and the learners. There is no scope for the learners to remain passive.
3. It helps the students to become good thinkers. They also acquire the habit of reasoning.
4. It develops in the learners love for self-study and independent learning.
5. It makes the teaching-learning process simple and easy as the matter is limited.

6. It helps in establishing a good rapport between the teacher and the learners.
7. In a good teaching-learning process, the role of the teacher goes on changing. Gradually the teacher goes in the background and the student carries on his studies. This is followed in the unit approach.
8. Here the learning is not just memorization. It rather leads to full understanding by the students.
9. Habit of writing is developed in the students. That helps them to think in concise and precise form and put it in a systematic way.

Disadvantages

1. It consumes a lot of time. More time is spent on limited teaching-learning.
2. This approach works well with the intelligent students. The average and the weak students find it difficult to pull on.
3. Every teacher may not be able to make use of the approach or teaching successfully.
4. The present day syllabus is heavy and it will be rather difficult to complete the syllabus in time.
5. All the students in the class will not be able to proceed efficiently.
6. Towards the end, this approach becomes dull and mechanical. It fails to achieve the desired end.
7. It is difficult to form meaningful and complete units and sub units for each lesson.

Evaluation Approach or Bloom's Approach

Another style of writing a lesson plan was given by B.S. Bloom. The basis of this style is evaluation which is one of the most important thing in the process of teaching-learning. Coming up of this new approach in the field of education has been welcomed by one and all. It is the result of new thinking in the process of teaching-learning and it has undoubtedly revolutionized the whole process of teaching-learning. According to this approach, education is considered as a tripolar process involving educational objectives, learning experiences and evaluation devices.

Main Steps

Evaluation approach to lesson planning involves the following three steps:

(1) Formulation of Educational Objectives.
(2) Providing Learning Experiences.
(3) Evaluating the Learning Outcomes.

Let us now discuss the three main steps fully.

Formulation of Educational Objectives

Education is a planned activity and it should be well cared for from the beginning. First of all objectives have to be formulated so that all efforts are made in some definite direction so as to achieve the desired goals. So in the process of education, identification and formulation of objectives is the most important thing.

The entry behaviour of the learner is seen and then desired behavioural changes are thought of and finalised.

Different teaching subjects have different objectives. Then the students may belong to different type of socio-economic conditions. These will also be cared for.

Educational objectives are broad based which are received through the process of education. Comparatively teaching objectives are very narrow and moreover they are specific. They are the teaching outcomes in the teaching process which goes on inside the class room. They may also be called the desired learning outcomes. They should be stated in terms of expected behaviour of the learners.

The structure of instructional objectives mainly consists of (i) the modification part (ii) the content part. Here modification part concerns the modification of the behaviour of the learner through teaching-learning experiences. And content part relates to the syllabus - etc. covered through instructions.

Writing an objective in behavioural terms is done in relation to the following:

(i) Nature of objective.

(ii) Area of domain of behaviour.
(iii) Specific content areas.

For example, the topic is Area of a Circle

Instructional

Objective (Cognitive -Domain)	**Objectives in Behavioural Terms.**
Knowledge......	The pupils are able to produce the formula for the calculation of the area of a circle.
Comprehension	The pupils are able to explain or prove the formula for finding out the area of a circle.
Application......	The pupils are able to apply the formula in other situations.

Providing Learning Experiences

In order to achieve the desired objectives, suitable learning environment is provided by the teacher. The learners are acquainted with son experiences so that they may also follow the procedure of learning. Some new experiences are also acquired by the learners through the situations created by the teacher.

In order to make this step successful, the teacher gives special attention to the selection of learning material, its organisation. Strategies, methods and devices which the teacher will be using are decided and planned by the teacher.

All the activities concerning the teacher or the learners are thought of different type of objectives require different types of objectives require different types of teaching learning strategies and experience.

Teacher Objectives	**Learning Wxperiences to be Provided**
Knowledge	Lecture, Assignment, Programmed Text, Demonstration.
Understanding	Question Answer, Group Discussion, Home Assignment.
Application	Project Method, Tutorials, Assignment.
Creativity	Problem Solving Method, Individual Experiment, Seminar/Workshop.

Evaluating the Learning Outcomes

Fixing up objectives, providing appropriate learning situations to achieve those objectives etc. are important but more important is to see how far those objectives have been achieved and how far those learning situations have been effective in bringing the desired changes. Evaluation need to be rightly done. To see to the changes in behaviour some suitable criteria will have to be adopted. Behaviour of the learner in different domains may be assessed by making use of appropriate, evaluating devices e.g.

Changes in Behaviour Evaluative Devices Suggested for Use:

1. Cognitive........ (Knowing) — Oral Examination, Written Examination (Essay Type, Short Answer Type, Objective Type) Interview.
2. Affective...... (feeling) — Observation, Interest Inventory, Essay Type Test, Situational Test ,
3. Psychomotor..... (doing) — Observation, Interest Inventory, Essay Student Demonstration, Interview.

Bloom's Evaluation Approach got modified gradually. The steps for writing the lesson plan were as under.

Teaching Point/Content : In this column of the lesson plan, the main teaching points contained in the subject matter are written.

Instructional Objectives : The instructional objectives are written in behavioural terms.

Teacher's Activities : All activities to be undertaken by the teacher for the realization of the objectives fixed up, are mentioned.

Student's Activities : Activities undertaken by the students are mentioned here.

Teaching Aids : Different types of aids both general and specific to be used in the lesson are written.

Evaluation : Evaluation techniques or devices used to assess the results of teaching are mentioned here. It provides feedback to the teacher and the students for bringing improvement in teaching and learning.

Bloom's approach has its good and bad points which are briefly given below:

Merits

1. It is founded on the basis of sound psychological principles and theories of learning.
2. The objectives are given in behavioural terms.
3. The activities concerning the teacher and the students are given separately.
4. The contents or the leaching points are stated clearly.
5. There is due emphasis on the evaluation of the desired objectives in behavioural terms.
6. It makes use of the teaching aids to make the lesson better learnable.

Demerits

1. Writing of objectives in behavioural terms is a big problem for the learners. Many weak and average students face problems here.
2. It makes the lesson planning dull and mechanical as the various steps are to be kept in view rigidly.
3. It is dominated by the teacher.
4. Integration of objectives, learning experiences and evaluation devices is a big problem for the teacher and the students.

RCEM Approach

A style of writing lesson plan was developed by Regional College of Education, Mysore. That approach is known as RCEM approach. It makes use of the concept of system approach to education. The three main steps involved in this approach are—Input, Process and Output. In the lesson plan developed by RCEM, the three aspects are known as-Expected Behaviour Outcomes (EBOS), Communication Strategy and Real Learning Outcomes (RLOS). That three aspects resemble the introduction, presentation and evaluator phases of a lesson plan. INPUT includes the identification of the entry behaviour of the learners. Instead of

Bloom's Taxonomy written in behavioural terms by employing 17 mental processes abilities (e.g. recognise, recall; seeing relationship, cite example classify, interpret, verify, generalize etc.) The second step represents the interaction process of the class room. It describes the learning experiences (Teacher's and student's activities) teaching strategy, A. V. aids etc. The third aspect is the evaluation phase of the lesson.

RCEM approach is an improvement over traditional lesson planning such as Herbartian approach, Unit approach and Bloom' Evaluation approach.

Advantage

1. The objectives are properly stated in terms of measurable mental processes or abilities.
2. Teaching-learning situations, strategies, aids, materials are properly stated.
3. Evaluation aspect is also cared for properly.
4. It is more suitable to Indian schools as it has been developed here.

Disadvantages

1. It is psychological and is too technical.
2. Formalities here consume more time.
3. Writing lesson plan of this type is more tedious.
4. It is rather difficult to see to learning in the light of seventeen mental processes. Which approach is better?

It will be wrong for anyone to swear by one method or the other and be dogmatic. A good teacher does not sell his freedom and be a slave to any method which he may find effective in particular circumstances. "Adoptur", 'don't adopt' is the general slogan of current language trends. None of the recognised methods is fool proof. The point was raised at the UNESCO International Seminar held in Ceylone in 1953. But even after a full week of lively discussion, there was certainly no general agreement on the infallible method.

There is thus a need to have an eclectic and pragmatic approach in the choice of methods and techniques of teaching. Each approach carries some of the standing features and the same must be incorporated in the teacher's method. Teaching method pre-supposes the 'Choice of material and technique of teaching.'

Eclectic Approach to Lesson Planning

Eclectic approach means the collection of all the plus points of various approaches and their compilation in a proper manner. Some factors should be taken into consideration while planning for teaching. Those factors are:

(a) Objective of teaching (b) Class from which the teaching of the subject is started (c) Age, ability and capacity of the pupils (d) Ability and training of the teachers (e) Size of the class (f) Location of the school (g) Availability of aids.

By adding the good points of the different approaches (Morrison's approach, Bloom's approach, Herbartian approach, RCEM's approach) the following steps of a lesson plan can be formulated:

Preparation

This step has been extracted from the Herbartian approach. The goodness of this step lies in the fact that preparation before teaching is very essential. I.A. Davies has rightly remarked. "Lesson Plan must be prepared, for there is nothing so fatal to a teacher's progress as unpreparedness. The teacher before going to his class collects subject matter and classifies it suitably formulates aims and objectives (general and specific) and he also thinks of the aids that he will be using. He also thinks beforehand the methods and strategy that he is going to use in the class.

Here two things need be emphasized (i) entry behaviour and ultimate behaviour. The entry behaviour may be determined by the assumed previous knowledge questions and the ultimate behaviour through recapitulation questions. (ii) Only one unit should be taken up at a time and it should be taught in details as in the case of Morrison's approach.

Exploration

This step has been taken from Morrison's approach or unit approach. The importance of this step lies in the fact that it gives sufficient information regarding the students to the teacher. The teacher tries to explore the background of the learner, his interest, attitude etc. Here a good rapport is formed between the teacher and the students. Some sort of interaction takes place between them. The teacher may explore indirectly also whether the students like his teaching method or not.

Presentation

On Unit Basis : This step has been extracted from Morrison's approach. The teacher takes up one unit of the subject matter for presentation gradually he takes up the other units out of the total subject matter. The unit is taught till there is full understanding. This type of teaching encourages the students and it promotes complete understanding in them.

Through Learning Situations : This sub-step belongs to Bloom's approach the teacher creates learning situations in order to make learning effective and simple. Ryburn rightly said, "To teach we must use experience." For example, if the teacher wants to give knowledge of our ancient art and culture, education tours and excursions need be organised to places of historical such as Taj Mahal, Ajanta and Ellora Caves, Elephanta caves etc. It will provide better learning to the students.

Evaluation

Bloom has given special emphasis to evaluation through this vital step. The teacher can know whether the objectives formulated by him have been achieved or not, whether the actual ultimate behaviour corresponds to the desired ultimate behaviour or not. Only this step tells us whether teaching is bringing in the desired results or not. Otherwise there is no sense in carrying out teaching if the results are poor and the children are not able to grasp anything. For this purpose, oral or written test must be held. Even observation of the students may reveal certain things about them. From the students point of view also, evaluation is very essential as it helps in maintaining the motivation level of the students. As far as possible, evaluation should be arranged quickly and the knowledge of results be prompted.

Application

This step belongs to the Herbartian approach. Learning is meaningful if the students are able to apply the learnt material in some different situations. The students should be able to use their knowledge in solving their day today problems. If an electronics engineer does not know how to replace a bulb, his knowledge is worthless. Similarly learning a language is useless if that person cannot write a telegram by the same language. The student of Social Study should be aware of his rights and duties when he faces the world.

Planning a lesson is a must for every teacher. It is all the more important for a teacher under training. While planning, the teacher should rightly choose, out of knowledge lesson, skip lesson and appreciation lesson as per his need and requirement depending upon his subject, topic and objectives. A suitably planned teaching results into good learning by the students.

QUESTIONS

1. Discuss the need and importance of lesson planning for a teacher.
2. What are the different approaches to lesson planning? Describe anyone of them in detail.
3. Discuss Herbartian Approach to lesson planning by giving an example.
4. What is Eclectic Approach to lesson planning. Develop a model lesson plan of this type by taking up any topic of your choice.
5. Write short notes on : (a) Lesson Planning (b) Importance of Lesson Planning.
6. Discuss in details the following: (i) Appreciation Lesson (ii) Skill Lesson.